THE HERO MAKER

THE HERO MAKER

A BIOGRAPHY OF PAUL BRICKHILL

STEPHEN DANDO-COLLINS

VINTAGE BOOKS
Australia

A Vintage book
Published by Penguin Random House Australia Pty Ltd
Level 3, 100 Pacific Highway, North Sydney NSW 2060
www.penguin.com.au

Penguin
Random House
Australia

First published by Vintage in 2016

Copyright © Fame and Fortune Pty Ltd 2016

The moral right of the author has been asserted.

All rights reserved. No part of this book may be reproduced or transmitted by any person or entity, including internet search engines or retailers, in any form or by any means, electronic or mechanical, including photocopying (except under the statutory exceptions provisions of the *Australian Copyright Act 1968*), recording, scanning or by any information storage and retrieval system without the prior written permission of Penguin Random House Australia.

Every effort has been made to identify individual photographers and copyright holders where appropriate, but for some photographs this has not been possible. The publishers would be pleased to hear from any copyright holders who have not been acknowledged.

Addresses for the Penguin Random House group of companies can be found at global.penguinrandomhouse.com/offices.

National Library of Australia
Cataloguing-in-Publication entry

Dando-Collins, Stephen, 1950– author
The hero maker: a biography of Paul Brickhill: the Australian behind the legendary stories The Dam Busters, The Great Escape and Reach for the Sky/Stephen Dando-Collins

ISBN 978 0 85798 812 6 (paperback)

Brickhill, Paul, 1916–1991
Fighter pilots – Australia – Biography
Authors – 20th century – Biography
Soldiers – Australia – Biography

940.544944092

Cover image © Hulton-Deutsch Collection/CORBIS
Cover design by Luke Causby/Blue Cork
Typeset in 13/17 pt Adobe Garamond by Post Pre-press Group, Brisbane
Printed in Australia by Griffin Press, an accredited ISO AS/NZS 14001:2004 Environmental Management System printer

Penguin Random House Australia uses papers that are natural, renewable and recyclable products and made from wood grown in sustainable forests. The logging and manufacturing processes are expected to conform to the environmental regulations of the country of origin.

TABLE OF CONTENTS

Acknowledgements		ix
Author's Note		xi
1.	Shot Down	1
2.	Ink in the Blood	13
3.	Peter and Paul, the Apostles of Individualism	28
4.	Wiped Out	36
5.	Flying Officer Brickhill	49
6.	Spitfire Pilot	60
7.	In the Bag	80
8.	Welcome to Stalag Luft 3	85
9.	The Tunnel Game	93
10.	In the Light of Day	106
11.	The Great Escape	121
12.	Counting the Cost	130
13.	March or Die	142
14.	A Friendly Interrogation	149
15.	The Man Who Came Back	171
16.	Back in England	200
17.	Enter the Author and Wife	213
18.	Bader, the Man with Tin Legs	233
19.	Reaching for the Sky	260
20.	The Dam Busters Crisis	280
21.	A Slap in the Face	294
22.	End of Exile	302
23.	Return to Oz	310
24.	John Sturges' Great Escape	327
25.	War of Nerves	343

26.	The Artful Dodger	350
27.	Back, for Good	355
28.	The Final Chapter	367
29.	Upon Reflection	373

Appendix – The Works of Paul Brickhill	381
Notes	382
Bibliography	392
Index	397

Dedicated to my dynamic co-pilot in life, my wife, Louise, who has been with me on every sortie into uncharted territory

Acknowledgements

MANY PEOPLE CONTRIBUTED to the creation of this book. First and foremost, Meredith Curnow, my publisher at Random House Australia for the past ten years, who guided me down the path that led to Brickhill. And Richard Curtis, my longtime New York literary agent, who has held my hand through many a book. My grateful thanks also go to the following . . .

SYDNEY: Denis Smith, President, Lane Cove Historical Society; former *Sun* journalist and Spitfire pilot John Ulm; Linda Ta of accountancy firm Winn Croucher Partners; Dr Philip Georgouras and his wife Tina, owners of 'Craig Rossie'; Allison Purdy, Media, Entertainment & Arts Alliance (successor to the Australian Journalists Assocation); Debbie Locke, North Sydney Boys High School; NSW State Archives' always helpful Kingsgrove staff; National Archives of Australia, Chester Hill staff. And my hard-working editor at Random House Australia, Patrick Mangan.

Acknowledgements

MELBOURNE: Christopher Widenbar, Shrine of Remembrance.

TASMANIA: Robyn Jones, Launceston Historical Society; David Parker, Beaconsfield, whose suggestion sparked this book.

PORT PIRIE: Greg Mayfield, *Recorder* editor.

WESTERN AUSTRALIA: Maria Lupp, Paul Brickhill's former nurse.

CANBERRA: Australian War Memorial Research Centre staff; National Library of Australia staff.

AUCKLAND: My guide Robert Kent.

LONDON: David Bickers, chairman of the Douglas Bader Foundation and son-in-law of Sir Douglas Bader; Robert Brown, Faber & Faber historian; Georgia Glover of Brickhill's literary agents David Higham Associates; Simon Gee, Elstree and Borehamwood Museum; Bob Redman, secretary, Elstree Screen Heritage.

TORQUAY, DEVON: John Tucker and Alison Willcocks, Torquay Library; Jean Bowden; and Torquay's *Herald*.

GLASGOW: Dawn Sinclair, HarperCollins archivist; Alma Topen and Gaby Laing, University of Glasgow.

NEW YORK CITY: Nick Minchin, stepbrother to Timothy and Tempe Brickhill; and Gloria Loomis and Julia Masnik, Watkins/Loomis Literary Agency.

AUSTIN, TEXAS: Richard B Watson and Ali Dzienkowski, Harry Ransom Centre, University of Texas.

Author's Note
Stalag Luft III or Stalag Luft 3?

As evidenced by German records from the camp, the Luftwaffe wrote the name of the Sagan POW camp as Stalag Luft 3. So too did the Royal Australian Air Force, and Paul Brickhill in 1945 press articles. By the time *The Great Escape* was published in 1950, Brickhill's editors had changed it to Stalag Luft III, which became the widespread usage.

The confusion arose because German POW camp titles varied between Roman and Arabic numerals. The title of the camp at Schubin, Poland, for example, officially, and confusingly, went from Oflag XXI-B to Oflag 64 in 1943.

In this work, I have chosen to remain faithful to the primary German source, writing the Sagan camp's name as the Luftwaffe did, Stalag Luft 3. Likewise, present-day Polish place names Zagan and Szubin are written as they were by the Germans during WWII, the form with which POW inmates were familiar, Sagan and Schubin.

1.

Shot Down

AT 12.40 PM on Wednesday, 17 March 1943, a dozen pilots of the Royal Air Force's Number 92 Squadron were sitting in their Spitfires on the coastal desert airstrip at Bou Grara, 360 kilometres southwest of Tunis, capital of Tunisia. On 'cockpit standby', with hoods open in the baking heat, they awaited orders. The enemy was expected to be active in strength in their sector, and 92 Squadron had been tapped to intercept them. Some pilots were relaxed as they waited. Others sat tensely behind their controls.

'Scramble, 92 Squadron!'

Chocks in front of the Spitfires' front wheels were whipped away, Rolls-Royce Merlin engines roared, and, in pairs, the Spits surged forward, bouncing down the sandy runway as they gathered speed. Buffeted by a strong southeasterly wind, they lifted into the air, their undercarriages retracting beneath them as they climbed. By 12.43, all twelve aircraft were airborne.

Flying Mark Vb Spitfire number AB136 in that scramble was Flying Officer Paul Brickhill, a twenty-six-year-old from Sydney, Australia. Just five feet six tall, handsome, with a pencil-thin Errol Flynn moustache, Brickhill was flying as wingman to a Briton, Flying Officer Mick Bruckshaw. Both were part of the squadron's B flight, led by Flight Lieutenant Peter 'Hunk' Humphries. As the Spitfires, engines straining, clawed for height, Brickhill concentrated on sticking to his number one like glue. This was Brickhill's thirty-fifth operational sortie. Up to this point, he had flown fifty-five combat hours. The fifty-sixth was to prove fateful.

Climbing to 10,000 feet, the squadron levelled out beneath a blanket of grey, featureless altostratus cloud, with the sun a dull white orb through the murk above. With cockpits closed and oxygen masks strapped in place, the pilots retained tight formation as they headed northeast, up the coast towards the Axis' Mareth Line. For fifteen minutes, they flew in silence, eyes constantly peeled for dots in the sky ahead, dots that would represent the 'Jerry' aircraft they were hoping to intercept.

Their course took the Spitfires over the opposition front line, and into enemy territory. From around the enemy-held town of Gabes, flak shells began to be flung up in their path, bursting in thick profusion. The black shell-bursts were too far away to worry about. 'When you see the red flash, you know it's too bloody close,' recalled John Ulm, who would later be shot down by flak while flying a Spitfire.[1]

An eagle-eyed member of 92 Squadron spotted Messerschmitt Bf 109s – known as Me 109s to Allied pilots – flitting through cloud behind the exploding anti-aircraft shells. They were flying several thousand feet higher than the Spitfires and heading south on a course that would bypass them. After the British pilot radioed the enemy's height and direction, the squadron's commander gave an order. One after the other, the Spitfires banked to intercept their opponents.

The enemy formation was made up of a dozen bomb-carrying Luftwaffe Me 109 fighter-bombers, escorted by six Me 109 fighters, plus three Macchi 202 Folgore fighters from Fascist Italy's Regia Aeronautica. In the past, the Luftwaffe had used Junkers 87 dive-bombers for ground attack, but they were too slow and too vulnerable against Spitfires, which had knocked them from the sky with ease. This was why some Me 109s had been converted into fighter-bombers. The bomb-laden Messerschmitts above today were on their way to attack Allied ground forces, while their escorts had the job of protecting them from opposition fighters.

Now, as the 92 Squadron Spitfires' new course saw them again cross the enemy's Mareth Line defences, the six covering Messerschmitts peeled away and came diving down at them, leaving the Macchis with the fighter-bombers. While B section continued on after the fighter-bombers, Hunk Humphries led Brickhill and the rest of his section in a climbing cross-over turn that took them across the top of the other Spits, and into the path of the oncoming enemy fighters.

The Luftwaffe fighter tactic was to fire during the dive, continuing on past their opponents, pulling up below them and climbing to attack again from below. As sand-coloured Messerschmitts came scooting by, flame and lead spurting from their guns, Hunk Humphries and his section got in a brief burst at them, and then the enemy had gone, scattering in all directions below the Spitfires like naughty schoolboys running from their teachers. Taking three Spitfires with him and leaving Bruckshaw and Brickhill as top cover, Humphries dived after the Me 109s.

Bruckshaw, with Brickhill tucked in beside and a little behind him, eased down to 9000 feet and flew on, looking out for the remaining enemy fighters and ready to dive down onto the tails of any Messerschmitts or Macchis that latched onto their comrades. As Brickhill scanned the sky beneath them, he spotted a pair of Me 109s.

'Couple at five o'clock, Hunk,' Brickhill warned section leader Humphries below by radio. 'Keep an eye on them.'[2]

Bruckshaw and Brickhill were three kilometres out to sea by this stage, flying south. As Bruckshaw scanned the sky above, Brickhill watched the two Messerschmitts below. Now, Bruckshaw saw three aircraft approaching head-on from the south, five hundred feet above. Bruckshaw identified them as Spitfires, apparently from 92 Squadron's B section and, oddly, flying in line ahead. What was to follow would take place in seconds.

With a glance at his watch, Bruckshaw noted the time: 13.05 hours. When he looked up again, he saw the first approaching Spitfire suddenly and violently turn to port. The second Spitfire in the line of three, flying just fifty metres behind the leader, immediately followed suit. The third aircraft, instead of tailing them, broke off and dived towards Bruckshaw and Brickhill. To his horror, Bruckshaw realised that the third aircraft was not a Spitfire, but an enemy Macchi 202, which had a similar profile to the Spit. At that moment, it dawned on Bruckshaw that the Macchi had been chasing the two Spitfires. He also realised that the Macchi's diving turn would bring it down behind Brickhill and himself. Craning his neck to track the descending Italian fighter's course, Bruckshaw yelled a warning.

'Paul! Behind you! Break! Break! Break!' As he spoke, Bruckshaw saw orange flame flicker from the Macchi's wings. He quickly threw his own Spit into a tight defensive turn.

Brickhill, looking over his right shoulder to try to spot the unseen enemy and mentally kicking himself for being careless, never caught sight of his attacker. Instead, he felt what he described as 'that dreadful jolting that shakes an aircraft like a pneumatic drill when cannon shells smack home in quantity'.[3] A series of explosions almost deafened him. His Spit was sent flicking into an uncontrolled turn.

Aware of shrapnel flying up between his legs, Brickhill expected a cannon shell to pierce the armour protecting his seat. His body 'tensed and shrank, expecting personal attention from a shell at any moment'. It was, he would later remark in a moment of understatement, a nasty feeling. Shattered cockpit fittings flew past his face. He felt pain in his back. More pain in the back of the head. Out of the corner of his eye he saw large chunks flying from his port wing. The cockpit filled with black smoke. And then the engine died.[4]

All was eerily silent as the crippled plane began to fall from the sky in a slow spin. Brickhill let it twirl a few times, figuring that would put his assailant off, before pulling the stick back into his stomach. The nose came up a little. But still the aircraft spun, rotating slowly. He tried to correct the spin and resume something approaching straight and level flight. Even if the engine was dead, he might glide down to the desert and make a belly landing. But now the stick simply fell forward, loose, floppy – like a broken neck, he thought. He no longer had control of the aircraft. It fell lazily from the sky in what Brickhill would describe as a curiously flat spin. He was struck by an incredulous realisation that it was doomed, and it was time he got out.[5]

Mick Bruckshaw had seen the bullets from the Macchi crash into the underside of the port wing close to Brickhill's cockpit and create several explosions. It was there that the shells for Brickhill's cannon were stored. The Italian's bullets had detonated Brickhill's own ammunition. Because Brickhill had not seen his attacker, with cannon shells clearly shattering his cockpit and controls, and because Me 109s were armed with cannon and Macchis were not – the Italian fighters were only equipped with machineguns, and a paltry two at that – the Australian firmly believed he had been done for by a Messerschmitt.

Bruckshaw quickly lost sight of Brickhill's aircraft once it was hit. He had his own problems, for the Macchi had left Brickhill to his fate and latched onto Bruckshaw's tail. The Briton was desperately attempting to throw him off. Although Macchi 202s were poorly armed, they were fast and manoeuvrable, and Bruckshaw had his work cut out.[6]

Brickhill, in his falling, slowly spinning fighter, reached up, grabbed the cockpit hood's twin toggles, and yanked, hard. The hood fell away. As the cockpit quickly cleared of smoke, cool air massaged his face when he ripped off his flying helmet and oxygen mask. But his left arm felt increasingly numb, and soon it was useless to him. With his right hand he unbuckled the Sutton harness holding him firmly in his seat, then shrugged off the straps. Summoning all his strength, he launched himself out the left side of the cockpit.

Halfway out, the slipstream drove him back. Heaving himself out a second time, he found that his parachute pack, strapped on his backside, had caught fast beneath the right-angled rear corner rim of the cockpit's little door flap. Once again the slipstream pushed him back. He found himself in the crazy position of lying with his back against the side of the fuselage, pinned there by a combination of slipstream and the trapped parachute, as the plummeting plane continued to spin. Kicking and struggling with the wind rushing by his face, he was like a bear caught in a trap. He tried to reach something, anything, that could be used for leverage. But nothing was within reach of his right hand.

Lying there, breathing hard, he looked over his left shoulder, to see the coastal foreshore below revolving slowly as if he were on an underpowered aerial merry-go-round, with the ground getting closer by the second. He estimated that he and his Spitfire were now at about 7000 feet. It occurred to him that he was about to die. 'There is no great fear in looking closely at death,' he would later say. At that moment, he would recall, he merely felt an angry irritation, the kind he'd experienced after spilling beer down the front of his tunic.[7]

But he wasn't giving up. Resuming his struggles, he twisted one way then the other, straining to get a handhold on the rim of the cockpit. With that, he would be able to pull himself back in, and free his parachute. But the forces against him were too great. Exhausted, he sagged back. Resigned to his fate now, feeling only disappointment that it was all going to end like this, he began to count off the swiftly decreasing altitude: 5000 feet; 4000; 3000; 2000.

And then, to his amazement, as the Spitfire spun, it suddenly released its hold on him. Falling clear, he felt curiously free and light. Looking down, he saw that his flying boots had been plucked from his feet, and he was in his socks.[8] Panic suddenly gripped him. Had his parachute been ripped away when he'd been flung clear? Reaching to his rump, he was relieved to find the bulky pack still in place. Without hesitation, he grabbed the ripcord's D-ring and yanked, praying that the shells that had come up through the cockpit floor hadn't shredded the chute. With a tug at the shoulders and a 'crack' above, the parachute opened. Undamaged silk filled with air, and the parachute successfully deployed, slowing his descent.

Thousands of feet above, still engaged in his duel with the Macchi that had shot up Brickhill, Mick Bruckshaw momentarily glanced earthward, saw Brickhill's Spit nosing toward the ground, then spotted a white parachute blossoming. Bruckshaw calculated that Brickhill's chute had opened at around 2000 feet.[9]

Brickhill thought it was closer to a thousand feet by the time it deployed. With increasing pain in his shoulder and back of the head, he hung uncomfortably beneath the shrouds. Looking down, he saw his Spitfire make one final rotation before ploughing headlong into the desert. There was a surprisingly violent explosion – much larger than if the fuel tanks alone had gone up. The wreckage began to burn furiously.

Above, Bruckshaw had shaken off the Macchi. As he banked, he saw Brickhill's Spitfire go into the ground, and saw his colleague's parachute descending not far away, to the southwest of the burning aircraft. Bruckshaw quickly noted the location's map reference, Z.6109. That put it on the northern edge of No Man's Land, closer to enemy lines than Allied lines. Rather than hang around any longer alone and invite the attentions of enemy fighters directed by Axis troops on the ground, Bruckshaw turned south and made a beeline for Bou Grara.[10]

Brickhill was coming down fast. He could see that he was about to land on flat, muddy sand extending several hundred metres to the Mediterranean shore, where low waves were breaking. The wind was still pushing strongly from the southeast, blowing him north, away from his lines and towards the enemy. He thought to himself that had it been blowing in the opposite direction it would have taken him to safety.

With the wind driving him backwards, he attempted to twist the shrouds to face the other way and see where he was going. He'd only succeeded in twisting part of the way before, unprepared, he hit the ground, hard. The impact forced an involuntary 'Aaah!' from his lips as he was slammed onto his back on the wet sand. That wasn't the end of it. Rolled over, he was dragged for a distance by his chute before coming to a stop. The abrupt landing had winded him. In pain from his wounds and gasping for breath, he struggled to his feet. But the breeze gusted again, the canopy refilled with air, and he was mobile once more, as he was dragged backwards across the sand, on a careering course over which he had no control.[11]

As he was carried along, feet trailing in the sand, he dazedly fumbled with the chute's quick-release box with his good right hand. Attached to the front of the parachute harness, this box featured a button that had to be turned, after which it was necessary to give the box a solid thump. The harness would then drop away, freeing him from the parachute. But after being hauled across the desert, the box had filled with sand. The button refused to turn. Continuing to struggle with the release mechanism, Brickhill was dragged at least two hundred metres.

Looking over his shoulder, he saw that he was being taken in the direction of a narrow waterway rippling towards the sea. Just beyond it, a line of entangled barbed wire marked the enemy's front line. As he reached the waterway, he finally succeeded in getting the release catch to work. The harness sprang open, and he fell free, landing on his back on the sand. Beside him, the chute emptied of air and gently collapsed into the stream.

He tried to stand, but, weak from exertions and wounds, he only fell back down on his rump. Sitting there, shaken and disconsolate, he became aware of the business end of a rifle pointing at him, no more than four metres away. Looking up, he saw the rifle's owner, an Italian soldier, splashing through the stream towards him. Ten metres beyond the stream stretched the barbed-wire entanglement, and standing in front of it, with a bunch of scruffy soldiers around him, was an immaculate Italian colonel with rows of decorations on his tunic and perfectly pressed riding breeches with a broad gold stripe down the sides. The soldier who crossed the stream took Brickhill's arm and hauled him to his feet, then helped him stumble across the water to the colonel, who made a courteous little bow to him.

'For you, the war is over,' the colonel declared in heavily accented English. This phrase, heard by tens of thousands of captured Allied servicemen during the war, was apparently the only English the officer knew.[12]

Brickhill would later say: 'The first few minutes after being shot down sometimes seem pretty unreal while the grey matter is trying to adjust itself to violently changed conditions.'[13] In his now wet socks, he was escorted through an opening in the barbed wire and along a series of low trenches to a dressing station. There, he stripped off his shirt and trousers and an Italian medic tended to the splinter wounds on his back and head, and contusions to his left leg. Handed a large 'dixie' mess tin half-filled with a brown liquid, he was urged to drink. Taking a wary sip, he found the tin contained cognac, fiery and warming. As he sat with the dixie in hand, an Italian corporal came to him.

'You are most lucky,' said the corporal in good English.

Brickhill didn't feel all that lucky, having just been shot down and become an unwilling guest of the Italian First Army.

'That was our minefield your parachute just dragged you across,' the corporal continued.[14]

That explained, Brickhill cogitated, why his plane had gone up with such a bang. It had landed smack dab on top of a mine! It had been a miracle that the parachute had dragged him all the way through the minefield without setting off another mine, a million to one chance that, like his plane, he hadn't been blown sky high. Even though he was now a prisoner of war, Brickhill had to agree with the corporal; he was a bit lucky after all. Raising the dixie to his lips once more, he downed the remaining contents in one go.

Brickhill hadn't been destined to die that day. Years later, he would be grateful to the anonymous pilot who shot him down and changed the course of his life. Now, the former Sydney journalist was about to be sent to a place he would make world famous, and which would make him world famous.

2.

Ink in the Blood

THE NEWSPAPER BUSINESS was in Paul Brickhill's blood, with his father, several uncles and grandfather involved with papers in five Australian states. Brickhill's Australian roots went back to the early 1840s. With the East End's silk-weaving industry in decline, London silk-dyer John Brickhill sailed as a free settler to the penal colony of Van Diemen's Land – renamed Tasmania in 1856 following the cessation of convict transportation from Britain. John Brickhill set up home at Launceston in the north of the island, working initially as a gardener. Within several years he was employed as a law clerk, before joining the Launceston post office and rising to a senior position. In 1844, John married Susannah Hutley.

John and Susannah Brickhill's third son, James, born in September 1846, would eventually do his father proud. As a boy of sixteen, James took up an apprenticeship at Launceston's daily newspaper, the *Examiner*. At nineteen, James made twenty-one-year-old local girl Rebecca Emms pregnant, and they were hurriedly married in May 1865. Their first child was born that September. James would father ten children in all, several of whom died young.

During nineteen years with the *Examiner*, James rose from office boy to journalist before ultimately becoming the paper's accountant. In December 1881, James left the *Examiner*, and the following January, at the age of thirty-five, entered into a partnership with a printer named Bell to take over the printery and masthead of the *Telegraph*. This then bi-weekly Launceston newspaper had been set up just a year before by three local businessmen with little newspaper acumen. James soon began churning out his paper three days a week, and within three months had bought out his partner. James built circulation so rapidly, and brought in so much additional business for his printery, including winning the Launceston Council's printing contract, that on 18 June 1883 he launched his paper as a daily, renaming it the *Daily Telegraph*.

Located in premises at 56 Paterson Street, just down the street from his old employer and around the corner from his parents' St John Street home, James now gave the *Examiner* a run for its money. Contemporaries admired the young newspaperman. 'Widely respected and honoured', said one, his 'disposition was unobtrusive and retiring, yet he possessed a great deal of enterprise, backed up by much perseverance'.[15]

'Very few people outside the precincts of a newspaper office have any conception of the care, toil, anxiety and expense that are involved in the management of a morning daily newspaper,' James declared.[16] Because of his care and toil, and despite the anxiety and expense, business thrived. Most of his sons joined him at the paper. The eldest, Walter, became a sports reporter. Another, Lewis, went into the printery as a compositor. Second youngest George also learned the business, as a junior reporter, joining the *Daily Telegraph* in 1894.

Then, to the surprise of many, at the end of 1894 James threw it all in. Selling the *Telegraph* to his general manager and a local consortium, Brickhill became a commission and mining agent. By the end of 1900, he was ready for yet another new adventure. His boys and one of two daughters were by then off his hands, so he took wife Rebecca and youngest daughter Daisy to the mining town of Zeehan, a cold, wet and miserable place in winter, deep in the wilderness on Tasmania's west coast. There, he became council clerk, and a justice of the peace. During his newspaper days, James had been urged to become involved in politics. His answer had always been that he was too busy. In 1903, his changed circumstances helped him change his mind, and he stood in Australia's second Federal Election in the newly-created seat of Darwin – renamed Braddon in 1955 – a sprawling electorate taking in Tasmania's west and northwest coasts.

In the seat of Darwin, James Brickhill had two opponents, chiefly the colourful King O'Malley, who was destined to become one of the most legendary figures in Australian politics. An American, an insurance salesman and an evangelist, auburn-haired, red-bearded O'Malley would during his career influence the policy direction of the Labor Party, play a hand in the foundation of the Commonwealth Bank, oversee the choice of the site for the new federal capital, Canberra, and hand that city's design competition prize to fellow American Walter Burley Griffin.

O'Malley had the advantage of having been one of four members sent to the first Federal Parliament representing Tasmania in 1901. Yet he was considered an outsider by many, not only for a murky North American background but because he'd previously served in South Australia's parliament. Brickhill, meanwhile, had the advantage of Tasmanian roots and an impeccable reputation in business and local government. The election campaign in the far-flung electorate proved tough, with the white-haired, white-moustached, fifty-six-year-old James Brickhill speaking to packed halls.

Opponent O'Malley was especially popular with the ladies, wowing them with his distinctive appearance, golden tongue and frequent biblical references. In a bid to counter this popularity with the fairer sex, an Ulverstone-based Brickhill supporter sent a lengthy poem to Burnie's *North Western Advocate & Emu Bay Times*, declaring O'Malley a 'mountebank and charlatan who insults the Book of Books', and urging women in the electorate, who would be exercising their newly won right to vote in a federal election for the first time:

> Mother, wife and daughter, by our side, come take your stand,
> Never let him beat us, and o'er his victory gloat,
> Help send this man O'Malley back to his native land,
> Give your support to Brickhill, and Vote, Vote, VOTE.[17]

The election result was close. While third candidate James Gaffney could only muster fifty-three votes, James Brickhill came in with 4354. Unfortunately for James' political aspirations, King O'Malley received 4483, and by the margin of just 129 votes the American was sent to Federal Parliament and a subsequent glittering career in the ministries of prime ministers Andrew Fisher and Billy Hughes. James Brickhill didn't venture into politics again, returning instead to the quieter life as Zeehan's town clerk.

Five years on, in the winter of 1908, he contracted pneumonia. A week later, on 10 July, James Brickhill passed away, at the age of sixty-one. After he was buried in Launceston, his wife, Rebecca, returned to that city. Cared for by unmarried daughter Daisy, Rebecca would live well into her nineties.

Most of James' sons had meanwhile scattered to the four winds. Only Lewis remained in Launceston, working now as a compositor with the *Examiner*. Frank was with the post office in Burnie. Walter and Hector had moved to Perth, Western Australia, where Walter wrote for the local press. Both Walter and Hector served in South Africa during the Boer War, settling there after the conflict. Running an ostrich farm in the Transvaal, Walter returned to journalism occasionally, writing articles about South Africa for Tasmania's *Weekly Times*.

Son number four, George Russell Brickhill, born on 26 January 1879, ninety-first anniversary of the arrival of Britain's First Fleet in New South Wales, had gone to Victoria when his parents moved to Zeehan and in 1901 joined Bendigo's *Advertiser* as a journalist. As early as 1899, in Launceston, George had attended a meeting of local journalists which discussed setting up a reporters' association. In Bendigo, he was often called out to work on his one day off each week at the *Advertiser*. There was no overtime pay, no set annual leave. Sick leave, if granted at all, was the prerogative of management. And the pay was abysmal. This was typical of the working conditions for journalists in newspapers across the country, and George was determined to correct the situation. That same year of 1901, he helped found the Bendigo Press Association, a social society for journalists which agitated for better pay and conditions for its members. George became the Association's inaugural secretary.

Perhaps influenced by his father's recent tilt at politics, a lust for adventure got the better of George in 1905. He ran away to join the circus, figuratively speaking, signing up with Wirth's Circus to travel the world in search of exhibits for them. His brief was to acquire elephants in particular; Wirth's then possessed just a single pachyderm. George's adventure took him to the Indian subcontinent, and, in April, Wirth's received a letter in which George advised he was having difficulties driving four wild elephants to the coast, but hoped to have them loaded aboard the Sydney-bound steamer SS *Ashbridge* at Calcutta.

George not only succeeded in getting the quartet of elephants to Wirth's, he also sent them several tapirs and a ten-metre python. In December, he despatched two more Indian elephants to Sydney aboard the SS *Gracchus*. Wirth's Circus elephant troupe increased to eight shortly after when one of their new elephants gave birth in Sydney.[18] So it was that the children of Australia in years to come had George Brickhill to thank for the sight of elephants in their home towns as Wirth's Circus toured the nation.

Elephant-catching did not a long-term career make. Back in Launceston to visit his mother on 5 March 1906, George spoke to the *Examiner*. 'Mr Brickhill has lately been travelling the world in search of circus novelties,' noted the paper the following day, 'but has completed his mission and purposes resuming his association with the newspaper world in Melbourne.'[19] Sure enough, in Melbourne, then Australia's federal capital, George joined the staff of the *Age*, the city's second-ranking morning daily after the *Argus*. Before long, George helped establish the Melbourne Press Bond, another pressman's social club with ambitions for improved conditions for journalists.

Over the next three years, George slaved away at the *Age*, making friends including *Age* parliamentary reporter Keith Murdoch, the future Sir Keith, father of eventual international media magnate Rupert Murdoch. With secure employment and good prospects, George's attention turned to affairs of the heart. The love of his life was Izitella Victoria Bradshaw, or Dot as she was known in the family. One of six children of Launceston accountant John Walbourn Bradshaw, a one-time associate of George's father, and Louisa Adelaide Bradshaw, Dot was six years younger than George. On his annual return visits to Launceston to see his mother, George would catch up with Dot. But by 1908 the Bradshaw family had moved to Sydney, where Dot's father worked as a travelling salesman and part-time accountant.

The added distance between George and Dot only made the heart grow fonder, and that year George popped the question. On 15 February 1909, the couple was married at the Methodist Church in Kensington, a pocket suburb of inner Sydney. The church was just a stone's throw from the Bradshaw family home in Elsmere Street. Following the wedding, George took his bride to Melbourne, where the couple's first marital home was a rented house at Auburn in inner Melbourne. Over the next several years, they moved around a number of rented addresses in the area.

A year after George's marriage, leading members of the Melbourne Press Bond agreed it was time to form a national organisation that would collectively bargain on behalf of journalists in the Commonwealth Conciliation and Arbitration Court. A trade union. At 8.00 pm on Saturday 10 December, Melbourne reporters gathered in a basement cafe in Flinders Street, usual meeting place of the Press Bond, to discuss the formation of the Australian Journalists Association. Newspaper proprietors were firmly against the creation of such an organisation, and had warned employees not to attend this meeting. The chief of staff of one paper even positioned himself in a basement billiard parlour next door to the cafe, trying to listen through the wall to what was said at the meeting.

Proprietors' warnings failed to prevent more than one hundred journalists, including George Brickhill, from attending, and George was one of eight elected to a steering committee. Two more December meetings followed, after which 147 journalists signed up as foundation members of the Australian Journalists Association. George was one of them, as was colleague Keith Murdoch. The Association was registered with the Arbitration Court, and, within months, George was elected the AJA's General Vice-President. In addition to keeping down his job with the *Age*, George worked long unpaid hours on behalf of the Association.

With the majority of newspaper proprietors across Australia opposed to the AJA and its objectives, a long and bitter fight was waged against the Association. Many press barons signed an agreement negotiated in 1911 with the AJA which initially put an extra £15,000 a year collectively into the pockets of journalists, but a number soon began to ignore the agreement. That same year, George and Dot's first child, Russell, was born. In 1913, another two-year agreement was negotiated with proprietors by the AJA. The following year, a second Brickhill son, Ayde Geoffrey, or Geoff as he became known, was born.

With a growing family and a pacifist outlook, George resisted the patriotic propaganda his paper and others peddled and declined to volunteer to fight in the Great War. This took courage, as relatives of the hundreds of thousands of Australians who did enlist frequently branded stay-at-homes like George cowards. From something his son Paul was to later say, it is likely George received a white feather in the mail. This was traditionally an anonymous – and as such cowardly – way of accusing someone of cowardice.[20] Some of George's newspaper colleagues, Keith Murdoch among them, went to the front as war correspondents. Feeling he had more important work to do at home, George didn't join war correspondent ranks either. Instead, he was to lead an important fight at home.

By 1916, with Australia's newspaper owners proving increasingly difficult to deal with, the AJA decided to take their wages and conditions campaign to a new level. George Brickhill was so passionate about the cause that he now left the *Age* to become the AJA's full-time general secretary. On 20 December, with the Brickhills renting at 'Elsmere', 133 Burke Road in Camberwell, Dot gave birth to their third son, Paul Chester Jerome Brickhill. George was a Methodist,

Dot an Anglican, and, although married in the Methodist Church, Dot was insistent that their children be raised in the Church of England. Baby Paul was accordingly baptised by an Anglican minister.

By early 1917, after six months of detailed preparation, George led the AJA's bid in the Arbitration Court for the introduction of an award scheme for journalists' pay and conditions. Two lawyers engaged by the Association would advise George, but, as the AJA's rules prevented the use of lawyers as advocates, he would put the case in court on the Association's behalf.

Just as the hearing, which was being contested by the collective newspaper owners of Australia, opened in Melbourne on 5 February 1917 before Justice Isaac Isaacs, a future knight of the realm and governor-general of Australia, the AJA's principal legal adviser was called away to urgent business in London. Without the legal eagle at his side, George went up against a team supported by senior barristers paid for by the press barons. The odds seemed stacked against the thirty-eight-year-old journalist as he put a case for set pay scales for each grade of journalist, for a forty-six-hour week, for three weeks annual leave and paid sick leave, and for equal pay and conditions for female journalists.

But, as the AJA's official history would record, 'Brickhill was brilliant. He developed the forensic style of a trained lawyer; he was respectful, imperturbable, candid and logical. He quickly won the respect of the court.' Most importantly, 'He made his plans well.'[21] Brickhill had spent the past six months reading every letter, document and minute book from every AJA branch across the country. He'd interviewed scores of potential witnesses in six states, preparing a list of eighty who could be called to give evidence. In the end, he called fifteen. As was to be proved, the press barons didn't come to court anywhere near as well prepared, and George humiliated several of their more arrogant witnesses during cross-examination.

Justice Isaacs brought down his decision in the case on 11 May. To the chagrin of the nation's newspaper owners, Isaacs ruled substantially in the journalists' favour, making their new awards retrospective to the beginning of the year. The only area where he didn't agree with Brickhill's case was in the length of a journalist's working week, which he set at forty-six hours. Nonetheless, George continued to fight, speaking for a day and a half attempting to convince Justice Isaacs to award journalists a forty-four-hour week, until he physically collapsed in court. The judge failed to relent. Still, the journalists' award resulting from this case was the most advanced in the world at that time, and as a consequence of the case George Brickhill became one of the best-known figures in Australian journalism.

The press barons didn't take the AJA's success with good grace. Although they agreed to meet the award's conditions, Sydney's four daily newspapers promptly sacked more than eighty journalists, and papers in Melbourne, Brisbane, Adelaide, Perth and Hobart also laid off staff. Collecting money for sacked colleagues, the AJA settled in for a long, hard war against proprietors. The court case sapped George's energy, and that Christmas he was glad to get away to Tasmania for a break. The Brickhill clan, including one-year-old Paul, made the storm-tossed steamer crossing of Bass

Strait to spend the holidays with George's mother, Rebecca, in Launceston.

In early 1918, Dot again fell pregnant. In October, she would give birth to another son, Lloyd. George continued to labour for the AJA that year, but as 1919 arrived, and with his fortieth birthday approaching, George felt it time to get back into harness as a pressman. One newspaper owner who didn't despise him was James E. Davidson, known as Jed among his peers. He offered George a job. Davidson actually supported the AJA, and admired Brickhill for what he had achieved for journalists.

Keith Murdoch considered Davidson 'one of the most noble characters in Australian journalism'.[22] A former editor of the Melbourne *Herald*, Davidson had acquired several regional newspapers in South Australia. In 1919, his latest acquisition was the *Recorder*, in Port Pirie. When Jed offered Brickhill the job of editor of the *Recorder*, George accepted. He left the AJA with the Association's gold medal for meritorious service, and in March 1919 the Brickhills moved to Port Pirie. George would continue to be an active member of the Association, and thirty years later would be made a life member.

The Brickhills moved into a house in Port Pirie's Stenness area, and George returned to the newspaper business with enthusiasm. Reporter Cecil Murn was given his full-time job at the *Recorder* by George. Murn would fondly remember 'the Boss' with pipe perpetually jutting from the corner of his mouth and running an ongoing feud with a night subeditor. George never raised his voice. Instead, he would conduct 'a wordy war', leaving notes.

'The politeness of some of these epistles was beautiful,' said Murn. 'And therein lay their sting.' For, said he, 'Mr Brickhill was the quiet, unostentatious type of editor. But his pen would be loaded to the nib with dynamite, and when he had some genuine grouse on behalf of the people, he poured it out.'[23] Murn would recall a young Paul Brickhill as a frequent visitor to the *Recorder* office, 'running around the place'. With workaholic George putting in long working days, Paul would also be sent by his mother, Dot, to fetch his father home for dinner with the family.[24]

In 1922, Jed Davidson acquired an Adelaide Sunday newspaper, the *Mail*, and the following year he offered George Brickhill the post of editor. George eagerly accepted this opportunity to edit a capital city newspaper. After publishing his last issue of the *Recorder* on 30 June 1923, and with Dot again pregnant, he moved the family to Adelaide and took over the editor's desk at the *Mail*. That same year, Davidson established Adelaide daily the *News*, creating the umbrella company News Limited to manage all his newspapers. This was the company which Sir Keith Murdoch would take over in 1949, and which, under Sir Keith's son Rupert, would become News Corporation, the international media giant.

Before George Brickhill took charge at the *Mail* it had been a sporting rag. From its new premises at North Terrace, he turned it into a quality publication with a news and entertainment focus. As a result, the paper's circulation rose, as did the *Mail*'s reputation. George was in his element. He employed Hal Gye, famous as illustrator of poet C. J. Dennis' bestselling *Sentimental Bloke* books, as the paper's cartoonist. And George initiated a comics page, starting with May

Gibbs' gumnut babies Bib and Bub as regulars. Circulation continued to grow. Meanwhile, the *Mail*'s burgeoning real-estate pages were generating healthy advertising revenue for News Limited. Jed was a happy man. And George was a happy man.

The Brickhills' fifth and last son, Clive, arrived in October 1923. The following year, when George was at the height of his success as a newspaper editor in Adelaide, he heard that Launceston's *Daily Telegraph*, the paper that had flourished under his father, and where George himself had launched his journalistic career, had gone under. As circulation haemorrhaged, the paper's proprietors had brought in a new editor from Melbourne to turn its fortunes around. Tom Prichard had previously edited Melbourne's weekly *Sun*, but not even he could save the *Daily Telegraph*. Prichard's daughter Katharine, who went to school in Launceston, would later gain fame as novelist and playwright Katharine Susannah Prichard. On the paper's closure, the Prichards returned to Melbourne, where Tom took the editor's chair at the *Mining Standard*.

By the second half of 1927, and with his fiftieth birthday just two years away, George Brickhill accepted the offer of a senior editorial position with the *Evening News*, considered Sydney's least serious daily paper. There were several factors in George's decision to move to Sydney. Louisa Bradshaw, Dot's mother, had been a widow since the death of Dot's beloved 'papa', John Bradshaw, at Lindfield in 1919. Louisa herself was in declining health, and Dot wanted to care for her. And George once again had itchy feet. Besides, if he was going to prove himself on a paper in the 'big smoke', it was now or never.

George was quite emotional when News Limited hosted his farewell function and Jed presented him with a travelling case and rug, plus a silver tea service for Dot. In a farewell editorial, George's successor at the *Mail* described him as 'versatile' and 'one of the best known of Australian journalists'.[25]

The relocation to Sydney was a move that would shape a spectacular writing career for one particular member of the Brickhill family. But it wasn't George.

3.

Peter and Paul, the Apostles of Individualism

In the second half of November 1927, just weeks before Paul Brickhill's eleventh birthday, he and his family arrived in Sydney. They moved into a house rented from Mrs Mary Colyer at 8 Mitchell Street on the Lower North Shore's picturesque Greenwich Point. For young Paul, this was the start of dual love affairs with residences by the water and Sydney's North Shore that would last the rest of his life. Already home to seven Brickhills – mother, father, and sons Russell, Geoff, Paul, Lloyd and Clive – the house would also accommodate Paul's widowed grandmother, Louisa, who would live with the family until her death. Dot's brother-in-law and sister, Mr and Mrs Fred Amos, lived nearby in the neighbouring suburb of Wollstonecraft, and the Brickhills had a close relationship with them.

Completion of the Sydney Harbour Bridge was then still five years away, and hordes of workers daily commuted across the harbour from the North Shore on fleets of ferries. George took the ferry from Greenwich Point each workday to get to the five-storeyed *Evening News* building in Elizabeth Street. Opened a year before, the premises had been purpose-built for the paper. It had frontages to both Elizabeth and Castlereagh streets, and huge new presses rolled six days a week in a massive print room thirty metres below the pavement. The editorial offices occupied the airy third floor. There was even a roof garden and cafeteria for staff. It looked like George had struck employment gold.

On the southern tip of Greenwich Point, foreshore swimming baths lay close to the ferry wharf, just a few minutes' walk from the Brickhill home. Young Paul was soon a member of the local swimming association, becoming a strong competitive swimmer. Before long, Paul noticed a boy who lived just a block away on the corner of Lawrence and George streets.[26] This boy was smallish, tawny-haired, grubby and solitary. Unlike other local kids, he never played in the local park. Every day, the boy could be seen walking a terrier dog around the district without ever exchanging a word or a glance with anyone.

Paul felt sorry for him. For young Paul was also different. Left-handed, he had stubbornly resisted attempts by teachers to make him write with the right hand. And, like the other boy, he lived in an isolated world. In young Brickhill's case, this was the result of a debilitating stutter. Paul was a sensitive child, and as an adult would retain painful memories of wetting his pants in childhood. Although he grew out of wetting himself, he would never entirely lose the stutter. At its worst, it made conversation difficult, and made him the butt of jokes of the insensitive. One device used by people who stutter is to avoid speaking unless absolutely necessary, limiting their interaction with others. Yet Paul was prepared to speak to the new boy, and risk being laughed at because of his impediment.

Throughout his life, Brickhill would display a generosity of spirit, reaching out to and for others, which showed itself most markedly for the first time when he saw that lonely boy in Greenwich Point. Feeling the other boy's isolation, Paul, as he would later recall, became determined to get him playing with the other children.[27] Approaching the new boy, Paul introduced himself, and learned that the stranger's name was Peter Finch. The new boy didn't laugh at him. He was grateful for the approach. And so was born a novel friendship.

Peter Finch was just three months older than Paul. Although a fifth-generation Australian, he'd been born in London and only arrived at Greenwich Point a few months before the Brickhills, landing in Australia the year prior to that. In an English accent that he before long smothered with the accent used by Brickhill and other Australians around him, Peter told Paul that he'd been born in England, lived in France, and been a boy priest in a Buddhist temple in India for two years before being sent to Sydney by his eccentric Australian-born grandmother. What was more, his physicist father George Ingle Finch had climbed Mount Everest almost as far as its summit in 1922. Paul, a boy with a fertile imagination, was immediately seduced by his new acquaintance's colourful background.

Peter, it turned out, hadn't even been able to read or write English prior to being despatched to Sydney in 1926 and consigned to a Mosman theosophical school as a boarder.

Peter was unaware that his itinerant life to that point was dictated by the fact that his father was not his father; Peter was the product of his mother's infidelity with an unidentified lover, although this was a closely held secret in the family. Subsequently taken out of the theosophical school by his New South Wales-born grandfather, Charles Finch, the retired chairman of the NSW Lands Board and a Greenwich Point resident, Peter had been placed with his great-uncle Edward Finch, also in Greenwich Point. To raise the boy, Edward, elderly and ailing, handed Peter over to his forty-year-old unmarried daughter Kate, who also lived under his roof.

Kate Finch was Peter's second cousin, but she made him call her Aunt Kate, and made his life a misery. Every day before school, Peter told Paul, he had to perform a range of household chores from washing up to making beds, which invariably made him late for school. Every day, too, Peter had to take Aunt Kate's terrier for a walk. Most days, Aunt Kate gave Peter a belting. Brickhill saw at firsthand how Kate Finch used young Peter as a personal slave. One afternoon, he was talking to his mate in the Finch garden, where Peter was at work, when Aunt Kate suddenly called out through an open window.

'Peter, go find my teeth.'[28]

Without comment, Peter turned into a denture-seeking robot. When he found the false teeth, in the garden, he silently handed them in through the open window, receiving not a word of thanks. Brickhill would say, years later, that, learning how hard done by Peter was by his uncaring Aunt Kate, he became all the more determined to help him, to rescue him from the friendless world into which he had fallen.[29]

Peter and Paul soon became best mates, yet they were the oddest match. Apart from small stature, blue eyes, fathers called George, and the ability to swim like fish, they had little in common. Paul loved competitive sports; Peter hated sport of any kind. Paul enjoyed reading; Peter could then barely read English. Paul was always neatly dressed; Peter was invariably dishevelled. But Paul would later rate himself an individualist. And Peter Finch was the exemplar of individualism. There were other attractions. Peter would prove increasingly daring, up for anything, heedless of risk. While Paul didn't lack courage, his new friend had more than enough bravado for the pair of them. Paul once watched Peter get into a fight with a much larger boy. Covered in blood, Peter fought bravely on until a draw was declared. And Peter had the gift of the gab. To spare Paul the trial of stuttering, he would do the talking for the pair of them.

In 1928, Peter was sent to North Sydney Intermediate High, an institution for the also-rans. Paul's grades were much better, and he was invited to sit the entrance examination for North Sydney Boys High School in Crows Nest. Then, as it is today, NSBHS was one of New South Wales' selective high schools, catering for the best and brightest students in the government school system. Paul passed the entrance exam and followed elder brother Geoff, who was a year ahead of him, in through the school's portals. North Sydney Boys High's creed was 'Vincit qui se vincit', meaning, 'He conquers who conquers himself'. It was an uncanny prediction of Paul Brickhill's future struggles in life.

Decades after leaving school, Brickhill would remark that it took him fifteen years to get over his education.[30] He didn't enjoy high school, or embrace it. His brothers did much better, Geoff becoming a school prefect and captain of the seconds cricket team, while younger brother Lloyd would pass his Intermediate Certificate exam at the same school with much better marks than Paul.

Not even English literature interested the future bestselling author. In his last year at North Sydney Boys High, Paul punched himself in the nose to make it bleed, just to get out of an English Lit class.[31] Ironically, it wasn't Paul who penned articles for *The Falcon*, the school magazine, it was Geoff. Paul lived for extracurricular activities, keeping up competitive swimming and diving and joining the Boy Scouts' 2nd Greenwich Patrol. He suggested to Peter Finch that he also join the Patrol, and, to Finch's amazement, Aunt Kate allowed him to sign up.

Young Finch was able to convince their patrol leader, Charles Butler, to put on a series of dramatic shows as fundraisers, and this was where Paul saw Peter's acting abilities on show for the first time. Peter wrote, directed and starred in these productions, staged at Chatswood Town Hall. In one play, *The Tragedy of the Romanoffs*, Peter played Tsar Nicholas of Russia, wearing his school army cadet uniform for the role. To add to the effect, Paul loaned him a recently won swimming medal, which Finch wore around his neck.

Peter cast Paul in the play, blessedly, as far as Paul was concerned, in a non-speaking role. As the Tsar's butler, Paul shuffled back and forth in the background as Peter embarked on a long discourse with another child actor. Paul would later judge the script a little over the heads of their audience. But two hundred people a night enjoyed Peter's performances, and the Patrol's new hall was built substantially from the proceeds from Peter Finch productions.[32]

As would become obvious in later life, Paul possessed an addictive personality. It showed itself early; he described himself as 'obsessional' in his younger years.[33] After a visit to Palm Beach on Sydney's Northern Beaches, he became obsessed with one day owning a grand home there where Sydney's doctors, lawyers and business elite spent their weekends. He loved fast cars, too. Sleek racing cars thrilled him, but he especially loved big, powerful British makes, and prestigious Jaguars and Bentleys above all.

While still at school, he fell in love with flying as well. His interest would be driven by the exploits of pioneer Australian aviators Sir Charles Kingsford Smith, Charles Ulm and Harold Gatty which filled the newspapers in the 1930s. Gatty, less well known than the others today, made the first around-the-world flight with American Wiley Post in 1931. Called the prince of navigators by Charles Lindbergh, then the most famous aviator on the planet, Gatty had been born in Tasmania, at Campbell Town, forty-five minutes south of Launceston, birthplace of Brickhill's parents. Both Kingsford Smith and Ulm perished separately while flying in the Pacific in the 1930s, but Gatty would live on to become an airline pioneer. Little did young Paul Brickhill know that he would one day number Gatty among his friends, and work with Charles Ulm's son.

Paul and Peter Finch became inseparable. On one occasion, they decided to adventurously paddle a leaky canoe from Mosman's Bradleys Head across Sydney Harbour to the eastern suburbs. When they were well away from land the canoe sank beneath them, and the pair had to be rescued by a passing boat. Probably as a result of this near drowning, Paul found himself banned from Peter's company.

'I'm not allowed to see you anymore,' Peter glumly advised when Paul came knocking at his door.

Paul, stunned, wanted to know why.

'You're a very bad influence on me,' Peter replied.[34]

Both must have burst out laughing at this. Neither of them took any notice of Aunt Kate's decree. They simply met up away from Peter's house. The firm friendship continued unabated.

4.

Wiped Out

IN 1931, BOTH Paul and Peter left high school. Paul passed the Intermediate Certificate examination with Bs in all his subjects. Peter didn't even bother sitting the exam. He was initially sent to work at a bank, but when this didn't work out a kindly Greenwich Point neighbour came to the rescue.

Norman Johnson was news editor with the Sydney *Sun*, an afternoon tabloid and member of the Associated Newspapers stable like the *Evening News*, where Paul's father worked. Johnson, who lived near the Finches, was a thirty-nine-year-old theatre and opera lover. Seeing something special in theatrical young Finch, Johnson offered him a place at the *Sun*, then Sydney's biggest-selling newspaper. Peter started deep in the print room as a 'printer's devil', a dirty manual job, before moving upstairs to become a copyboy, the first step on the ladder to becoming a journalist. At least as a copyboy he had a window to look out when he daydreamed about an acting career.

Meanwhile, for the Brickhills, 1931 was a bitter year. On 21 March, the owner of the *Evening News*, Sir Hugh Denison, closed the paper down, and George Brickhill lost his job. The Great Depression was biting, and newspaper circulations had plummeted. Through mergers and acquisitions, by the start of 1931 Denison had owned two morning newspapers, two afternoon papers and four Sunday papers in Sydney. By the end of the year, he had reduced this to one of each, leaving the city awash with unemployed newspapermen. More grief beset the Brickhills shortly after. In June, after a long illness, Grandma Bradshaw died under their roof.

George had been determined that his sons receive the education he had not. Eldest boy Russell graduated from the University of Sydney with a degree in civil engineering. Working with the Main Roads Board, Russell studied part-time, gaining further qualifications including an economics degree. With their father now unemployed, Paul, seen as the least academic of the Brickhill boys, was despatched to join Russell in the workforce while Geoff completed high school and Lloyd and Clive also continued their studies. By way of compensation, Paul's father arranged for him to attend night classes at the University of Sydney in 1932.

Paul's working career began rockily as he went through several jobs in short order. The stutter was his undoing. His first job was at an accountancy firm. Paul was doing fine until the boss heard him stumbling over his words. Paul was sacked. The same thing happened in his next job, at an advertising agency. When the boss heard him stammer, he terminated the fifteen-year-old's employ.

The Sydney Harbour Bridge opened in March 1932, with much fanfare and a little controversy as a political activist rode up and cut the opening ribbon with his sword. Several weeks later, the unemployed Paul was wandering around the harbour's northern edge when he noticed that the Adelaide Steamship Company was reconditioning an old ship moored nearby. Reasoning that, if the company had money for that, they could afford to employ a new office boy, he boldly fronted up at the company's downtown offices in Bridge Street and offered his services. Impressed by his initiative, the office manager took him on. Paul started work in May.

Two weeks later, Edward Wareham, head of the company's Sydney branch, arrived back in the office after taking his wife and daughter on a month's holiday to his native Queensland. And when he heard the stuttering voice of this young man who had been hired in his absence, the boss was furious. Wareham, a stern-faced man with a walrus moustache, had been with the company thirty-eight years. A lawyer, justice of the peace and president of the Interstate Steamship Owners Association, he was well-to-do, living in a mansion called the Ritz at Cremorne. He was also a perfectionist, and couldn't abide young Paul's affliction.

Wareham was about to dispense with the stuttering teenager's services when other staff members ganged up in Brickhill's support. Relenting, the boss gave Paul a new job – lift boy, riding the lift up and down the floors of the company's offices, pressing buttons. Young Paul was happy to be contributing to the family coffers, but unhappy about his boring dead-end job. Peter Finch, full of sympathy for his mate, and having only recently been promoted to the copyboy ranks at the *Sun*, took up Paul's case with his own champion, Norman Johnson, hounding him to also take on Paul as a copyboy.

Even though Johnson, a native of Port Pirie, knew George Brickhill well, he refused Finch's requests at first. But Finch kept on at Johnson until he agreed to see his friend. As a result, Paul was summoned for an interview at the *Sun*'s grand offices in Elizabeth Street. Built just three years before in the Skyscraper Gothic style, this tall, impressive building would have been at home in Manhattan. Undaunted by the surroundings, Paul impressed Johnson, despite his stutter, and was offered a position as a copyboy. Paul was able to return to the Adelaide Steamship Company and politely tell Mr Wareham to stick his lift boy's job up his funnel. That winter of 1932, Paul Brickhill joined the staff of the *Sun*, becoming, via the agency of Peter Finch, the only one of George Brickhill's five sons to follow their father's and grandfather's footsteps into journalism.

'If it hadn't been for Peter making Johnson hire me,' Brickhill would later say, 'I would never have become a newspaperman or a writer. I owe Peter a lot.'[35]

So, now Paul and Peter crossed the harbour together by ferry each day on their way to work at the *Sun*. In modern day terminology, copyboys were 'gophers', at the beck and call of senior journalists, carrying freshly typed copy to and from subeditors and editors, and doing any errand required. In the process, they learned the journalistic ropes, and how a big city newspaper ticked. Paul embraced it. Peter was not so enamoured with his job. 'I was an indolent lead-swinger of a copyboy,' Finch would say years later, 'cheeky and untidy.'[36]

As they steamed from Greenwich Point to Circular Quay and back, Paul and Peter would share their dreams for the future. Peter had no plans to become a newspaper hack in the long term. And neither did Paul; his ambition was to be a pilot. Peter was single-minded in his ambition to go into acting. But the Depression had closed down Sydney's professional theatre companies, and local film companies had suspended production while they waited to see what impact the new-fangled overseas talking pictures had on the film business. Peter was convinced that talking pictures weren't going to last, while Paul felt they were the future. Peter's only outlets for his acting ambitions were then the amateur theatre groups and social clubs which ran theatrical productions on Sunday nights.

On the ferry one morning, Peter and Paul, daydreaming as usual, shared a fantasy. Peter unexpectedly received a cable from a theatre company in London's West End. There was an emergency. The actor playing the lead role in a play about to open had been struck down. Only one person in the world was capable of taking his place – Peter Finch! But, wait. How would Peter get to London?

'I'll fly you there in my plane!' Paul chimed in.[37]

Brickhill's parents were progressively wiped out by the Depression. By the end of 1932, George could no longer afford to pay for Paul's university night classes. Paul quit after just a year. He didn't mind. He was fed up with university, finding it dour. By 1933, George Brickhill's worsening financial situation had him seeking a cheaper place for his family to live. He was still calling himself a journalist when the census-taker for 1933 called, but no man in his position with any pride would volunteer to be listed as 'unemployed'. The Brickhills' new residence was not far from Mitchell Street. At 30 George Street, it was rented from Mrs Josephine Harrison.

At the *Sun,* Paul was impressing his superiors with his conscientiousness. Within a year of starting as a copyboy, he was made a cadet journalist. His first assignment, compiling the shipping list, was wearisome, but he knew that if he applied himself he would be moved on to more interesting work. Quickly mastering touch-typing and shorthand, he found he could remember large slabs of detail without having to write everything down. As his abilities were appreciated and rewarded, his confidence grew, and his stutter faded, only to reappear at times of emotional stress.

Peter Finch, meanwhile, still a copyboy, was frequently in trouble with his superiors. He fell asleep on the job at the annual wool sales. On a visit to the Supreme Court with court reporter George 'Doggie' Marks, he was called to the bench by Justice Frank Boyce. Finch had kept his cigarette burning in court, hiding it under his hat. And the judge had spied the trail of smoke emanating from beneath the hat.

'In future,' growled Justice Boyce, glaring down at Finch, 'when you gentlemen of the press come to court, would you mind putting your hats out!'[38]

Finch did manage to impress his workmates with an ability to mimic anyone and everyone with great skill and wit. One Friday afternoon, chairman of the board Sir Hugh Denison walked in on sixteen-year-old Finch standing on a table and doing an impression of him, to the great amusement of gathered colleagues. Peter had even borrowed Denison's own hat and cane for the performance.

'Boy, do you work here?' boomed Denison.

'Yes, sir,' Finch replied.

'Well, you don't anymore!'[39]

Norman Johnson managed to get Peter his job back, but the young man's days at the *Sun* were numbered. Peter was repeatedly running away from Aunt Kate's house and sleeping rough at sleazy Kings Cross, which he adored. The Finches would bring him back, but when he ran away yet again in 1933 and refused to return, Norman Johnson gave him an ultimatum – return home, or lose his job at the paper.

'Sack me!' Peter challenged, calling the editor's bluff.

When Johnson declared that young Finch was making things very difficult for him, Peter decided to make it easier. Taking up a full water pitcher, Peter emptied the contents over the benevolent Johnson's head. On his way out the paper's door, Peter stopped to tell Paul Brickhill what he'd done.

'That took guts!' Paul declared, impressed by his friend's bravado. 'Now what are you going to do?'

'I'm going to the Cross!' Peter happily announced, before marching out of the newspaper for good.[40]

After that, Paul would regularly catch up with Peter at the Arabian House coffee lounge in Kings Cross, a popular meeting place for members of Sydney's arts scene. Peter was sleeping wherever anyone would give him the space to lie down. Over coffee paid for by Paul, Peter said that an amusing 'older man' of twenty-five had invited him to move in with him.

Two weeks later, back at the Arabian House, Peter confessed that the arrangement with the twenty-five-year-old wasn't working, and he was moving out. He'd found a room to rent in Woolloomooloo for five shillings a week. The only problem was that he didn't have five shillings. Generous to a fault, Paul offered to help. For several months, Paul would pay Peter's rent from his weekly pay packet of twenty shillings. There is no indication that Finch ever repaid him. Paul didn't seem to mind. But the pair would grow apart over the coming years. Finch's arty friends like gay artist Donald Friend, with whom Finch would live for some time, were not young Brickhill's kind of people.

As Peter embarked on a career as a sometime actor and full-time scrounger, Paul's career at the *Sun* went ahead in leaps and bounds. He regularly won two-shilling prizes for the best stories in competitions the *Sun* ran for young members of staff. Over the next few years he graduated to fully fledged reporter on the crime beat, doing the coroner's court and police rounds, then the starting point for all journalistic careers on big city papers. It didn't go unnoticed at home or in the office that he'd achieved promotion much more quickly than his peers.

Hearing of a bank robbery on one occasion, Paul rushed to the scene to find he'd even beaten the police to the bank. This allowed him to interview the teller involved without interference. But Brickhill felt there was more to the story. So, to capture what he called 'the living moment', he interviewed every witness he could find, building a bigger picture of the event. His report went down well with the paper, and this encouraged him to take the same detailed approach to future reports.[41]

He came unstuck when his quest for detail and drama led him to miss a deadline. At the scene of a safe-blowing at Botany, he found everything very routine, with no witnesses and little to write about. Walking around the corner, he located several people who lived above a shop and had received a rude awakening when the safe was blown. They had subsequently seen the safe-blowers making their escape. These witnesses were afraid to talk at first, but the affable young reporter with a ready smile eventually got them to open up. Feeling pleased with himself, Brickhill sought the nearest public telephone armed with his dramatic story.

'I telephoned it through to the office,' he would recall several decades later, 'and got my pants kicked off for having missed the first edition with the colourless report that the safe had been blown.'[42] The *Sun*'s competitors ran reports of the safe-blowing in their first edition, beating Brickhill's paper to the punch. No editor likes missing a news story, no matter how bland the copy might be. The person kicking Brickhill's pants was news editor Norman Johnson, Peter Finch's one-time mentor, who remained at the *Sun* until 1938, when he left to become secretary to the board of the David Jones department stores.

Here was a salutary lesson for Brickhill on how to think like a newspaperman – get the story in, and worry about the colour later. The problem was, this wasn't an approach Brickhill the writer appreciated. 'That was really the first division between newspapers and me,' he was to say. 'I liked to take my time with a story, uncover the drama in it, bring the drama out.' He delivered on time in future, but that didn't stop him looking for the inherent drama in a news event, or, as he put it, 'the guts of a story'.[43]

Paul was still living at home with his parents and brothers, when, in 1936, the Brickhills moved house yet again, this time renting at 2 Greendale Street, still in Greenwich Point, from the estate of Esther Quaife. In 1937, Paul's elder brother Russell, who was a member of the Australian Militia, the country's part-time army, encouraged him to join the Militia. Paul joined the 7th Brigade's field artillery, and his after-hours military training provided good background for feature articles he was soon writing as a military reporter for the *Sun*. By 1938, the family moved house again, this time to 132 Greenwich Road, a property rented from Mrs Louisa Martin. The move coincided with the departure of Russell Brickhill in late 1938 to work in England as an engineer.

Mary Callanan featured in Brickhill's life during these pre-war years. She may not have been his first girlfriend, but he would later rate her as the love of his life. Little did young Brickhill know that the Callanans, Irish Catholics, would never permit him to marry their precious daughter. But, for the sake of harmony, the Callanans always made young Paul welcome. By 1939, it had become clear to Paul that there was no future in pursuing the relationship, and, broken-hearted, he began looking elsewhere for love.

Come late 1939, with World War Two several months old, Paul had been one of the Sydney *Sun*'s two military reporters for over a year. The other was Lionel 'Bill' Hudson, under whom Brickhill had trained. Paul even carried a military pass complete with his photograph, giving him access to military offices and bases. At this time he was leading an active social life as a member of his swimming club, of a squash club and a golf club – all of which, as it happened, involved primarily individual sports rather than team sports. Into his busy life came a new female individual who took his fancy.

Del Fox was a slim, long-faced brunette with the good humour of her Irish forebears. A secretary with a Sydney company, Del came from a good Bellevue Hill family in the posh eastern suburbs. Through his swimming connections, Brickhill secured two tickets to the annual Speedo Ball, and resplendent in dinner suit and bowtie he escorted an equally spruced-up Del to the ball. Brickhill paid for several photographs to be taken of the couple on the night, and sent copies to Del a few weeks later, apologising for the delay and blaming what he called his 'congenital procrastination'. He thought one picture of her an absolute 'clinker', saying she looked 'very willowy and graceful'. Brickhill was still living at home with his parents, and before he sent the photos to Del he showed them to his mother. 'Mother is quite impressed,' he told Del.[44]

The main topic of conversation at the ball had of course been the war in Europe. In the letter to Del that accompanied the photographs, Brickhill made it clear he had no interest in fighting the Hun for king and country, unlike many young men he knew. 'Chaps seem to lose their minds and think there is honour and glory in it still. They can have it on their own. I have no intention of going 12,000-odd miles to stick a bayonet in the insides of a man to whom I have never even been formally introduced – or more to the point, have a total stranger stick a bayonet into my insides. The only way to get me into uniform is for the defence of Australia – which is an unlikely necessity.' The war was, he declared, 'a damn silly show'.[45]

*

On 3 January 1940, Paul's paternal grandmother, Rebecca Brickhill, passed away in her Launceston home. She was ninety-six. By this time Brickhill's father and mother had relocated to Newcastle, where George was working with the *Newcastle Sun*. On their departure, Paul moved into a flat in another 'Elsmere', in Lawrence Street, Manly, still in sight of Sydney Harbour.

This same year, Sir Henry Gullett, Federal Minister for Information and a former journalist of note, created the Department of Information, intended to be the agency which controlled war information reaching the Australian public. To run the department, Gullett recruited George Brickhill's former colleague, Sir Keith Murdoch, and put together a list of top journalists to work under Murdoch. One of the pressmen chosen by Gullett was Lionel Wigmore, a former *Sun* journalist and aviation writer who would become one of the department's senior men. *Sun* prodigy Paul Brickhill was the youngest of the journalists on Gullett's list.

The *Sun* refused to release Brickhill, valuing his skill and potential too much. Bill Hudson, his colleague at the *Sun*, rated him 'an exceptional journalist'.[46] To placate the disappointed young man, his superiors promoted him to subeditor with the *Sunday Sun*. His place as a military reporter with the *Sun* was taken by another young journalist of promise, who, like Brickhill, had come through the ranks from copyboy. This was John Ulm, son of Charles Ulm, the famous pre-war aviator. Like Brickhill, young Ulm had a passion for flying, in his case with a very obvious motivation. In a series of coincidences, Ulm would continue to follow in Brickhill's footsteps over the next few years.

Despite the additional pay, the subeditor's job locked Brickhill in the office and kept him away from the sources of the news. To the peripatetic Brickhill, who enjoyed being out and about, this was a restriction he didn't enjoy. The Department of Information, meanwhile, was going through a rocky beginning. First, Gullett was killed in a plane crash in August 1940. By year's end, Murdoch would resign his director's post after federal cabinet refused to give him the censorial powers over the media he'd demanded.

As the Nazis overran western Europe and the Battle of Britain began in British skies, Paul's younger brother Lloyd surprised everyone by joining the Royal Australian Air Force in Brisbane. He would train to become a pilot, and be commissioned an officer. This may have spurred Paul's decision, in June, to resign from the Militia and join the RAAF Reserve. At least that way, if he was to put hours into military training, he would be learning about flying, his real love. Brickhill's parents returned to Sydney from Newcastle at year's end, with George now Sydney correspondent for the *Newcastle Sun*. For the time being, George and Dot moved in with Paul at his Manly flat.

With Britain pounded by the Luftwaffe's aerial 'Blitz' and German U-boats taking a heavy toll on shipping in the North Atlantic, in Asia the invading Japanese Army was fighting nationalist and communist armies in China. At that time there was no hint of 1941's dramatic Japanese drive into South Asia and the Pacific. There appeared no threat to Australia, whose national focus was on the war in Europe, a war in which Paul Brickhill had expressed no interest in participating.

5.

Flying Officer Brickhill

ON MONDAY, 6 January 1941, twenty-four-year-old Paul Chester Jerome Brickhill fronted up at the RAAF's Number 2 Recruiting Centre at Sydney's Point Piper. The shambolic withdrawal of the British Expeditionary Force from France at Dunkirk in May and June of the previous year had profoundly shocked young Brickhill. He was to say that news of this reverse brought home to him that the war was a serious business; a war that was not going to be over by Christmas as some suggested.[47] When Christmas did arrive, a Nazi invasion of Britain seemed on the cards, although Brickhill's primary interest was still the defence of Australia. Bored stiff in his subeditor's job, he saw no future for himself in the newspaper game. He also probably envied younger brother Lloyd's tales of training to be a pilot. Patriotism, boredom and pilot envy combined to send him to Point Piper that Monday morning following the Christmas holidays.

In signing up, he was going against his pacifist parents' wishes. George hadn't served during the First World War, and had no desire to see his sons serve in this one either. It was bad enough that his eldest boy, Russell, had ended up on active service for Britain via his membership of the Royal Navy Volunteer Reserve in England, and then Lloyd had joined the RAAF. So, when Paul was required to write down his next of kin, he named his favourite uncle, Fred Amos.

Brickhill was interested in flying, not fighting, and it seemed a pretty good deal if the RAAF would teach him to fly, and pay him to do it. To bolster his application, Paul included his three years' service in the Australian Militia. Recording his employment with the *Sunday Sun*, he wrote that he'd spent two years as defence and aviation writer with the *Sun*. In case the Department of Information heard that he was free of the grasp of the *Sun* and again tried to snaffle him, he failed to mention the department's earlier interest in his services.

With the paperwork out of the way, Brickhill was given a medical by an Air Force doctor, a flight lieutenant who passed him as fit for service and noted his vital statistics. Stripped down, the recruit was five feet six inches (167 centimetres) tall, weighed 148 pounds (66.6 kilograms), and his chest measured 33½ inches (84 centimetres). The doctor also recorded an appendectomy scar, small scars on his arms and a scar on his right leg. Brickhill was now accepted for service in the RAAF. That same day, he happily signed his life away, enlisting for the requisite period – the duration of the war plus a further twelve months following war's cessation.

With the rank of aircraftsman second class, lowest of the low in the Air Force, Brickhill went through two months' basic recruit training at Number 2 Initial Training School at Lindfield, with much marching and early morning rises. Because of his six months in the Air Force Reserve and three years in the Militia, he had a head start on many other recruits. Next, he was sent for flight training, which began on 6 March at Number 8 Elementary Flying Training School at Narrandera in southern New South Wales. He arrived with an induction of trainees which included sporting celebrity Stanley Sismey, wicketkeeper with the New South Wales state cricket team. Narrandera's local paper noted the arrival of Sismey at No. 8 EFTS, along with 'Paul Brickhill, late of the Sydney *Sun*'s editorial staff'.[48]

Initial RAAF pilot training was in the De Havilland DH 82 Tiger Moth. First introduced as a basic trainer in 1932, this slow, forgiving biplane had open tandem cockpits for trainee and instructor. Many who flew the Tiger Moth would fall in love with the graceful old bird, and Brickhill was one of them. He was not as fond of his time in the classroom. After spending fifty-four hours in Tiger Moths over twenty-four days, Brickhill completed basic flight training at Narrandera on 30 April with 'excellent passes', achieving promotion to Leading Aircraftsman, the equivalent of a corporal in the army.[49]

On 5 May, he arrived back in Sydney, marching into the RAAF's Number 2 Embarkation Depot in Bradfield Park on Milsons Point. Sitting beside the Sydney Harbour Bridge's northern pylon, the depot had a grandstand view of the harbour and of the city centre across the water. Australia's flying schools could not keep up with the demand for aircrew, and since 1940 a percentage of Australian trainees had been sent to Canada to complete their training under the Empire

Flying Training Scheme (EFTS), after which they would be allocated to squadrons in Britain.

Fate decided that Paul Brickhill would be among those sent to Canada. That decision would set the course for the remainder of his life. It would mean he would end up fighting the Nazis in the Northern Hemisphere, not defending his homeland in the Pacific as he had originally intended. But now that he was in the military he had no say in the matter. No leave was granted the cadets. Fifteen days after arriving at No. 2 ED, Brickhill and other trainees sailed from Sydney aboard a troopship bound for Vancouver, to undertake the next stage of their training. In Brickhill's case it would be a ten-week advanced flying course provided by the Royal Canadian Air Force as part of the EFTS. The day he sailed, Brickhill was made a temporary sergeant.

Disembarking in Vancouver on 13 June, the trainees spread out to training schools across Canada. Brickhill was in a group that travelled by train to the Canadian capital, Ottawa, then on to the nearby Royal Canadian Air Force base at Uplands, Ontario, home to Number 2 Service Flying Training School. With paved runways, massive rectangular brick hangars and administration buildings, and more than one hundred aircraft, Uplands was a major training establishment. Ever since the EFTS had commenced the previous year, several staggered courses were run at any one time at Uplands. Brickhill and his Australian contingent joined Course 31, which commenced on 17 June.

The aircraft used by trainees here was the North American Harvard II. In Australia, it was built under licence as the Wirraway. A two-seat monoplane with an enclosed cockpit, the Harvard had a top speed of 318 kph and the characteristics of a fighter plane. Brickhill would spend eighty-six hours in canary-yellow Harvards, initially with an instructor, later flying solo. In addition to spending time in the air, the budding pilots had to put in long, hot hours in lectures, taking copious notes on everything from the theory of flight to cloud formations. In the main, their instructors were Canadians and Americans. Warned that Ontario's summer was baking hot, the Aussies came equipped with shorts and slouch hats.

Brickhill lived for the hours in the air, and when he was supposed to be studying the theory of meteorology he had his head in the clouds, daydreaming about flying. The night before the meteorology test he 'crammed', reading the textbook from cover to cover. As he'd demonstrated while working for the *Sun*, he had a fine memory for detail, and he passed the test next day with flying colours. Then, midway through Course 31, a surprise written test was sprung on cadets about the reflector gunsight. Brickhill hadn't been paying attention when the armaments instructor explained the details, and all he knew was that the gunsight worked with mirrors. Paul would later say that he decided to apply the BBB principle – bullshit baffles brains. He wrote a turgid paper, full of pseudo-scientific jargon. 'I just hoped I'd get away with it,' he said.[50]

Two days passed. Into another lecture strode the armaments instructor. Interrupting proceedings, he announced that he had the results of the reflector gunsight test, before looking around the classroom.

'Brickhill, where are you?' he demanded. 'Stand up, Brickhill.'

Fearing that he was in for a rollicking, Brickhill slowly came to his feet. The instructor asked him if he'd ever been a writer, and Paul confessed to having been a journalist before enlisting.

'Well, you might like to know that your paper on the reflector gunsight has been forwarded to Air Force headquarters – with a recommendation that it becomes the standard training manual.'

Brickhill would feel guilty for years over this. But at least he passed the test.[51]

There were numerous distractions for the Uplands trainees. Occasional leave passes saw the Australians flood into Ottawa, looking for local bars and local girls. Back at base, there was great excitement when King George VI's younger brother, Prince George the Duke of Kent, paid a visit in July. Two Australians on Course 31, Rex Marre and Bill Williams, found themselves chatting with the duke. Within several years, all three would be dead, the Australians killed in action and the duke killed in Scotland when the Sunderland flying boat he was aboard mysteriously crashed on a secret 1942 mission to Iceland.

There was even greater excitement when Hollywood came to Uplands. Warner Brothers were filming a movie, *Captains of the Clouds*, at several RCAF bases. Starring Jimmy Cagney, the film was being produced by his brother George. At this stage America was still neutral, but, by the time *Captains of the Clouds* was released in 1942, the United States would be at war with Japan and Germany. While Australians on Course 32 would be roped in as extras for several scenes, Course 31 members saw the activity from the sidelines when eighty members of the film crew descended on Uplands.

Learning to fly a military aircraft was a dangerous business. Several trainees and instructors had been killed during previous courses, and on 15 August, just two weeks before Brickhill's training ended, Course 31 was marred when cadet pilot Harry Long from Balgowlah in Sydney's northern suburbs ploughed his Harvard into the ground on a solo flight, and was killed.

By 31 August, Course 31 was over, and the chief examiner's results were posted. Paul Brickhill, who had dreamed of being a flyer since childhood, turned out to be a born pilot. He was dux of the class, passing Course 31 with special distinctions. He learned that he was to be posted to Britain for advanced fighter training, on attachment to the RAF. Some of the course's less talented pilots would be sent to train in bombers or transport aircraft, which would make them, in the eyes of fighter pilots, little more than bus drivers. But Brickhill was destined to learn to fly the famous Spitfire fighter, the sports car of the sky; a sports car designed to kill.

That evening, the thirty-nine Course 31 graduates went into Ottawa for a celebratory dinner at Chateau Laurier. Standing next to Parliament House, this massive limestone hotel with turrets and masonry mimicking a French chateau was a centre of Ottawa social life. Brickhill, even though he had topped the class, shied away from the limelight, and from public speaking. He'd gone a long way towards mastering his stutter, but it would re-emerge when he was nervous. So it was that another Aussie graduate, Flight Sergeant Harry Dimmock, gave the speech on behalf of the students of Course 31 that night, and proposed a toast to their hosts, the RCAF.

The next afternoon, 1 September, the graduates, in dress uniform, fell in for their Wings Parade. A large crowd of instructors, trainees and civilians from Ottawa, including attractive young ladies who'd formed friendships with some of the Australians, gathered to watch as the graduates lined up in front of the RCAF's Wing Commander Joseph de Niverville, Officer Commanding, Uplands Training School. A French-Canadian from Montreal and a World War One flyer, De Niverville would present each man with the treasured golden wings emblem that he would wear with pride to show he was a qualified Air Force pilot.

'You have set yourselves two objectives,' De Niverville told Brickhill and his colleagues. 'The first is to qualify as pilots. The second is to do your part in the greatest struggle the world has ever seen. You have obtained the first of these objectives. These wings will be the symbol that you have done so.'[52]

Brickhill was first to be called forward to receive his wings. With an exchange of crisp salutes, the presentation was made. Once all graduates had their wings, Brickhill led the parade in a march-past, with Wing Commander De Niverville taking the salute. And then it was all over. The cadets were officially pilots. That same day, Brickhill received a commission from the RAAF as a pilot officer, equivalent of a second lieutenant in the army.

Friends crowded around to congratulate the graduates, and reporters from the *Ottawa Citizen* and the *Ottawa Journal* threw questions at them. The reporters were particularly intrigued to find two young Tasmanian flight sergeants among the graduates, William Waddell from Hobart and Fred Wilmot from Launceston. The Tasmanians were frequently the butt of jokes from their mainland colleagues, who told the reporters that Tasmania was 'the pimple on the pumpkin' as far as Australians were concerned. Kidded by the Australians into believing that Tasmania was a separate country Down Under, the journalists singled the Tasmanians out. Brickhill was in the bunch of mainlanders who clustered around the Tasmanians as they were interviewed.

'We're proud to represent the pimple,' said a grinning Wilmot to the press. 'But we could do with a few more from the island. We need 'em among all these Aussies.'

This brought laughter from the bunch, and slaps on the back for Wilmot and Waddell.

'Don't worry, they'll be in there before this show's over, old chaps,' a mature mainlander assured them.[53]

Brickhill joined in the fun, but self-consciously failed to volunteer that his parents and grandparents were Tasmanians. His Tasmanian connections were not overlooked on the pimple, however. The Launceston *Examiner*, reporting the 1 September graduation at Uplands, would note that top-of-the-class Paul Brickhill was 'a nephew of Miss D Brickhill of Launceston' and 'a descendant of two generations of newspapermen'.[54]

The fledgling pilots now left their Uplands nest and travelled east to the port of Halifax, Nova Scotia, where a convoy was assembling to cross the North Atlantic to England. The Australian pilots spent five days at an RCAF depot in Halifax, and what a dry city it turned out to be. Nowhere could the Aussies find an open bar. In desperation, on 8 September, Brickhill and several mates scoured the city looking for a cooling glass of the amber liquid. By late afternoon, unsuccessful, they decided to settle for a cup of tea, and trooped disconsolately into a cafe crowded with noisy military personnel.

After they'd sat down, Brickhill noticed a Royal Navy lieutenant at another table, two metres away, who eyed him with a quizzical expression. It occurred to Brickhill that the fellow looked a bit like big brother Russell, who he hadn't seen in three years. When he first landed in Canada, Brickhill had written to Russ in Bermuda, where he'd been stationed with the Royal Navy since 1939. Receiving no reply, he'd subsequently heard from home that Russ had probably left Bermuda in July, England-bound. Deciding that this fellow opposite was a bit too plump to be his brother, Brickhill looked away. But something made him look back. His eyes dropped to the lieutenant's hands. Russ, in his youth, had lost half a thumb in an accident with a chaffcutter. Sure enough, this lieutenant was minus half a thumb. Lifting his eyes, Brickhill saw a smile spreading across the naval officer's face.

'Gosh!' Brickhill exclaimed. 'It *is* Russ!'[55]

As if spring-loaded, both came to their feet. Taking a step forward, they firmly shook hands, grinning like idiots. After the initial shock of their reunion subsided they became locked in a conversation which, in Brickhill's words, 'bubbled with explosive pops of surprise like porridge on the boil'.[56] It turned out that Russ' departure from Bermuda had been delayed, and he was only now going on to England to a new posting at the vast Royal Navy base at Scapa Flow in Scotland. The auxiliary merchant cruiser he was allocated to was sitting in Halifax's harbour, and would sail in the same convoy that his little brother was joining.

Russ was a private and conservative individual, yet in comfortable company he could be quite sociable, giving rein to a wicked sense of humour. Meanwhile, the little brother he found here in Halifax had changed from the youth he had known back in Sydney. Not so shy as in his younger days but still loath to stand out, Paul smoked heavily, enjoyed a beer and had a cheeky self-deprecating sense of humour. Yet, despite being surrounded by hard-swearing fellow Aussie servicemen, the strongest curse words Paul would ever use would be the occasional 'Christ', 'damn' or 'bloody'. And here, for the first time, their similar rank and situations made the brothers equals, despite their age difference. After chattering away all evening, catching up on what each had been doing, laughing and reminiscing, the pair agreed to meet up again next day.

But just as fate had thrown the brothers together, it rudely drew them apart again. The next morning, Brickhill and his Air Force comrades were awoken before dawn. An hour later, they were embarking on a small troopship lying in Halifax harbour. The convoy sailed for Liverpool later that day, with the warship carrying Russ located in the same column as Brickhill's troopship. Now, both brothers would get a taste of the war that had seemed so unreal from Australia's distant shores.

6.

Spitfire Pilot

The brothers Brickhill survived the North Atlantic crossing and went their separate ways. As Russ went north to Scarpa Flow, Paul headed south to Bournemouth in Hampshire on England's south coast. Paul's destination was the RAF's Number 3 Personnel Dispatch and Reception Centre (3PDRC), where he would await posting to a fighter training school. Quarters for newly minted airmen flooding in from around the Dominions were in Bournemouth's many seaside hotels, and after early-morning parade and rollcall Brickhill was free to do whatever he pleased.

During this period he found his way to Torquay in Devon; 3PDRC had an annexe there. In Torquay he made a new friend, Matron F. M. Rimmer, who ran the Cripples Home and Industrial School for Girls, which had been transferred from London in 1940 to avoid German bombing. Matron Rimmer was a single motherly older woman.

In the second week of October, Brickhill received a posting to the RAF's 53 Operational Training Unit, located at Llandow in the Vale of Glamorgan, twenty-four kilometres west of Cardiff in South Wales. There, in grim wintry temperatures and soaking Welsh rain, Brickhill joined a select band of Britons and men from the Dominions on Course Number 10, learning to master the legendary Supermarine Spitfire. But first, he had to go up in a Miles Master trainer to prove to his instructors, mostly 1940–41 Battle of Britain veterans who were often younger than Brickhill, that he could fly like an eagle.

With a few flights in the Miles under their belts, trainees progressed to the star of the show, the Spit. The aircraft they trained in were Mark I Spitfires, 'clapped out' superseded models that had flown during the Battle of Britain, slower and less well armed than the Mark Vb currently in operational use. But that didn't matter to Brickhill and his colleagues. Flying a Spitfire of any type was a joy. The first thing Brickhill had to become accustomed to was the claustrophobic smallness of the Spitfire's cockpit. Once the hood was closed, it was like sitting in a coffin. Johnnie Johnson, who would end the war as the RAF's top-scoring fighter ace, was so uncomfortable in the cockpit the first few times he flew a Spitfire he had to leave the hood open throughout.

In the Spitfire, pilots certainly felt like captains of the clouds. They revelled in the gut-throbbing power of the V-12 Rolls-Royce Merlin engine, with the power of a thousand horses dragging them through the heavens. They savoured the serenity of flying alone in bright sunshine above oppressive grey clouds at 20,000 feet; the responsiveness of the controls; the joyous agility of the 2.5 tonne machine as they threw it about the sky.

Roald Dahl, who later, like Brickhill, became famous as an author, flew RAF Spitfires. At the time that Brickhill was training in Britain, Dahl was flying ops in North Africa. According to Dahl, a good Spitfire pilot 'flew his aircraft not with his hands but with the tips of his fingers, and the Spitfire was not a Spitfire but a part of his own body . . . For the body of the Spitfire was the body of the pilot, and there was no difference between the one and the other.'[57]

Every moment in the cockpit of a Spit was a delight to natural flyers like Brickhill. At the same time, instructors made the rookies, many no more than nineteen years of age, aware of the responsibility being handed to them. The Spitfire cost the equivalent of several suburban houses. Woe betide the pilot who lost a Spit through negligent or irresponsible flying. But, despite his conscientiousness, Pilot Officer Brickhill still possessed an Australian tearaway streak. Soon supremely confident in a Spit, he buzzed a Bournemouth pub at treetop height to impress RAAF colleagues below. His stunt was reported, resulting in Brickhill being hauled before his superiors, charged with 'low and dangerous flying'.[58] He escaped with a reprimand.

Brickhill learned fighter tactics from his instructors. He also learned the RAF lingo. An aircraft was a 'kite', or a 'crate'. 'Gen' was information. 'Recce' was reconnaissance. 'R/T' was radio transmitter. Ground crew were 'erks'. An air battle was a 'scrap'. A successful outcome was a 'good show', an unsuccessful outcome a 'bad show'. Anything really good was 'wizard'. To attack by surprise from above, out of cloud or with the sun behind, was to 'bounce' the opposition. A low-flying attack, or a stunt like Brickhill's at Bournemouth, was a 'beat up'. A flying accident was a 'prang'. A difficult situation, especially in a dogfight, was a 'sticky' one. If someone was killed while flying, they'd 'gone for a burton', or 'bought it', or 'got the chop'. A captured airman was 'in the bag'. To exaggerate, or talk a complete load of bull, was to 'shoot a line', while the perpetrator of such a crime was a 'line-shooter'. This lingo would stay in Brickhill's vocabulary for the rest of his life.

Come January 1942, after spending his first Christmas away from home and putting in forty-two hours in Spitfires, Pilot Officer Brickhill was declared ready to fly in combat. On 16 January, he received a posting to an operational Spitfire squadron, Number 74. Known as Tiger Squadron, it had made a name for itself in the Battle of Britain. Before Brickhill left Llandow, the students and instructors of 53 OTU's Course 10 gathered for a group photograph. For the picture, while the majority of his colleagues stood behind him, Brickhill sat on his rump on the ground in the front row. It was a typical position for Brickhill, repeated throughout his life – to the forefront, yet keeping his head down.

With a week's leave pass, he headed for London to see the sights before joining his unit on 23 January at Long Kesh, Maze, in Northern Ireland – which, decades later, would become infamous as the location of a British prison housing IRA prisoners during 'the Troubles'. While in London, Brickhill went for a fitting for a new uniform at Gieves Ltd in Old Bond Street. Today, as Gieves and Hawkes, the store occupies number one Savile Row.

Going back to 1775, this bespoke and military tailoring firm had made the uniforms of a young Winston Churchill, the Duke of Wellington and Captain, later Admiral, William Bligh – famous for the mutiny on the *Bounty* and less well known as the only British governor in Australia deposed in a military coup. The tunic worn by Admiral Horatio Nelson at the Battle of Trafalgar had been made by Gieves; it was pierced by the French sharpshooter's round that killed him. Brickhill, always a dapper dresser, couldn't resist the temptation to have a uniform made to measure by such famed tailors – damn the cost, in cash and clothing coupons! Made from the finest wool, the tunic of Brickhill's Gieves Ltd uniform would be lined with satin.

On joining 74 Squadron at Long Kesh, Brickhill upgraded to the Mark Vb Spitfire, in which, over the next six weeks, he clocked up another twenty training hours. Much faster than the Mark I he'd trained in, and armed with four machineguns and a formidable 20mm cannon in each wing, the Vb was a significant improvement. Yet, for all its features, the Spitfire then lagged behind the Luftwaffe's Messerschmitt Bf 109F, which was faster. The Spitfire could turn more tightly, but as Johnnie Johnson was to remark, you couldn't turn forever.[59]

To survive in a dogfight, a Spitfire pilot had to find other ways of outflying and outfoxing his German opponents. A keen eye and lightning reflexes were the best attributes for any fighter pilot. But, even though they were ostensibly part of a team, Brickhill reckoned that all successful fighter pilots were individualists. Now an RAF Spitfire pilot, Brickhill could put on the airs and graces that went with his qualifications – the swagger, the unofficial right to wear the top button of his uniform jacket undone and to wear a silk scarf, or, in winter, a rollneck pullover with his uniform.

When late March arrived, Brickhill had yet to fly in combat. By that time, 74 Squadron was busy packing up to go out to the Middle East to join the Desert Air Force in the fight against General Erwin Rommel, the 'Desert Fox', and his Afrika Korps. Before they left Britain, the men of 74 Squadron were granted a week's leave. Brickhill had been in touch with brother Russ in Scotland, who arranged to get leave at the same time so they could meet up. Paul set off from Long Kesh on 31 March, and the pair reunited in London.

It turned out that Russ was quite envious of Paul. Bored with naval station life at icy Scapa Flow, Russ wanted to be where the action was, as he imagined Paul was shortly going to be. Russ told his little brother that after he'd requested a transfer to the army for active duty, and been rejected, he'd applied for a transfer to the RAF. Three times. And on each occasion, he'd been knocked back by the aircrew medical board, because of his thumb. Trying a fourth time, he had been accepted by the Air Force, only for the Royal Navy to counter with an offer to send him home to Australia as a liaison officer with the Australian military. But that wasn't what he wanted at all. He'd rejected that, and was still determined to join Paul in the RAF.

'Good luck,' said the younger Brickhill as they firmly shook hands on parting, and Russell in turn wished him luck in North Africa.[60]

In the middle of 1942, 74 Squadron sailed from England for the Middle East aboard a Mediterranean convoy. Now it was the younger Brickhill's time to be frustrated, as, once he landed in Palestine in July, the prospect of action seemed to slip further and further away. The ship carrying 74 Squadron's cherished Spitfires had been sunk by the Germans as it crossed the Mediterranean.

With no means with which to fight, the squadron was transferred to Tehran, capital of Iran, where, after several weeks, it was given a handful of Hawker Hurricane IIb fighters, and sent to North Africa's Western Desert. Rapidly retraining on the Hurricane, 74's best pilots managed to get in some flying time escorting sea convoys and strafing German-occupied Crete. But there was no opportunity for Brickhill to fly. In August, Tiger Squadron finally received replacement Spitfire Vb and Vc aircraft, but by this time Brickhill had applied for a transfer. While a new home was found for him, he was sent to the RAF's 22 Personnel Transit Centre at Almaza, just outside Cairo.

From Almaza, on 28 August, Brickhill was posted to Number 145 Squadron as a replacement. But Number 145 also had many more pilots than it had planes after a disastrous summer. Out in the desert, Rommel's German and Italian forces were driving the Allies back, and the Desert Air Force, like the British Army, was in retreat. Brickhill had no plane to fly and nothing to do. Another transfer brought a wasted week with 127 Squadron, with no flying, before he was informed he was being sent to join 274 Squadron, to fly Hurricane fighter-bombers.

This was a comedown for a Spitfire jockey, the Hurricane being considered the inferior of the Spitfire by friend and foe alike. The RAF had twice as many Hurricanes as Spitfires, and to the Hurricane fell the majority of the tough fighter assignments of the air war. Proven the inferior of the Me 109, during the Battle of Britain the Hurricane had been assigned the task of going after German bombers, leaving their Spitfire cousins to intercept German fighters and keep them off the 'Hurri's' tails. Now, the demands of the desert war meant that the Hurricane was being thrown into the ground-attack role.

This meant that when Brickhill joined 274 Squadron he had to retrain, firstly learning to fly the Hurricane, and secondly learning the techniques of ground attack with bomb, shell and bullet. He spent twenty hours in Hurricanes as a result, until, by the Second Battle of El Alamein in September 1942, he was flying his first operational sorties, swooping down on German and Italian tanks, vehicles and troops, dropping bombs and strafing with his guns. For the first time he saw the enemy, close up, and killed them.

Rommel's army was in full retreat following Second El Alamein, and 274 Squadron pursued them across Libya and Tripolitania towards Tunisia, jumping from one captured German airstrip and rough landing ground to another. This became known within Allied ranks as the Big Push. Before 274 Squadron left Alexandria for the desert chase, Brickhill received a letter from his big brother. The bad news was that Russ' application for a transfer to the RAF had been turned down by the possessive Royal Navy. The good news was that the navy was posting him to North Africa, to manage harbour clearance operations. And, what was more, he was being sent to Alexandria. Russ arrived before Paul departed

Alexandria, but neither could get leave. Hopes of a reunion in the city were dashed.

Months of desert bombing and strafing operations passed without pause until, in the second week of December, Brickhill was transferred to 244 Wing's Number 92 Squadron, which was equipped with Spitfires. Making a name for itself flying out of Tangmere and Biggin Hill during the Battle of Britain, Number 92 was the most celebrated, top-scoring RAF fighter squadron in North Africa, and its cocky pilots were considered the 'bad boys' of the Desert Air Force. That this posting was a deliberate upgrade for the Australian, and a reward for meritorious flying with 274 Squadron, was confirmed a week later with his promotion to flying officer (first lieutenant), just three days shy of his twenty-sixth birthday. He arrived at 92 Squadron bearing a bottle of Scotch whisky and a cheeky grin. A beer drinker himself, Brickhill had found that a gift of a bottle of Scotch was a sure way to win friends and influence fellow officers at new squadrons.

Among the first 92 Squadron pilots Brickhill met was Flying Officer Neville Duke, one of the squadron's aces – an RAF 'ace' being a fighter pilot who'd shot down five or more enemy aircraft. The USAAF also made five 'kills' the qualification for ace status, but allowed its pilots to include aircraft destroyed on the ground in their tally. The Luftwaffe, meanwhile, only gave its pilots *Experte* or ace recognition with the downing of ten enemy aircraft. Twenty-year-old ace Neville Duke was a tall, skinny-as-a rake native of Tonbridge in Kent. His facial features put some in mind of the male members of the British Royal Family. Duke's favourite word was the well-used RAF superlative 'wizard', and he was particularly keen to welcome Brickhill, and his 'wizard' gift of Scotch – the squadron mess had been drunk dry the previous day.

Brickhill was now back in Spits, his first love, and flying with the best of the best. The heavy-smoking, hard-drinking, quick-witted Australian swiftly made friends with his two dozen fellow 92 Squadron pilots, who included several other Aussies as well as Canadians. Most Australians quickly fitted into the British squadrons. Brickhill's former workmate at the Sydney *Sun*, John Ulm, was one of them. 'I thoroughly enjoyed being on a RAF squadron,' said Ulm, who later flew Spitfires with 145 Squadron, which, as fate would have it, would then be commanded by Neville Duke. What Ulm liked most was the cosmopolitan mix of nationalities populating the Spitfire squadrons: fellow Australians, New Zealanders, Canadians, Americans, South Africans and Britons.[61] In the desert, too, Desert Air Force officers and non-commissioned ranks ate in the same mess, a breaking down of British class structure which suited Brickhill and fellow egalitarian Australians.

By this time, back in Australia, Brickhill's father, George, was continuing to scratch a living as Sydney correspondent of the *Newcastle Sun*, and Paul knew that his parents were still struggling financially. He also knew that his father was too proud to take handouts directly. So Brickhill wrote home and told his parents that he was arranging for the difference between his old pilot officer's pay and his new salary as a flying officer to be sent to his mother each payday.

Brickhill spent his second lonely Christmas away from home, this time at a bleak tented base in the desert. Beer, spirits, cigarettes and rations were in short supply. Water for washing clothes was almost non-existent. When he'd first arrived in the desert, Brickhill had been repelled by the sight and smell of 'dirty Arabs'. Now, with his clothes filthy and his aroma rich, he felt he was 'no longer entitled to haughty scorn' of the locals. No one in the squadron minded how he looked or smelled. They were all in the same dirty boat, and took their situation in good spirits. Brickhill would write home, 'The desert isn't so bad, and we have a fair bit of fun in one way and another.'[62]

In early January, 92 Squadron relocated to a landing ground near Hamrat in Tripolitania. The squadron was engaged in almost daily battles with the German and Italian air forces, several of whose pilots were well-known aces. The new year's battles started out even on 8 January with 92 Squadron bagging two Me 109s but with two of their Spitfires being shot down, one piloted by an Australian, Geoffrey Rose. The next day the score was one loss for each side, and once again the squadron's commanding officer was writing a condolence letter to a bereaved family. On 10 January, high-flying pilots from the squadron excitedly reported they were able to see enemy-occupied Tripoli, the Libyan capital, in the distance.

The next day, a Monday, the squadron was on standby from the moment the sun rose. After a morning sweep of the desert and a quick bite of lunch back at base, Brickhill took off as wingman to Neville Duke to intercept two enemy aircraft reported to be active in Libya's Tamet area. As wingman, it was Brickhill's job to protect his leader. Past wingmen had failed to adequately protect Duke, who'd been shot down twice during his short career, parachuting to safety each time. While the leader did the attacking, the wingman was supposed to stick to his number one like glue, all the time keeping a lookout for the enemy. Sometimes the wingman would get in a burst at the foe, but often came home without firing his guns.

Near Tamet, Brickhill and Duke spotted two Me 109s way below them. Duke immediately dived to the attack, and Brickhill followed him down. But Duke's dive was too steep, and he nearly passed out from lack of oxygen. By the time Duke had cleared his head and levelled out, with Brickhill dutifully close behind, the pair of Messerschmitts had disappeared. After the evening meal, Duke went up again, with another pilot as his wingman this time. Encountering five Italian Macchi 202s coming in from the sea, Duke shot down two of them. It happened to be Duke's twenty-first birthday that day. As his squadron comrades remarked as glasses were raised in the mess that night, it was a hell of a way to celebrate a twenty-first.

Duke's latest two 'kills' brought his aerial victories to twelve. Flying Officer Brickhill, meanwhile, had yet to notch up a single kill. In all the months he'd been flying, Brickhill had not shot down a single enemy plane. The best he could manage was damage to a single Me 109, which had succeeded in escaping. Another Australian fighter pilot flying in North Africa, Flight Lieutenant Jack Donald of the RAAF's Number 3 Squadron, was to observe that many pilots during the war were there merely to make up the numbers while the few real killers among them did the dirty work. Donald, who would be shot down and taken prisoner, ranked himself among those making up the numbers.[63] Brickhill seems to have been in the same category, acknowledging that, as good a pilot as he had become, he was not the RAF's best shot.

Blinding sandstorms frequently grounded 92 Squadron over the next ten days, but on 21 January the unit moved to Wadi Surri, from where, in a sweep over Tripoli, it shot down three Stuka Ju-87 dive-bombers. Looking down on the Libyan capital during this mission, Brickhill was hoping to soon make close acquaintance with the city. Later that day, Neville Duke was appointed leader of A flight, one of 92 Squadron's two flights of six aircraft.

After dinner, to celebrate his appointment, Duke adjourned to the trailer of 242 Wing's commanding officer, Wing Commander William Darwen. They were joined by 92's CO, Squadron Leader John Morgan, and three Australians with the squadron, Brickhill among them. According to Duke, they all proceeded to get 'legless'.[64] The British 8th Army fought its way into Tripoli on 23 January, and two days later Number 92's Squadron Leader Morgan was the first Allied pilot to land in the city.

'Liberated' Tripoli beer and Italian Chianti found their way into the dry 92 Squadron mess, to the delight of Flight Lieutenant Duke and Flying Officer Brickhill, who hadn't seen liquor in the weeks since the party to celebrate Duke's promotion. Brickhill got stuck into the Chianti. He would write home that it was good while it lasted, 'But, oh, the ginormous hangover!!!'[65] The few gallons of Chianti were swiftly liquidated by thirsty pilots, but in their opinion the staple Italian wine was no match for English beer or Scotch whisky.

The weather closed in as January ebbed away. With no flying possible, Brickhill and several other pilots from Number 92 drove into Misrata, Libya's third-largest city,

200 kilometres from Tripoli on the Mediterranean coast. Under Italian government since 1911, Misrata had recently been wrung from Axis control. For Brickhill, this proved an entertaining day. Some Italian colonists still living in the town treated the RAF pilots nervously, while others ingratiated themselves. Native residents happily bartered. 'Arabs will sell their souls for tea,' Brickhill observed. In exchange for several handfuls of tea, the pilots came away from Misrata with 160 eggs and a large sack of greens, the first vegetables Brickhill had seen in three months.[66]

On 28 January, with rain pelting his tent, and suffering from a cold, Brickhill had time to catch up with mail that had remained unanswered over the last few hectic and sometimes uncertain weeks. One of his letters home, on Australian Comforts Fund notepaper, was in answer to an unexpected missive from one-time love interest Del Fox. Feeling lonely and a bit sorry for himself, he was uncharacteristically affectionate, calling Del 'my pet' and signing off this letter, 'Yours, with a big kiss.'

His previous correspondence to Del had ended much more formally. It seems that their relationship had cooled several years before because of Del's dislike of Brickhill's penchant for getting drunk when they went out. He wrote now that he was confident that Del would be 'pitilessly amused to hear that such essentials as beer and spirits' had become matters 'of fond memory only'.

He told Del that his war was sometimes quite good fun, but could also be horribly frightening. He confessed that he had only recently escaped being shot down. 'I should have been clobbered cold one day through my own utter dimwittedness, but the Jerry was as rotten a shot as I am, so I'm still here – and hoping to stay.' As he wrote, he became nostalgic. He missed England, he told Del, and would give anything to go back there, even though the country was cold and wet. 'The sheer beauty of the countryside grabs you by the throat and shakes your heart up into your mouth.'

And he'd fallen in love with English pubs, which he'd found warm, friendly and comforting. He preferred them to the 'cheap, repetitive personality of the chrome, tile and new bricks' of Australian pubs. Yet, he was homesick for Australia and keen to help defend his homeland from the Japanese threat. 'I wish to Hell I was back there, but blokes like us here can't get home for love nor money. I guess it's the same war anyway.'[67]

February was a hellish month for flying. Storms lashed and shredded the squadron's tents, soaking everyone and everything inside. The atrocious weather kept the air forces of both sides on the ground, and Brickhill had his CO authorise seven days' special leave so he could go back to Alexandria to catch up with his brother. On the last day of February he hitched a ride with a Beaufighter flying to Cairo, and from there he sent a telegram to Russ in Alexandria, urging him to come to Cairo to meet up.

The following day, Brickhill received a message from Russ' secretary – an hour before Paul's telegram arrived, Russ had left Alexandria for Cairo, bound for Tripoli. Brickhill tried to track his brother down in Cairo, but had no luck.

Despondently, he decided he would have to return to his squadron in Tripolitania. Picking up a telephone, he called RAF Transport Command to book a place on an aircraft heading in that direction.

'Didn't we fix your passage a few minutes ago?' said an RAF clerk on the other end of the line.

'No, you couldn't have,' Brickhill responded.

'Did you say your name was Brickhill?'

'Yeah, that's right.' He spelled it out for the clerk.

'Well, I booked a Brickhill a few minutes ago. It's an unusual name, and I was wondering . . .'

'Hell's bells! That's my brother. Well, I'm damned! Have you got his address? Well I'm damned!'

Suggesting he not shout quite so loudly down the line, the clerk asked him to wait, and after a pause came back with the information that Lieutenant Russell Brickhill was staying at Cairo's Victoria Hotel. Thanking the clerk, Brickhill rushed off to locate his brother. Crossing the lobby of the Victoria Hotel a little later, he walked right into an astonished Russ, who was coming out of the dining room. Once again, fate had brought them together in the most unlikely of ways. They spent the rest of the evening together in the bar.[68]

Both had heard from home that their nineteen-year-old brother Clive had followed Lloyd and Paul into the RAAF, enlisting the previous December. The Air Force would dash Clive's hopes of emulating Paul and Lloyd as a pilot. Because he'd worked as an optical instrument maker, he became an Air Force mechanic. Clive's fine eye for detail would later see him become a meteorological assistant. He would end the war in Darwin, a corporal.

When Russ left for Tripoli early the next morning, Brickhill stayed on in Cairo an extra day waiting for a flight, and then he too flew to Tripoli, where the brothers again got together. On 6 March, Brickhill rejoined his squadron. He arrived to mixed news. The previous day, four of 92 Squadron's Spitfires had mixed it with seven Messerschmitts, and had come off the worst, with two Spitfires being downed by Luftwaffe ace Hauptmann (Captain) Heinz Bar, for no loss to the Germans. These kills had brought Bar's total to a daunting 166. Bar would survive the war, racking up 220 kills. Yet, he was not the Luftwaffe's top-scoring ace. That title would go to Erich Hartmann, who would amass a staggering 352 aerial victories, making him by far the top air ace on either side. A number of other Luftwaffe pilots would notch up more than 100 kills. This put the score of top British ace Johnnie Johnson, of thirty-four kills, well in the shade.

One of the two 92 Squadron pilots brought down by Bar in this 5 March scrap was Pilot Officer Bernard 'Happy' McMahon. A Canadian from Ottawa, McMahon had laughed his way through life and had been highly popular with his comrades. The good news was that in Brickhill's absence Neville Duke had added to his total, which now stood at seventeen kills. Young Duke, whose nickname was 'Hawkeye' because he was frequently the first to spot the enemy, also had a growing tally of decorations. Before long, the total number of aircraft downed by the squadron as a whole since the war began reached 250.

In the mess two days after his return from leave, Brickhill heard concerned pilots tell of encountering the Luftwaffe's Focke-Wulf 190 fighter for the first time. They'd been dismayed when the Fw 190s drew away from them with ease at 14,000 feet, with the Focke-Wulf's BMW engines outperforming the Spitfires' Rolls-Royce power plants. On Saturday the 13th, the squadron relocated to a landing ground at Bou Grara – the pilots called it simply Grara. This was a desolate landing strip on a salt flat by the sea, and far from ideal; aircraft sank into the salt in places. But the breeze off the Mediterranean was cooling and healthy.

Late that same day it was announced that Number 92 would soon be re-equipped with the new and improved Mark IX Spitfire. Pilots would be progressively sent to Algiers in coming weeks to collect them. There were cheers all round, for the Mark IX was reputedly 110 kilometres an hour faster than the Vb at 30,000 feet, and would put the pilots of Number 92 on a more equal footing with the formidable Fw 190.

On 16 March, Brickhill watched as a Pathé Gazette cameraman shot footage of ace Neville Duke and his Spit for a newsreel to be shown in cinemas across Britain and the Empire, glorifying his exploits. In the mess that night, Brickhill and others ribbed Duke and asked him what all the fuss had been about.

An embarrassed Duke tried to shrug it off, claiming he'd talked a load of bull for the Pathé man's benefit. 'I put on the usual line shoot for a movie type who would insist on taking shots.'[69]

That same evening, Brickhill learned that he was rostered to fly the next day. After weeks out of the saddle, he would have a chance to get back into the air and grab a little of the glory.

*

On the afternoon of 17 March, Mick Bruckshaw landed back at Bou Grara without his wingman. Lodging a mission report, he told of seeing Brickhill shot down. It had not been a good day for 92 Squadron. The enemy fighter-bombers had got through, and while Hunk Humphries and another 92 Squadron pilot damaged one Me 109 in the scrap over the Mareth Line, it escaped and no enemy aircraft had been shot down. The scoreline for the day's contest was Axis 1, Number 92 Squadron 0.

At that point, neither Bruckshaw nor anyone else in the squadron had any idea whether Brickhill was alive or dead. The next day, Number 92 received a message from Eighth Army headquarters: 'Friend says pilot safe, but not on our side.'[70] The 'friend' was a Long Range Desert Group patrol lying, camouflaged, out in the desert near the Italian front line. Its men had seen Brickhill come down and taken prisoner by the Italians. Another Spitfire pilot with 242 Wing was downed that afternoon. It was not until that other pilot was accounted for that 92 Squadron knew that Brickhill was the one in enemy hands.

In a 21 March report to his superiors, 92 Squadron's latest commanding officer, Squadron Leader William Harper, passed on Bruckshaw's account of Brickhill's downing, adding that all efforts over the past four days to trace the whereabouts of the Australian had failed, and he was accordingly being listed as 'missing'.

The sun hadn't long risen when, lying in an army cot in an Italian hospital in Tunis, Brickhill was astonished when one of his fellow prisoners, a Guards officer in the British Army, and a lord of the realm, what's more, demanded marmalade for breakfast. His lordship and his demand caused considerable consternation among their excitable Italian hosts.[71]

Over the days immediately following his capture, Brickhill, weak from his wounds and drained emotionally after being shot down, had been shunted from one Italian field hospital to another. First it was Sfax. Then Sousse, 140 kilometres south of Tunis. Finally, he'd been sent around the Gulf of Hammamet to Tunis. The British Eighth Army's long-expected assault on the Mareth Line began two days after Brickhill's capture. The battle for Tunisia would rage until late May, with Tunis falling on 5 May, the day the Luftwaffe would pull its last aircraft out of North Africa. Rommel, the Afrika Korps' commander, now promoted to field marshal by Hitler, had meanwhile been recalled to Germany for 'consultations' with his Fuehrer, thus preventing the humiliation of his capture. By May's end, more than 275,000 German and Italian prisoners would be taken by the Allies. But Brickhill would be long gone by that time.

After six days in captivity, Brickhill, in boots provided by the Italians, was loaded with other prisoners into an aircraft on 23 March, to be transported to Italy. The usual Italian practice was to put Allied POWs aboard large three-engine Cant Z506B floatplanes for the transfer across the Mediterranean. Painted entirely white, the Cants had large red crosses emblazoned on wings and fuselage to identify them as 'hospital' aircraft. Brickhill's plane flew him to Naples. There, he was bundled aboard a train. Destination: Germany, and a prisoner-of-war camp.

7.

In the Bag

OBERURSEL, JUST OUTSIDE Frankfurt, was home to Dulag Luft, the Luftwaffe's central receiving and interrogation depot for captured Allied airmen. In 1943, with RAAF and USAAF bombing raids into the Reich intensifying, and the number of bombers being brought down consequently increasing, Dulag Luft was a very busy place. From here, after questioning, prisoners would be dispatched to various prisoner-of-war camps to wait out the war. On 25 March, Brickhill arrived at Dulag Luft by train from Naples.

The RAF routinely lectured its aircrew on what to expect in the event they fell into enemy hands, so Brickhill had a fair idea what he was in for. The Luftwaffe's reception process for new prisoner arrivals at Dulag Luft tended to follow a pattern. First, Brickhill was given a hot shower, after which a medical attendant changed the prisoner's dressings. His clothes were taken away – to be X-rayed, one RAF prisoner was told.[72] Then, to soften him up for questioning, he spent several days in solitary confinement, naked, in a wooden cell.

The cell's only furniture consisted of a cot and an ablutions bucket. Twice a day, a silent guard would pass in a bowl of cabbage soup and a chunk of black bread, and replace the bucket. Brickhill's clothes and few possessions were meanwhile examined minutely by his captors. Everything from the maker's label on his uniform to the content of a prisoner's pockets was noted: train-ticket stubs, cinema tickets, personal photographs in wallets. No clue to the life he'd led up until his capture was overlooked by the thorough Germans.

On 27 March, as Brickhill was languishing naked in a cell at Dulag Luft, in Sydney his parents were preparing for a week's holiday in early April, at the Jervis Bay Hotel at Huskisson on the New South Wales south coast. That afternoon, a telegram boy knocked on their door. For the past few months, George and Dot had been once more renting a house at Greenwich Point, this time from engineer James Robertson. They were back in George Street, at number 41, a cute two-storey gabled abode in the heart of Paul's teenage stomping ground. With several sons in the military, it was with trepidation that George opened a telegram from the government, to learn that Paul was missing in action.

Despite the concerning news, or perhaps because of it, George convinced Dot that they should still go on their holiday, and he cabled the RAAF to tell them where he would be between 5 and 12 April, in case there was more news of Paul while they were away.

*

In late March, a Luftwaffe captain, an intelligence officer, came to pay Paul Brickhill a visit in his Dulag Luft cell. Sitting on the end of the cot, the captain lit a cigarette and chatted away in excellent English. One of the approaches used by Dulag Luft intelligence officers to gain prisoners' confidence was to tell new arrivals that they secretly believed that Germany was going to lose the war, and as a consequence had sent their family to safety in South America. They would go on to say that Russia was the common enemy of the German people and the British people, and this made Germans and Britishers allies. When this failed to elicit anything other than name, rank and serial number from the prisoner, the interrogation moved to a new stage.

The following day, a guard unexpectedly came and marched Brickhill, still entirely nude, down an echoing corridor, through an office occupied by German girls pounding away at typewriters, and into a large meeting room. The prisoner was made to stand at attention in front of a panel of six Luftwaffe officers sitting at a long table. From behind him, a female stenographer slipped into the room and took a seat, pencil and pad at the ready. For the next hour, the officers threw questions at the naked prisoner, about his squadron, his wing, the Spitfire, about attitudes to the war among his squadron comrades. The following day, this was repeated. When the prisoner revealed nothing under questioning, he was returned to his cell, again via the room full of women.

A new day brought a new approach. His chief interrogating officer brought Brickhill's battledress and other clothes to his cell and laid them out on the bed. The battledress had been cleaned and pressed, the rents in the back, made when Brickhill was wounded over the desert, sewn up. The captain even presented him with a long, flowing, military greatcoat and a scarf. It would still be wintry where he was going, he was told. At that time, newly captured RAF prisoners were being given the greatcoats of Polish officers, probably from a stockpile created by the Russians after massacring 10,000 Polish officers in the Katyn Forest in 1940, and seized by the Germans when they invaded Russia the following year.

Once the prisoner had dressed, his interrogator took him to an office. Opening a filing cabinet, the captain took out a file with the prisoner's name on it. The captain proceeded to astonish him by reading aloud accurate details of his military career, from pilot training to war service, even talking about the exploits of men in his squadron. Dropping the folder back into its drawer, the captain closed the drawer with a bang.

'Name, rank and number?' he exclaimed, with practised disdain. 'Bah! Who needs it?'[73]

The captain was trying to get the prisoner to relax his guard. A more gullible prisoner might reason that if the Germans knew so much about him, he needn't worry about giving away information they already knew, and subsequently reveal more than he should. Brickhill found his captors soon being very chummy indeed. In his last days at Dulag Luft, he was informed that the pilot who'd shot him down was going to pay him a visit, as a friendly gesture between fellow knights of the air.

At Dulag Luft, RAF navigator and future Stalag Luft 3 escapee and author Eric Williams met a Luftwaffe oberleutnant who claimed to be the Junkers 88 night-fighter pilot who'd shot down his Wellington bomber. Williams became convinced the man was an intelligence officer, or, at the very least, was working with the interrogators.[74] Brickhill was less suspicious. In North Africa, several German pilots shot down by 92 Squadron had been taken to meet the men who'd downed them. Brickhill's generosity of spirit would show itself when, years later, he said he felt no bitterness towards the man who'd shot him down. 'There were no hard feelings. It was done without anger. There was just a job to be done.' Besides, Brickhill felt he'd been careless in allowing himself to be jumped by an unseen opponent over the Tunisian desert.[75]

As it turned out, Brickhill was moved from Dulag Luft before the projected pilot's visit took place. That pilot and Brickhill never met. Brickhill would have been disappointed, if not horrified, to learn that he'd been the victim of an Italian, 'Eyties' being considered inferior pilots to those of the RAF. Worse, an Italian flying an aircraft rated the technical inferior of the Spitfire.

Brickhill spent just a week at Dulag Luft. Other downed Allied airmen, especially bomber aircrew with knowledge of radar developments, could spend up to thirty days under interrogation. On 2 April, with a group of other RAF prisoners, Brickhill was discharged into the hands of Luftwaffe men armed with MP40s, or, as he habitually called all submachine guns, 'Tommy-guns', after the American Thompson submachine gun. Under the watchful eye of their escort, the prisoners transferred to the local railway station and were loaded into a third-class European day coach with hard wooden seats. They, and their guards, set off on an arduous two-day rail journey east, dodging Allied air raids, to German Silesia, and the camp that Brickhill would one day immortalise. The most formative period of his career was about to begin.

8.

Welcome to Stalag Luft 3

ALONG THE TREE-LINED road the 400 metres from Sagan station tramped a group of sullen Allied airmen in ragged formation. Around them marched their guards, alert German Air Force men armed with the neat MP40 submachine gun. In the middle of the group, swathed in a greatcoat and scarf against the sharp spring cold, trod Paul Brickhill. Almost all his companions were bomber aircrew, and most were several years younger than the Australian. It was 4 April 1943, and the captives were being herded towards Stalag Luft 3, a prisoner-of-war camp for captured Allied flyers in Silesia, 150 kilometres southeast of Berlin.

In front of them, the vista of close-packed fir trees opened up to reveal a large clearing in Sagan Forest containing a camp sprawling behind barbed-wire fences. Dotted along the outer fence were guard towers, each containing a sentry with a heavy machinegun and searchlight. The new arrivals were marched to a gate on the northwest corner of North Compound. Fourth and latest of the camp's compounds, it had only been open for business for three days. Here, at the North Compound gate, Brickhill and his companions came to a halt, waiting as an attractive German girl in Luftwaffe uniform passed out through the gate from the *Vorlager* – literally, the 'fore camp' – which contained the Luftwaffe administration area immediately inside the compound gate.

As Brickhill was to learn, female Luftwaffe personnel were among 100 censors working in the nearby *Kommandantur*, the camp command centre, under intelligence officer Hauptmann Günther von Massow, censoring the mail of all Stalag Luft 3 prisoners. Men of the new batch of captives were beginning to shuffle through the open outer gate, but Brickhill had turned to watch the well-formed censor bicycle away. Suddenly, with a grunt, he felt the business end of an MP40 being jabbed into his ribs.

'If you are ever found with a German girl,' threatened the Luftwaffe man at the other end of the submachine gun, having apparently read the Australian's thoughts, 'you will pay for it with your life.'[76]

Looking over his shoulder, Brickhill saw the guard's finger resting close to his trigger. With another shove of the MP40, Brickhill stumbled forward and through the gate to join his travelling companions. Inside the Vorlager, to his left Brickhill could see a low guardhouse. To his right there was a distant coal dump and, closer, what appeared to be a compound hospital and another administration building, a grey concrete structure with bars on the windows. The latter was the solitary confinement block, or 'Cooler' as both prisoners and guards called it, where prisoners were sent to cool off for weeks at a time after breaking camp regulations or attempting escape. Ahead stood another three-metre wall of barbed wire, and, beyond it, North Compound itself.

One by one, the new prisoners had their photographs taken, standing in the open with their backs to the guardhouse wall. Brickhill posed with an expression that mixed a scowl with an amused tug at the left corner of the mouth. He was weighed, coming in at 72 kilograms in boots and heavy garments. His minute details were recorded by efficient English-speaking Luftwaffe clerks. Height. Hair colour. Eye colour. Date of birth. Pre-war occupation. For his religion, Brickhill gave Church of England, but after the wartime horrors he'd witnessed he was no longer a believer. Asked for details of next of kin, Brickhill gave his father George's name and Greenwich Point address.

A guard roughly pressed the Australian's index finger into an ink pad before applying the print to a *Personalkarte*, the record card devoted to Brickhill that would sit in camp files for the rest of his incarceration. Each prisoner was issued with a new dog tag, replacing their own, which had been removed after capture. The new metal, oblong neck tag was stamped with the word *Kriegsgefangener* – prisoner of war – and a number. From now on, these men were 'kriegies', as English-speaking prisoners of the Germans called themselves, and they were entering 'kriegiedom'.[77]

Marched to the inner gateway, the new arrivals were admitted to their new home. Taking little notice of the latest arrivals, hundreds of Allied airmen in bits and pieces of often-threadbare uniform strolled around 'the circuit', a walking track inside the wire, hands in pockets, in small groups. Many looked far from military, with stubbly beards and shaggy hair. Others had shaved their heads shiny bald. Not a few were hollow-eyed. A lot of these men had been prisoners for more than three years.

The double gate was shut and locked. The Germans were now on the outside, prisoners on the inside. Several RAF officers came to meet Brickhill's group. The new men were divided up and instructed to follow the welcoming committee, in turn, to various accommodation blocks in the camp. Brickhill was taken to 103 Block. Like the other fifteen blocks, it was a long single-storey wooden building divided into fifteen rooms each capable of housing eight men in four double bunks, plus three two-man rooms for senior officers.

Accommodation blocks had a washroom with concrete floor, a toilet and a basic kitchen with a two-plate coal-burning stove. Apart from the bunks, furnishings in the bunk rooms were basic: a bare wooden table surrounded by eight chairs and stools, wooden lockers and a small coal-burning stove set on tiles in the corner. A bunk in one of these rooms was assigned to Brickhill. The room was devoid of occupants when the welcoming committee brought him in. Here, he was grilled in private, to establish that he was who he said he was.

'This is just routine, old boy,' said one of the welcoming committee once the questioning had ended satisfactorily. 'We have to make sure the Hun isn't trying to put a "plant" in here on us.'[78]

The Germans were known to try to infiltrate spies into POW camps posing as prisoners, to obtain information. One such spy discovered in the Russian compound had been strung up by the genuine prisoners, who told the Germans he'd committed suicide. Having passed the test, Brickhill was welcomed into the camp community. Shortly, he was told, he would be taken to be officially greeted by the Senior British Officer, or SBO, Group Captain Herbert Massey. The welcoming committee departed, and before long Brickhill's roommates began wandering back in, to look him over.

Brickhill quickly befriended a fellow Australian in 103, a prisoner who'd been 'in the bag' twelve months by this time. Albert 'Al' Hake was his name, and his voice wafted from a northern room in the block as he sang 'Waltzing Matilda' and strummed a guitar provided by the International Red Cross. Handsome, a little taller than Brickhill, and stockier, Al Hake had thick dark hair and remarkably bushy eyebrows. He and Brickhill had a lot in common. Both were from Sydney, were the same age, had been members of the RAAF Reserve before enlisting, had ended up Spitfire pilots attached to the RAF, and had both been shot down flying Spits – in Hake's case, over France in 1942 after a tussle with five Focke-Wulf 190s.

Hake had enlisted in the RAAF at Sydney just two days before Brickhill signed up. Their paths hadn't crossed back then. While Brickhill trained as a pilot at Narrandera and in Canada, Hake had done all his pilot training in Wagga Wagga, and once he'd gained his 'wings' he'd been sent direct to Britain. Just a month after Brickhill commenced his training at the RAF's 53 Operational Training Unit at Llandow in South Wales, Hake arrived to also train in Spitfires. They'd passed each other in corridors and on the tarmac at Llandow without becoming friends, but now, in Stalag Luft 3, the two Aussies quickly became good chums.

Brickhill was soon taken to meet Group Captain Massey in a two-bed end room. The tall, slender, forty-eight-year-old SBO was crippled by a foot injured on multiple occasions, the last time when he'd bailed out over the Ruhr. Regularly in and out of the compound hospital, Massey spent the rest of the time with his foot up or hobbling painfully about with the aid of a stick. As North Compound's SBO, he dealt directly with the Luftwaffe's camp commandant, who was of similar rank.

After Brickhill came to attention before Massey, who sat behind the small table serving as his desk, the SBO proceeded to have an amiable chat with the Australian about camp life and the German regulations that governed it. Once the formalities were over, Massey informed Brickhill that Squadron Leader Roger Bushell would also want a word with him over the next day or two. Intriguingly, the SBO didn't say what the meeting with Bushell would be about.

Once Massey dismissed him, Brickhill went for a wander around the 'circuit', to take in his new surroundings. The warning wire, a barrier of low strands set ten metres in from the initial fence, could be easily stepped over. But, do so without permission, and you could be shot by one of the 'goons', or guards, stationed in the 'goon boxes', the towers standing every fifty metres outside the fences. Around the camp perimeter ran a pair of high wire fences two metres apart. Brickhill, a man with an eye for detail, counted an average of twenty rusty strands of barbed wire to each fence. Coils of barbed wire filled the gap between the two fences. From the outer fence to the close-packed trees that surrounded the camp and sealed it off from the outside world there was an open space – a hundred feet wide, in Brickhill's estimation.

Inside the compound, apart from the accommodation blocks there was a kitchen, used primarily to boil water and potatoes, and a parade ground. Covered with dry grey earth and dotted with tree stumps, this open space was where prisoners had to assemble twice a day in five ranks, in all weathers, to be counted by their guards. The Germans called this parade *Appell*. The Appell ground also served as the prisoners' recreation area. Within a few months a wooden theatre would be thrown up on its northern edge by prisoners. In addition, there was a large square pool in the middle of the compound, its water to be used in case of fire. This bleak camp, 'innocent of luxury' as Brickhill was to put it, was now his home; a desolate, Godforsaken place in his opinion.[79]

The day following his arrival, Brickhill responded to a summons to 110 Block. Roger Bushell was waiting for him. The Australian knew of Bushell, a thirty-two-year-old South African-born Brit who'd gone to school in England and been a barrister in London before the war. When Bushell was shot down in May 1940, he'd been commanding officer of Brickhill's last squadron, Number 92, although that had been some time before Brickhill joined the unit. Brickhill was impressed by Bushell when he met him, and a little intimidated. 'He was a big tempestuous man,' he was to say, 'with broad shoulders and the most chilling pale blue eyes I ever saw.' Bushell had injured his right eye in a skiing accident before the war, and that eye drooped a little, giving him a slightly sinister appearance.[80]

Behind his closed door, Bushell informed the newcomer that he was 'Big X', chief of 'the X Organisation', the camp's secret escape committee. And Bushell told Brickhill that every inmate of the compound was expected to participate in a mass escape plan first conceived the previous Christmas and which, since North Compound's inmates had only been transferred here three days before Brickhill's arrival, was just now coming together. When Brickhill expressed a desire to be involved, Bushell asked him what special skills he possessed. What, for example, had been his pre-war occupation?

'Journalist, with the Sydney *Sun*,' Brickhill replied.

Bushell wasn't overly impressed. He was looking for specialised skills: men who could dig tunnels, produce escape equipment, tailor escape clothes, or forge German documents. Still, because Brickhill was trained in shorthand, he could join the team rostered onto listening, via headphones, to the BBC News, on a secret camp radio nicknamed the 'Canary'. That radio had originally been smuggled into the camp in a soccer ball, by a Brit captured at Dunkirk in 1940. The job of the shorthand boys was to note down every word of the nightly news bulletins. The following day, war news would be quietly spread through the compound by word of mouth.

Brickhill went away from his first meeting with Big X excited by the possibility of being a part of a big breakout. Little did he or Bushell know that his journalistic talents, while of small value to the X Organisation, would eventually help the Australian shape some aspects of the history of World War Two, and make both Brickhill and Bushell famous.

9.

The Tunnel Game

Sagan would become the Polish town of Zagan in the post-war redrawing of European borders. Paul Brickhill estimated that, when he arrived there, the town had a population of 25,000. Northeast of Dresden and west of Breslau – today's Wroclaw – Sagan was an important rail junction. German trains heading to and from the Russian front passed through here. From his Stalag Luft 3 bed in North Compound's 103 Block, shivering beneath two blankets on a thin mattress stuffed with wood shavings, Brickhill could nightly hear the wheeze and puff of shunting locomotives, and the clang of buffer hitting buffer, as freight trains were marshalled in the Sagan yards.

Stalag Luft 3 was run by the Luftwaffe, which provided all the officers, guards and administrative staff – 1200 men and women by late 1944.[81] The German Air Minister and chief of the Luftwaffe, Reich Marshal Hermann Goering, had told one Stalag Luft 3 inmate in a meeting following the man's capture in 1940 that his policy was to look after Air Force prisoners well.[82] Compared to the way the Japanese looked after prisoners of war generally, and the way the Germans looked after Russian prisoners specifically – the Soviets were not signatories to the Geneva Convention on the rights of prisoners of war, so their men were not protected by its provisions – the prisoners at Stalag Luft 3 were cared for relatively well, at least up until the closing stages of the war.

As Brickhill settled into life as a kriegie, he learned camp etiquette. Apart from the SBO, everyone referred to each other by first name or nickname. Food etiquette was all-important. The Germans daily issued each prisoner with a small hunk of black bread, from which three or four thin slices were made to stretch over three meals. Plus, either a few potatoes or a cup of sauerkraut. Once a week, a small ration of sausage was handed out, together with a tablespoon of jam made from sugar beet and a tablespoon of margarine per man.

Once a week, too, welcome Red Cross food parcels from home were distributed, one for each prisoner. The Australian and New Zealand parcels were popular, for, in addition to bully beef, powdered milk, raisins or prunes, sugar, tea or coffee, a chocolate bar and a pack of cigarettes, they contained a tin of prized Australasian butter. Roughly every three weeks, minced horsemeat was made available by the Luftwaffe, and occasionally, too, a few vegetables, a little barley, and soup bones. Under rules established by the prisoners themselves, all food went into a community fund, with the eight men per room cooking and eating their shared rations together.

Brickhill, a heavy smoker, had to learn to get by on a reduced ration of cigarettes. As for regular intakes of booze, he would crave that for six months, along with female company, before adjusting to the privations of prison life. A typical Aussie who'd grown up on a meat diet, he never adjusted to the lack of nutrition, flavour or variety in camp food, and his dreams were frequently about food.

The worst aspect of camp life was boredom, so the inmates did their best to keep mentally occupied. Theatrical types produced shows in the camp theatre. Sporty types organised games on the Appell ground. There were bridge tournaments, an active debating group and an international relations society to integrate North Compound's various nationalities. Many men also took advantage of the opportunity to improve their education while in camp, taking lessons in a variety of subjects using textbooks provided by the Red Cross and taught by inmates with the requisite skills. Brickhill took up French and Spanish lessons.

Above all, the one activity that was guaranteed to keep prisoners from becoming bored was the covert planning and execution of escapes. In this game, Paul Brickhill would be an enthusiastic player. He, like everyone else in North Compound, was oblivious to the fact that, in East Compound, Englishmen Eric Williams and Michael Codner had teamed up with Canadian Oliver Philpot to execute an ingenious plan. They would disguise the entrance to a tunnel brazenly dug from their Appell ground by using a hollow wooden vaulting horse – over which inmates vaulted while a man was inside, digging. A digger was carried to and from the tunnel entrance inside the horse, returning with the soil he'd dug. He covered the entrance with a wooden trapdoor which was in turn covered with earth. When the horse was carried away, there was no sign of the entrance. On the day of their break, all three escapees would be carried to the tunnel site in the horse.

Williams and Codner knew all about tunnelling, having participated in a March 1943 underground escape from the Oflag XXI-B POW camp at Schubin in Poland. As clever as the wooden-horse scheme was, at best only three prisoners would be able to escape via it. Nonetheless, the inventive trio received approval from their compound's SBO and X Organisation, and the cooperation of men who vaulted over the horse. Through the spring and summer, East Compound's wooden-horse tunnel crawled towards the wire.

In North Compound, Big X Roger Bushell had grander ambitions. He was intent on a mass escape, one potentially capable of almost emptying the compound. Within a week of the transfer of prisoners to North Compound, and just three days after Brickhill arrived at the camp, Bushell had completed planning for what would become the Great Escape. Like Eric Williams and his colleagues, Bushell felt that tunnelling offered the best chance for a successful escape. But Bushell planned a break so large it would give the Germans enormous headaches and, in the furore that followed it, give the escapees the maximum opportunity to get back home.

Bushell astonished his escape-committee colleagues when he announced his plans in the second week of April. To achieve his big break, he said, they would dig not one tunnel, but three. And, to gasps, he declared that 600 men should be able to escape via these tunnels in one night. But, for

The Tunnel Game

reasons of security, the word 'tunnel' must henceforth never be uttered carelessly in the compound.

Codenaming his tunnels Tom, Dick and Harry, Bushell designated their routes. Tom was to be dug from 123 Block, which housed seventy Polish RAF officers, out under the west wire. Dick would go from 122 next door, also to the west. Harry would go from 104, tracking under the Vorlager and, cheekily, under the Cooler, to the woods on the camp's northern edge. Harry would be by far the longest – roughly 130 metres. But Bushell also felt that Harry might have the best chance of success, because the logical Germans would think no one would tunnel such a distance, and beneath their very feet.

Treating the escape as a business enterprise, Bushell set up a series of X Organisation departments to execute escape plans, choosing heads of department from among his fellow prisoners according to their skills. The tunnelling department would be headed by Wallace 'Wally' Floody, a bearded Canadian who had mined for gold on the Yukon. Brickhill, who came to know Floody well, reckoned the slight, gaunt Canadian looked like a consumptive. When Floody told Bushell of his gold-digging background, Bushell assumed he was a qualified mining engineer. Floody didn't have the heart to tell Bushell he'd been a self-taught miner without any formal training. But, as it would turn out, Floody's work underground would prove inspired. To support him with tunnelling equipment, the engineering department would be headed by South African Johnny Travis.

To give escapees the maximum chance of evading capture, Bushell dictated that escapers be sent out completed tunnels with specially tailored clothing to enable them to blend in with the population, and forged papers to get them across Germany and occupied Europe. Tommy Guest set up the tailoring department, recruiting men who could sew. His sixty tailors would work in their rooms throughout the compound. The gentlemanly Gilbert 'Tim' Walenn had operated an art studio in London before the war, and he took charge of the forgers. Because so many of the fakes his team would produce would be travel documents, Walenn named his department after a well-known British travel agency, Dean and Dawson.

Paul Brickhill's new Aussie friend, Al Hake, had a reputation as a skilled tinkerer, and Bushell gave him the task of creating 200 small hand compasses. Jerry Sage, a gregarious, twenty-five-year-old, six-foot-two American paratroop major from Spokane, Washington, was put in charge of organising diversions to distract guards away from X Organisation activities. John 'Willy' Williams, a curly-headed Australian, became supply supremo, or chief scrounger. Williams' task was among the most difficult, with a long list of items for procurement including a camera and photographic materials for ID photos, special paper for the forgers, copies of German military and government documents, even German money.

Some items would be stolen from under the Germans' noses. For the rest, German speakers under the intelligence department's Czech chief Arnost 'Wally' Valenta were assigned the job of befriending the less dedicated 'ferrets', the overall-wearing German guards whose job it was to prowl through the camp, day and night, armed with torches and probes, looking for suspicious activity. Valenta's team had to pick their marks carefully. The two most senior ferrets were avoided like poison. Methodically efficient Sergeant Hermann Glemnitz earned the grudging respect of his charges. An engineer by profession, he had worked in Yorkshire before the war. Not only did Glemnitz speak excellent English, he had a good understanding of how the British mind worked.

Glemnitz was not averse to sharing a joke with prisoners, unlike his humourless deputy Corporal Karl Griese, who earned the kriegies' intense dislike for his unrelenting hate of the British and a dogged determination to prevent escapes. Because of his long neck, which he tended to poke into their business, prisoners nicknamed him 'Rubberneck'.

While Glemnitz and Griese were beyond corruption, several of their subordinate ferrets were seduced into friendships with prisoners, who then became their X Organisation handlers. In return for a discreet cup of Red Cross coffee, some chocolate, a cigarette and a friendly chat, these ferrets began doing their new RAF friends small favours. Gradually, the handlers of these German 'contacts', as they became known, upped the ante, asking for more and more outrageously illicit items. When a ferret backed off, his kriegie 'friend' would remind him of the other things he'd brought into the compound for him. If a prisoner were to tip off the ferret's superiors about this, the incautious German would face severe punishment – probably a posting to the dreaded Russian front.

When one ferret was asked to bring in a camera, he rejoined that he'd be shot if he did. Roger Bushell told his handler to tell the already compromised German he'd be shot if he didn't. A tiny camera found its way into the compound, plus photographic paper and developer. In most cases, the blackmailed ferrets came up with the goods. One guard even proved sympathetic to the prisoners and got his wife in Hamburg to help with material needed by Tim Walenn's department.

The most senior German collaborator was Hans Pieber, an Austrian Luftwaffe captain and *Lageroffizier* in day-to-day charge of North Compound. Hauptmann Pieber carried out his superiors' orders to the letter, but, convinced that Germany would lose the war, he covertly helped the prisoners wherever he could. He had even smuggled the prisoners' radio into North Compound for them during the 1 April transfer from East Compound. Despite this, following the war Pieber would be convicted as a Nazi and imprisoned, losing all his property.

Bushell decided that overall compound security would be headed by Albert 'Bub' Clark, a toweringly tall, ginger-headed United States Army Air Force lieutenant-colonel still in his twenties. Paul Brickhill nicknamed him 'Junior', because he looked so young. Designated 'Big S' by Bushell, security chief Clark instigated a system of 'stooges', prisoners who 'stooged around' acting as lookouts. With a number of deputy security officers reporting to Clark, each block had its own Little X in overall charge of escape activities on the block and a Little S in charge of block security.

By 11 April, Bushell and Floody had jointly chosen the locations for the three tunnel shafts and their entry trapdoors. To prevent prisoners from digging tunnels, the Germans had erected each accommodation block 20 centimetres off the ground. But they'd built solid foundations beneath the washrooms and stoves in each block, and that was all Floody and his team needed. Tom would go from near a chimney, Dick from a drain sump in a washroom floor and Harry from beneath a stove. Tunnelling began with the sinking of three shafts, firstly by chipping through the brick and concrete foundations. The shafts were then sunk into the dry Silesian soil underneath, neatly shored up with timber slats removed from bunks.

It took just two weeks for Tom to go down ten metres. It was necessary to dig this deep because the Germans had installed microphones around the fences to detect the sounds of digging. Floody and company reckoned that, at ten metres, their tunnels would avoid sound detectors. As it happened, a listening device would pick up digging sounds near 104, but the Germans would put it down to activity in the nearby coal store. Progress on Dick and Harry was a little behind Tom, but they too soon reached the required ten-metre depth.

As digging continued, a major problem emerged. The deeper soil proved sandy. Much lighter in colour than the topsoil, it would be easily spotted if spread on the ground above, tipping off ferrets that tunnelling was afoot. Peter 'Hornblower' Fanshawe, a Fleet Air Arm navigator, had tunnelled at Schubin, and Bushell put him in charge of dispersing their mining spoils, with the formidable Jerry Sage rounding up 'volunteers' for dispersal work. Initially, tunnel earth was removed in pots, jars and anything else that could do the job, and Fanshawe came up with the idea of digging vegetable gardens outside every block to hide it. Block gardens sprang up overnight. Bordered by low stone walls, they permitted tunnel soil to be covered by a layer of disguising topsoil. Jerry Sage was digging the garden outside 105 when a ferret appeared and asked him what was going on.

'We're just beautifying the Third Reich,' Sage replied with a grin, before asking the German for white paint for the border stones. Scoffing at the request, the ferret moved on.[83]

Before long, the increasing amounts of tunnel earth demanded a more industrial-scale dispersal method. Hornblower solved that problem, too, inventing trouser bags, made from woollen 'long john' underpants, which would be filled with tunnel soil and suspended inside prisoners' trousers. Once the wearer had filled up, he would amble out to a block garden, pull strings inside his pockets, and release the soil from the bottom of the trouser bags. The soil which oozed out over his shoes was then casually spread into the garden with the toe. Not surprisingly, these soil-distributors became known as 'penguins'. Men not involved in other X Organisation activities were roped into Fanshawe's penguin brigade; ultimately there would be 150 of them.

Meantime, upwards of 300 prisoners would work for the security department as stooges. Paul Brickhill was among the first, joining the roster of men keeping watch at assigned stations throughout the compound, or tailing ferrets as they did their rounds. It was important work, but it was boring. Brickhill told Roger Bushell that he was also keen to be involved in digging. Only the chosen few worked as diggers, men who were physically fit and who could be trusted implicitly. Many prisoners in North Compound knew that tunnels were being dug. Only those who needed to know were aware in which blocks the tunnels started, and only a few dozen knew the precise locations of the trapdoors – the X

The Tunnel Game

Organisation's most senior men, and the diggers. Because Brickhill was doing important work on the Canary team and had Bushell's trust, he received approval to tunnel.

In preparation for digging work, Brickhill was briefed by Floody. Digging shifts lasted four hours, with enough time after each for a digger to wash down in the block washroom and appear at Appell. Men dug in long johns, or naked. Because of the soft soil, there was a constant risk of cave-in. Brickhill would have to work fast, all the while listening for the sound of shifting earth above, after which hundreds of kilograms of sandy soil could suddenly come tumbling down, smothering him.

'There's a shaven second to get out,' Floody told him.[84]

Down one of the shafts went Brickhill. Which shaft, he never revealed, but he described it as having a west-facing tunnel, so it was almost certainly Tom, the most advanced of the three. After squeezing through the trapdoor in the washroom floor in 123, he climbed down a wooden ladder nailed to one side of the neatly timber-lined shaft, to the dispersal area below. At the shaft's base he found a series of chambers hacked from the earth, all shored up with timber stripped from bunks throughout the compound. One chamber, about two metres long, housed a carpenter who shaped the bed-boards used to shore up the growing tunnel. Opposite, another small chamber was used to store sand until it could be hauled to the surface by dispersers working at the trap.

On the third side, another chamber would in time contain one of the most ingenious aspects of Floody and company's work, the air-conditioning plant, and its operator. This was a hand pump with home-made bellows which pushed air from the surface along a pipe made from Klim dried milk cans linked together, with tops and bottoms removed, and run beneath the tunnel floor. (The catchy manufacturer's Klim brand name was 'milk' backwards.) An air vent would come up where two tunnellers lying full length worked at the tunnel face, the first facing forwards, his number two facing back to the shaft. Each day's last shift would extend the underfloor air pipe to allow the first shift next day to get straight to work digging.

Into the tunnel crawled Brickhill to commence his shift with another digger. Lighting was provided by home-made lamps: Klim tins containing pyjama-cord wicks sitting in margarine. 'They were a bit smelly,' Brickhill later recalled.[85] Subsequently, electrical wiring would be pilfered to create a tunnel lighting system patched into the camp's electricity supply. The air down here was thick and hot, and the diggers were soon bathed in perspiration as one dug with a trowel at the tunnel face and then pushed earth back to the man behind. Every metre, they would pause to shore up around them.

'No one ever spoke much down below,' said Brickhill. 'You were too busy listening.'[86]

In his writings, Brickhill gave the impression that, as he dug, with one ear to the tunnel's roof, he heard the telltale sound of wood creaking above, and began back-pedalling, fast. But not before being caught in a cave-in and covered in earth. He was hauled back by his feet by the man behind, with sand in his mouth, eyes and ears. Panicking, he became desperate to get out of the coffin-like confines. Once he returned to the surface, gripped by claustrophobia, Brickhill couldn't bring himself to go digging again.

Perhaps being caught half in and half out of his falling Spitfire had contributed to his fear of being trapped. He was not alone; several others also panicked underground, and, like Brickhill, had to beg to be excused from tunnelling duty. Still, with no history of claustrophobia, Brickhill was devastated by his reaction. Ashamed by what he clearly perceived as a flaw in his character, he would never write about his debilitating panic attack underground, or speak about it publicly.

10.

In the Light of Day

IN MAY, ONLY weeks into the digging of Tom, Dick and Harry, two dramatic things occurred on the same day. Work was proceeding slowly in Dick. Three men including Wally Floody were still completing the tunnel's dispersal area when there was a massive cave-in. Two men shot up the shaft's ladder as the sandy soil poured into the hole behind them like water at the flood. Floody, last man out, was caught on the ladder, trapped, and overwhelmed. He was almost suffocated. Luckily for him, the two men above were able to reach down, grab the unconscious Floody, and pluck him to safety. Floody proved to possess nerves of steel. The next day, he went back down the 'rat hole', as Brickhill called it, and in just four days he and his team had repaired the damage caused by the fall, and resumed tunnelling.

The day of Dick's cave-in, Wing Commander Harry 'Wings' Day arrived back at Stalag Luft 3. Wings had been

In the Light of Day

one of the camp's original inhabitants, after his Blenheim bomber had been shot out of the sky on a reconnaissance flight over the Rhineland on Friday the 13th of October, 1939. Transferred by the Luftwaffe from Stalag Luft 3 to the Schubin camp in April 1942, becoming Senior British Officer there, Day had been one of thirty-four RAF officers in the Schubin tunnel break. Although all got out of the camp undetected, two escapees had drowned in the Baltic trying to cross to neutral Sweden. The remainder, including Day, had soon been recaptured. After spending weeks in the Schubin Cooler, Day had been sent back to Sagan as part of the transfer of all British prisoners from Schubin. The Germans turned their old camp into Oflag 64, a camp for US Army officers.

Day was offered a bunk in 104, but when he learned that a tunnel was being dug from there he recoiled from the idea. He well knew that a man's life wasn't his own when a tunnel was being dug from his block; too much inconvenience and too many security precautions to be able to relax. Day ended up moving into Brickhill's block, 103. Brickhill was to describe Day as looking like a hungry and unfriendly hawk. But Day had his congenial side, and the pair would over time become firm friends, with Brickhill respecting this determined and resourceful man who'd been a POW for almost the entire war. Because of Day's seniority, Group Captain Massey appointed him his deputy, and let him run the show day-to-day. From this point forward, Day was North Compound's SBO, in effect if not in name.

Wings Day knew how to run a compound, and knew all about daring escapes. Apart from the Schubin break, along with sixteen others he'd earlier dug his way out of Dulag Luft via the first completed RAF tunnel in the Reich. All seventeen escapees had been swiftly recaptured, but Day had learned much from that experience. He would guide X Organisation's executive, which consisted of Roger Bushell, Norman 'Conk' Canton serving as Bushell's adjutant, senior Fleet Air Arm officer Norman Quill, who'd been at Schubin with Day and been involved in the tunnelling there, and security boss Bub Clark. Collectively, the executive members were known as the Big Four, and Wings got solidly behind their mass escape enterprise.

Day would later say that no more than five per cent of prisoners were like him, spending every waking hour thinking about escape. In fact, contrary to the picture painted by Paul Brickhill and other authors, not every prisoner in North Compound was behind the Great Escape. And, contrary to a later popular belief, there was nothing in King's Regulations that required a British officer to attempt to escape. Of the 1200 men soon populating North Compound, only half became involved in one aspect or another of the mass escape, and a number of those only did so reluctantly. Day was to reckon about 250 POWs were genuinely up for escape.[87] Jerry Sage felt that, in South Compound, the number was no more than 150.[88]

Many Stalag Luft 3 inmates didn't want to know about escape, and flatly refused to be involved. Content to await war's end, they felt escape attempts potentially fatal for participants and likely to bring reprisals on other POWs. Canadian Eddy Asselin, who'd led the Schubin tunnel break – that tunnel had been named 'Asselin' after him – had given up escaping and would spend much of the rest of the war running a highly profitable East Compound card game based on IOUs payable post-war from back pay. Some POWs went 'wire happy', their behaviour ranging from weird eccentricities to total delusion. A traumatised few who'd survived being shot down in horrific circumstances, or had received 'Dear John' letters from wives or girlfriends, attempted suicide. One threw himself on the wire, and was machine-gunned to death. Some, gripped by chronic depression, spent all day in bed, only rising to eat. Brickhill called these men the NI, the not interested.[89]

By contrast, some POWs were actually enjoying incarceration, organising and participating in sporting contests or putting on regular shows in each compound's theatre. A number of those involved in these dramas and musicals had been actors and musicians before the war. Not a few relished the opportunity to go on the stage, and some happily put on dresses and make-up to play the female roles among all-male casts. One or two in fact made quite fetching girls. A minority of the kriegies who did work for X Organisation, Paul Brickhill among them, participated voluntarily and with unbridled enthusiasm. Others had at times to be strongarmed into involvement. When Jerry Sage one day urgently called for fifty volunteers from 105 Block for a hurried diversion, only three men stepped forward. Sage had to get tough on other inhabitants, physically dragging another forty-seven men outside for the diversion.

Some prisoners didn't even know they were being used as a diversion when a hundred-strong choir was formed under the tutelage of forty-seven-year-old Major Johnny Dodge. The choir was assembled in the open to rehearse outside a particular block window. Behind that window lay a secret engineering workshop whose men needed to bash Klim cans to make escape apparatus, and the singing covered the sound. Dodge, an American and cousin by marriage to Winston Churchill, was nicknamed the Dodger for his frequent escape attempts; he knew precisely why this choir was required. But one peeved squadron leader not in on the secret called in through the block window, telling the bashers to pipe down so he and his colleagues could sing undisturbed.

Under Day's influence, X Organisation became even more efficient, and even more security conscious. Wings suggested that someone be appointed with specific responsibility for tunnel security. Wally Floody said he knew just the man. Floody and American George Harsh had become firm friends in camp. Harsh was a big man, grey-haired despite only being in his early thirties, and with the squashed nose of a regular pugilist. Floody knew that his intimidating friend George was Harsh by name and harsh by nature. From Georgia, Harsh had gone to Canada to join the Royal Canadian Air Force in 1941. Attached to the RAF, he became a tail gunner with exceptional night vision. His eyesight hadn't helped him when his Halifax had been locked in searchlight beams over Cologne in 1942. With his bomber crippled by flak, Harsh had bailed out, parachuted to the ground and was captured.

Roger Bushell knew all this. But what he didn't know, and Wally Floody and two other Georgia natives in the compound did know, was that, not long before he'd gone to Canada, George Harsh had been serving a life sentence in a Georgia prison, for murder. One winter's day in that prison, a fellow prisoner needed to have his appendix urgently removed. With the prison snowbound, a doctor couldn't get through, so George had operated, and saved the man's life. The prison governor had pardoned George for that deed. But George was still a murderer. Not only had he shot dead a clerk in a grocery store robbery that went badly wrong when he was a youth, in prison he'd been in a fight with another inmate over a bar of soap. Disarming the other man of a knife, Harsh had sliced him to death with his own weapon.

In confidence, George had confessed all this to Wally Floody, who thought that such a background made George the perfect candidate for enforcing strict security over his tunnels. Harsh disagreed. He thought any mass escape doomed to fail, and likely to get them all shot. He had absolutely no desire to be involved, and told Floody so, in no uncertain terms. Floody told Bushell, and the next thing Harsh knew he was summoned to a meeting with Massey, Day and Bushell.

Wings Day informed Harsh that he was putting him in charge of security for Tom, Dick and Harry, and, if he met obstructions in the prosecution of that duty from any man in the compound, they would face court martial after the war. The implication was, of course, that Harsh could look forward to a similar fate if he refused his appointment. SBO Massey drummed home this point by telling Harsh that just because men were now behind the wire, this didn't mean they were no longer subject to King's Regulations. Bushell admitted that a mass escape was likely to only get a few men back to England. But that wasn't the point, he said. It was important to cause the enemy as much disruption as possible.

'We're going to give these Huns as much trouble as would a division of assault troops landing on the beaches of France,' Bushell declared.[90]

Harsh's resistance buckled, and he agreed to do the job. Secretly, he still thought a mass escape crazy, and would get people killed. Yet, despite his grave misgivings, which he only shared with Floody, Harsh would do his job, with cool efficiency. He recruited two well-built deputies, Canadian George McGill and South African Neville McGarr. The trio went everywhere together. Like Chicago gangsters, they became fearsome enforcers – of tunnelling security. All new prisoners arriving in North Compound were warned by the security trio to completely ignore anything unusual they saw going on around them.

Brickhill overheard Neville McGarr tell a new arrival bunking down in 103, 'If you see me walking around with a tree trunk sticking out of my arse, don't stare. I'll be doing it for a good cause.'[91]

Harsh also administered a 'duty pilot' or DP system. Every day, a different stooge sat near the front gate keeping a log of who came through the gate and when, and the time they left, so that X Organisation knew which German ferrets or officers were in the compound at any time. The ferrets soon cottoned on to this, with some jokingly 'reporting in' to the duty pilot as they came and went. What they didn't know was that Harsh had set up a signalling system, inspired by US baseball team signals from dugout to players on the field, to warn men working in tunnels and workshops of enemy approach.

If ferrets were on the prowl, a stooge reading a book outside 110 would relay a warning from the duty pilot by adjusting shutters on the nearest block window. A man lounging outside 120 would blow his nose, and Harsh in 123 would warn the men working on the tunnel beneath that block to pack up. The same warning process applied to digging operations at 104 and 122, and to activities in the workshops, all of which operated in blocks on the compound's western side, the SZ or Safe Zone, a good distance from the gate. The eastern side was designated the DZ, or Danger Zone.

Several weeks later, Tim Walenn politely complained to Big X that his forgers had nearly been sprung several times by wandering ferrets looking in windows. The Dean and Dawson artists needed to work together to share scant resources and their knowledge and skills, in good light, near windows. George Harsh decided he required a security deputy whose sole focus was safeguarding the forgers and their work – not a muscleman like himself, but a quick-witted fellow good at organisation and deception. The prisoner appointed as security chief of the forgers' department was Paul Brickhill.

Brickhill, acutely embarrassed by his panic attack down Tom, readily accepted this responsible post, taking charge of the stooges allocated to Dean and Dawson, becoming one of just a small number of kriegies who knew everything about the mass escape. Working closely with chief forger Walenn, Brickhill devised a complex system of stooge locations and signals that allowed the forgers to work undetected in a library established in 110 Block. Forgers, who included Dicky Milne, a nephew of *Winnie the Pooh* author A. A. Milne, put in three to five hours a day on their meticulous work. Copying printed documents by hand, they stopped before they tired. A tired forger made mistakes. Dean and Dawson couldn't afford mistakes. The more complex passes took a month to complete. A mistake meant starting again from scratch.

In his new role, Brickhill became a good friend of his security associate George Harsh. It would be many years before he learned about Harsh's murderous past in Georgia. Harsh simply told Brickhill that prior to the war he'd been a journalist in Chicago. Brickhill considered him 'a wild, wild man' and a 'rambunctious soul'. When Brickhill asked Harsh how he'd been shot down, the American, lounging on the edge of his upper bunk with his legs dangling over the side, responded, 'I was sitting on a barn door over Berlin and some bastard shot the hinges off.'[92]

With Tom just short of the wire, the Germans began clearing the forest beside North Compound, for a new South Compound to house US airmen, including those currently housed in North Compound. To the frustration of X Organisation, this meant that Tom would have to go even further to reach the trees. It also meant that American X-men would miss out on the escape. To enable the Yanks to go out with the rest of the escapees, the Big Four decided to close up Dick and Harry and concentrate on Tom, hoping to complete it before South Compound opened. Soon measuring thirty-five metres in length, with a 'halfway house' chamber midway, Tom was resplendent with a little wooden railway running its length to haul earth back to the dispersal chamber.

Meanwhile, the growing quantities of tunnelled earth could no longer be accommodated in the gardens, and the dispersal department took to storing it in emptied Red Cross ration boxes kept beneath beds in barrack blocks. This was risky, and before long a ferret discovered stored earth in Red Cross boxes in 103, Brickhill's block. Glemnitz and his ferrets turned the compound upside down, without locating a tunnel. But now aware there was one somewhere, they were on heightened alert.

As work continued on Tom, its soil was hidden down Dick. Before long, German sound detectors picked up indications of digging near 123, starting point of Tom. Yet repeated searches of 123 by Glemnitz found nothing. And then the kriegies' luck ran out. A conscientious ferret named Hermann stumbled on Tom's entrance. The game was up. The triumphant Germans blew up Tom with explosives. Its loss sent a pall of gloom through the compound, but, at a mass meeting in the newly completed theatre, Massey and Bushell told kriegies that it was business as usual for X Organisation. The Big Four decided now to concentrate all efforts on Harry and break out to the north.

On 6 August, Brickhill wrote a postcard addressed to the International Red Cross in Cairo. In it, he requested that clothing he'd left behind in North Africa be sent to Matron Rimmer in Torquay, for her to send on to him at Stalag Luft 3. He listed the items he wanted: two uniforms, including the one made by Gieves Ltd, heavy brogue shoes, a forage cap, shirts, tie, socks and his RAAF greatcoat. He was insistent that he be sent at least one complete uniform, not the tunic from one and the trousers from another, which would not match. To those who knew how particular Brickhill was about his dress, this would not have seemed an unusual request.

Although it was still summer in Silesia, the camp's German censors well knew that winter at Sagan would be bitter, and come November prisoners would need all the clothes they could lay their hands on. The censors put Brickhill's card in the post, unaltered, and it duly reached the Red Cross in Cairo, who passed it on to the RAF. After Brickhill was confirmed as a POW, his belongings had been shipped to the Central Depository at RAF Colnbrook, at Slough, Buckinghamshire. His request was forwarded to Colnbrook and his clothing released to Matron Rimmer, who arranged for the items to be sent to Brickhill at Sagan via the Red Cross.

Brickhill had sought all these items primarily for use as escape clothes. With skilful cuts and tucks and the application of shoe polish as dye, Tommy Guest's tailors were converting spare uniforms into civilian clothes to wear on the run, and even creating near copies of German military uniforms for some bolder German-speaking kriegies. Brickhill's Gieves Ltd uniform, with its expensive cloth and satin lining, was ideal for transformation into a smart businessman's suit. The brogues would complement it nicely.

When the clothing parcel reached Brickhill, he kept most items for himself, donating several pieces to colleagues for their escape rig. It seems his surplus blue RAAF greatcoat went to Dutchman Bram 'Bob' van der Stock, a pre-war medical student who helped out in the compound hospital, where Brickhill befriended him while hospitalised with severe bronchitis. The trousers from the parcel's second uniform went to another escape candidate.[93]

In late August, to the chagrin of all prisoners, the three hundred USAAF personnel in North Compound were marched out to the new South Compound. Fresh RAF prisoners would soon fill their emptied blocks, 105 to 108. Americans who, like George Harsh, were members of the RAF remained in North Compound, but valuable X Organisation members such as Bub Clark and Jerry Sage were lost to South Compound. With Big S gone, George Harsh moved up in the X Organisation hierarchy, becoming security supremo. Clark and Sage departed vowing to dig their own tunnel and beat the Harry crew to freedom, with Clark becoming South Compound's Big X and Sage his Big S.

Sage didn't want to escape to get home. He had other plans. A member of the OSS (Office for Strategic Services), forerunner of America's Central Intelligence Agency, Sage, like Brickhill, had been captured in Tunisia; in his case, during a behind-the-lines operation. The Germans never discovered that Sage was an OSS operative, codenamed Dagger. And he was itching to use his espionage skills in occupied Europe.

Later, Brickhill would learn that, on 1 September, the RAAF had promoted him to flight lieutenant, the equivalent of an army captain. By this time, he'd befriended another 103 inmate on BBC News-taking duty, Conrad Norton, a South African journalist. A civilian, Norton had been a war correspondent attached to the RAF when captured in Italy. In 1941, Norton had co-written a book, *Vanguard to Victory*, with fellow war correspondent Uys Krige, about South African victories against German colonial forces in East Africa during 1940–41.

Brickhill and Norton were instructed to keep their Canary transcripts absolutely exact. As the pair learned, the BBC news contained coded information sent to POW camps throughout occupied Europe by a secret British government outfit, MI9. This was, like the better known MI5 and MI6, part of the British War Office's Directorate of Military Intelligence. Based initially at London hotels and later at Wilston Park in Beaconsfield, Buckinghamshire, MI9 had the task of facilitating and supporting escapes by British POWs and downed aircrew. It also gathered intelligence from POWs, those who'd found freedom and those still in camps. Several North Compound prisoners including Hugh Rowe and Henry Stockings had been briefed in England on the workings of MI9 prior to being shot down. Day appointed them the compound's 'code users'.

By day, Henry Stockings was one of Fanshawe's penguins. At night, by the low light of a candle, Stockings and Rowe decoded messages coming in via the BBC News transcripts. They also coded texts for selected British prisoners to send messages to MI9 in their letters and postcards home. That code related to page numbers in a standard English-German dictionary.[94] Outgoing messages would contain militarily important information from new prisoners, relating to what they'd seen on their way to the camp, and from X Organisation contacts on the Stalag Luft 3 staff.

Incoming messages included requests from London for specific information. In 1943 London particularly wanted to know about German rocket development, and X Organisation member Sydney Dowse, who'd been at Schubin with Day and Fanshawe, had befriended a German contact in the

Stalag Luft 3 censor department who let it slip that rocket development was going on at Peenemunde on the Baltic. This information was passed on to London via coded mail from North Compound.[95] Later in the year, the RAF mounted a 600-bomber raid on the Peenemunde complex which put Nazi rocket weapon development back by months. After the war, the work and very existence of MI9 remained a classified secret, in case it had to be activated again in another conflict. For that reason, Brickhill and other writers would for decades be prevented from mentioning MI9.

Among his inbound cards and letters, Brickhill had heard from Del Fox. Writing a card in reply on 27 November, he lamented that he was 'extensively browned off' and voiced the hope that he would see Del sometime in the future. He told her that the first snow had fallen at Stalag Luft 3, and it was getting mighty cold there. By that time there had been several shows put on by the kriegies in the compound theatre, and Brickhill reported that he'd enjoyed one or two of these. He also mentioned that he was involved in the fermentation of raisin wine for Christmas.[96]

Even Roger Bushell was contributing to the wine-making process, pilfering sugar from colleagues to go into the pot. The last big brew had been for riotous Fourth of July celebrations led by the Americans. This latest concoction would end up being consumed on New Year's Eve, with near-tragic results. Most wine drinkers would come off with crushing hangovers, but one drunken young Englishman would stagger out into the snow after lights-out, and be shot by a guard, although not fatally. The SBO would ban the making of raisin wine after that.

Brickhill also told Del that he was studying French and Spanish intensively. He didn't tell her that he had chosen to learn these two languages because his intended escape route would take him through the south of France to neutral Spain. Likewise, he failed to mention that in October the men of North Compound had been heartened to learn that the Williams trio had escaped from East Compound using their wooden-horse tunnel. All three would succeed in reaching England.

This break was encouraging news for North Compound's X Organisation. The men of North Compound needed geeing up. While Harry's progress had been steady, the tunnel was still well short of the woods, and digging had been suspended until the new year, when the worst of winter had passed. The Gestapo, Germany's secret police, were seething that three POWs had escaped to England, and security in the Reich had tightened. As the X Organisation learned through its contacts, the Gestapo was now talking about shooting POWs caught on the run.

When Roger Bushell was told this, he dismissed it as a bluff, reminding colleagues that the Geneva Convention prevented the execution of POWs. And hadn't Germany been the first nation to sign the Convention, in 1929? Bushell remained gung-ho about his big break. As tunnelling had forged ahead the previous spring, he'd trumpeted the motto 'Home by Christmas'. Now, as the Christmas of 1943 came and went and he was still a prisoner, he was forced to revise that goal.

11.

The Great Escape

COME 7 JANUARY 1944, the weather was mild enough to consider recommencing work in Harry. After an initial inspection and running repairs, digging resumed a week later, after a two-month hiatus. At this time of year the perennial problem of tunnel-soil dispersal was exacerbated by the fact that snow lay throughout the camp. It would be impossible to hide earth coming up from Harry on the ground. The solution proved simple. There was a gap beneath the sloping floor of the compound's theatre and the ground. Penguins paid regular visits to the theatre while rehearsals for the latest show were underway, depositing their loads. The theatrical kriegies protested vehemently. Should the ferrets find tunnel soil there, they said, their theatre would be closed down. They were overruled by Wings Day. Escape came before entertainment, he proclaimed.

As digging progressed in Harry through February it was freezing down below, and all thirty diggers involved continually suffered from colds. It was estimated the tunnel would reach the woods within a few weeks when Roger Bushell called in star forger Flight Lieutenant Ley Kenyon and gave him a special assignment. Bushell wanted a permanent record of X Organisation's amazing feat of engineering. Previously, their precious camera had been taken down into Harry in an attempt to take photographs. Due to regular Allied air raids in the vicinity, the Germans had cut the power supply, blacking out the camp, and Harry. The candlelight used in the tunnel proved insufficient for successful photography, and some bright spark had suggested that Kenyon be sent into Harry with his sketchpad. An art teacher before the war, Kenyon was a fine artist, and Bushell commissioned him to draw what was going on below.

'Prepare to go down for four hours,' Bushell instructed, 'and make your drawing board a small one.'[97]

At the change of tunnelling shift, Kenyon clambered down into Harry, remaining until the next shift change. In candlelight, he sketched men working in the dispersal area, in the workshop and air-conditioning pumping station, and in the tunnel itself, where, lying on his back, he used the wooden ceiling as his drawing board. Returning to the surface, Kenyon packed his drawings into an airtight container made by the engineering department from Klim cans. The container was taken to 122 block and secreted down Dick's dispersal chamber along with forged escape documents awaiting use.

In late February, X Organisation received a blow. Twenty men were called out by Rubberneck, chief ferret now that Glemnitz was occupied elsewhere.[98] Considered troublemakers, these men were immediately transferred to the maximum-security punishment camp at Belaria, thirty-five kilometres away. Among the purged group were Floody, Harsh and Fanshawe. Harsh didn't mind so much. He still considered the mass break harebrained, and at least he and best friend Floody would still be together. Bushell regretted their loss, but nothing would deter him from his big break.

By 14 March, Harry measured almost 130 metres in length, and three kriegie mathematicians calculated that the tunnel was beneath the forest on the northern fringe of North Compound. Sure enough, digging an exit shaft straight up, tunnellers reached tree roots 30 centimetres from the surface. Bushell ordered further operations suspended until a night with good weather and no moon. On that night, the final breakout would be made.

Excitement ran high in X Organisation ranks. Escape kit was readied – forged documents, clothing, accessories, and high-energy 'Fudge' escape food in 4-ounce cocoa tins. Concocted by pre-war dietary expert David Lubbock, Fudge was high in fat and sugar. Big Four members reviewed escapees' fake identities and cover stories, sending some away to revise when holes were found. The Big Four now also chose the escape order for breakout night. Wings Day's policy was to top the list with men who'd dug the tunnels and worked in dispersal at the head of the shafts, followed by X Organisation's senior men, with all others coming next.[99]

Bushell nominated the first thirty names, which included Day and himself, with their order of escape dictated by a draw from a hat. After this, seventy more names from a list of 190 were chosen from the hat. Brickhill was to say that his name was chosen for a privileged position. Once these first 100 were selected Bushell nominated another thirty, after which a further seventy names were drawn from the hat. That made 200 names. Bushell estimated that between lights-out and dawn at least 220 men could use the tunnel to escape. Another twenty names were drawn.

Brickhill was excited at the prospect of adventure as he fled across western Europe. Equally, he was terrified at the prospect of going back into a rat hole ten metres underground, then crawling for a hundred metres with the possibility of another cave-in burying him. Roger Bushell soon called in Brickhill and four others who had panicked while underground, and informed the little group that he had summarily removed them all from the escape list. X Organisation was worried that, should any of these men again panic while in the tunnel and try to back out, they would cause chaos, perhaps even bringing the roof down in their blind desperation to regain the surface. Either way, they would block escape to those waiting behind.[100]

Bushell tried to soften the blow by telling the delisted quintet that at least they would get to see, and enjoy, the aftermath of the break. 'I can promise you plenty of entertainment later,' he told Brickhill and his equally disconsolate comrades.[101]

Brickhill acknowledged that, for the sake of all, being dumped from the list was the right decision. But that didn't prevent him from feeling angry and frustrated. After all the work he'd put in, to lose his privileged place in line and be barred from escape was a kick in the guts. Two additional men were also prevented from taking part in the break, this time by order of SBO Massey. Cronk Canton and dour Scotsman Robert 'Crump' Ker-Ramsey had been chief tunnellers with Floody, and that was why Massey ordered them to stay behind, to form the nucleus of the X Organisation that would resume tunnelling once the big break was history. For no one knew how many years this war would last. Likewise, no one knew how many more escapes it would be necessary to engineer at Stalag Luft 3 before it was all over.

Friday 24 March was chosen for the breakout. There would be no moon that night. In addition, according to escaper Sydney Dowse, the ferret rostered onto Friday nights was lazy and unlikely to bother entering the compound for a spot check.[102] In the lead-up to breakout day, a team of kriegies not on the escape list checked the papers and equipment of the 220 who were. When the escape clothes of Dutchman Bob van der Stock were checked, a Gieves Ltd label was found in the roll-neck sweater he intended wearing, while his real name was on his socks. Off came the labels. Even Big X himself made a slip-up; Bushell had packed a hairbrush labelled 'Kent of London'. Out came the hairbrush.

Throughout escape planning and preparation, Bushell had been forbidden by SBO Massey from being physically involved because he was closely watched by the Germans, and he'd kept well away from tunnels and workshops. The Germans considered Bushell an arch-escaper after he'd bolted from a train when being transferred from Stalag Luft 1 at Barth on the Baltic. He'd succeeded in spending months in hiding with a Czech family in Prague before being recaptured. His Czech helpers were arrested and shot. Partly to keep the Germans thinking he'd since become a model prisoner, Bushell had taken part in the compound's theatrical shows, and leading up to the break he rehearsed the lead role of Professor Henry Higgins in the upcoming production of *Pygmalion*. Not expecting to be around for opening night on 25 March, Bushell had encouraged his understudy to prepare to take over at short notice.

At Sagan on the morning of 24 March the sun shone weakly, but snow lay fifteen centimetres thick on the ground. This was not ideal for an escape. Snow would make walking cross-country extremely difficult, and tracking of escapees extremely easy. There was the danger of frostbite. And, if driven to find overnight shelter, escapees risked being captured in outbuildings. At 11.30 that morning, Bushell hosted a meeting of X Organisation's executive. It was only a short meeting. After sounding out his colleagues about making the break now or waiting for April and better weather, Bushell, impatient to get on with it, made a decision, and a decree.

'Tonight's the night.'[103]

Feverish preparations proceeded through the afternoon. Men on the escape list gathered up escape kit from hiding places. Fake travel documents were stamped with the current date using a date stamp fashioned from a rubber boot heel by Al Hake. And men began slipping in and out of 104 by circuitous routes. Those coming in were escapers. These going out were 104 occupants remaining behind. Giving up their rooms to kriegies down for escape, they would spend the night in the blocks and bunks of escapees. Among those moving out of 104 was code user Henry Stockings. His eyesight had become so bad he was rated unfit for an escape bid.

In 103, Brickhill tried to be upbeat as he shook the hands of Al Hake, Wings Day and others on the escape list as they moved next door to 104 in preparation for going out. In 104, escapers reported to escape 'controller' Dave Torrens, who marked their names off a list. By sundown, 104 Block was packed with 220 nervous men. Anxiously they waited their turn to climb down the block's narrow shaft then propel themselves along Harry's rail lines full-length on the little trolleys that had been used to bring out soil.

The first fifty men were considered to have the best chance of success. Most of this first batch had foreign-language skills and were given a share of the small cache of German money collected by X Organisation, to enable them to buy railway tickets. The remainder would have to make their way overland – Bushell called them the 'hard-arsers' and he frankly gave them almost zero chance of getting home.

Come early evening, in 104's room 23, the hot stove covering the entrance to Harry was lifted aside and tunnel king Ker-Ramsey went down to check that everything was in order after weeks of neglect. He seemed to be gone forever, but eventually he reported back and gave the OK after making minor repairs. At 8.45, Leslie 'Johnny' Bull and Cuthbert 'Johnny' Marshall descended into the gloom. Along with Floody and Ker-Ramsey, the two Johnnies had made up X Organisation's tunnelling subcommittee, and they'd been at the forefront of digging over the past year. It was their job to open up the tunnel at the woods. For their efforts, they would have the privilege of being first men out. They were followed into Harry by fifteen others including Big X.

It took quite a while to trolley one at a time along the tunnel. Finally, at 9.30, Bull, standing on a ladder built up one side of the exit shaft, dug the last 30 centimetres of earth away from above him, and stuck his head out into the cool night air. He was horrified to discover that the tunnel's surveyors had blundered – the exit shaft had come up in the open, three metres short of the trees and just fifteen metres from the legs of a goon tower. Fortunately, the guard up in the tower routinely looked into the compound, not out to the surrounding woods. Meanwhile, close to the tunnel's exit, two patrolling guards were walking by in opposite directions, crossing midway on their beat. Withdrawing back down into the tunnel, Bull had a whispered consultation with Bushell and Marshall at the base of the exit shaft.

They considered closing up the entrance and digging further until Harry reached the woods, postponing the break until the next month. Then Bushell remembered that their travel documents, which had taken many months to forge, were date-stamped for this weekend. They had to go now, he declared. The trio quickly agreed a system to get escapees across the snow-covered open ground beyond the exit hole. The first man out would trail a rope to the woods. When all was clear, he would jiggle the rope for the next man to exit. Succeeding men would briefly take over his role, then make their escape into the woods. A request was passed back along Harry to 104 for a twenty-metre length of rope.

The Great Escape

More time ticked by as the rope was acquired. Johnny Bull then went back up the exit ladder and looked out. When the patrolling guards were out of sight, he clambered up into the snow and scurried to the trees, trailing the rope. Using this, he signalled the all clear. Marshall appeared, and scuttled to join him. After wishing Bull good luck, Marshall played the rope out into the trees, then hunched down as he waited to be joined by the next few men out. Like a nervous mole, another man popped his head up and looked anxiously all around. The rope quivered. The mole sprang from his hole.

The Great Escape was underway.

12.

Counting the Cost

LYING IN HIS bunk in 103, Brickhill could only imagine what was going on down below, and at Harry's exit. Just after 10.00 pm, he heard the German guard who closed up the blocks for the night doing his rounds. The men in 104 held their collective breath as their block's outer door banged shut and the wooden bar that locked the occupants in for the night was slid into place. The guard trudged away. Midnight was lights-out time in the blocks, and camp rules meant that all blackout shutters had to be open so that guards could look inside. Even in 104, escape central, the shutters were opened when the witching hour arrived. Out in the compound, a Luftwaffe *hündefuehrer* was on the prowl with a fierce German shepherd on a leash.

Brickhill lay listening for sounds that would indicate the break had been detected. It was impossible to sleep. Not long after midnight, the camp's air-raid sirens began to wail.

The RAF was bombing Breslau, fifty kilometres away. In the Kommandantur, a guard threw a switch, and the camp's lights were abruptly dowsed. Stalag Luft 3 was thrown into darkness. Only later would Brickhill learn that this caused a lengthy delay in the breakout. Escapees could get by without the electric lighting strung along much of Harry's length because it was supplanted by candles. But because the blackout also closed down the camp's perimeter lights and tower searchlights, the Luftwaffe doubled the guard. With twice as many vigilant sentries walking the perimeter, it was judged too risky to try to make the move from tunnel exit to woods. Only after the sirens sounded the all clear and the guard was reduced could escaping resume. By 2.45, the blackout had ended and roughly thirty men had made it out. In 104, men continued to file to the trap to follow their colleagues in the slow, jerky exit from Harry.

A little before 5.00 that Saturday morning, a rifle shot rang out on the northern edge of North Compound. It was heard all the way back at 104. A guard had stumbled on an escapee emerging from the tunnel exit, then spotted two others on the edge of the woods. The guard blew his whistle, then, shining a torch down Harry's exit shaft, found a fourth man on the ladder. All hell broke loose, above and below ground. Armed troops came dashing from the guardroom, and inside the tunnel scores of frantic kriegies attempted to retrace their way back to 104. In the block itself, small fires broke out as escapers tried to burn forged papers – which might get them shot for espionage.

Some escapers launched themselves out 104 windows and tried to run back to their original blocks. A Spandau machinegun chattered from the goon tower near the Cooler, and 9mm bullets whistled over running men's heads, putting an end to their flight. Retreating to 104, they awaited their fate with their comrades.

Outside the guardroom in the Vorlager stood the Kommandant of Stalag Luft 3, the tall figure of Oberst Friedrich von Lindeiner. He was raging at the four kriegies captured at the tunnel exit. Heads bowed, they stood in line in front of him as he blasted them. Von Lindeiner was actually liked by SBO Massey, and Brickhill and other prisoners felt sorry for him because he'd been a fair man and they knew he would be punished by his overlords for allowing a mass escape right under his nose. The colonel had even passed warnings into the compound that the Gestapo would shoot escapees caught on the run. Now, his mouth was flecked with foam as he raged at the captured quartet.

'So, gangsters, you do not like my camp? I will hand you over to the Gestapo. They will finish you all!'[104]

As the compound filled with Luftwaffe troops, all camp inmates were ordered out into the snow and searched. The 140 men from 104 were formed up and kept apart from the others, who were ordered to line up in ranks on the Appell ground. As guards attempted to count the prisoners, some POWs slipped from rank to rank to confuse the count. Shaking with anger, Oberst Von Lindeiner drew his automatic pistol.

'I shall personally shoot the first man that moves!' he shouted.[105]

It was clear he was in deadly earnest. No one moved after that. The final headcount made the commandant turn grey – seventy-six prisoners missing. Seventy-six! It was the greatest RAF prisoner escape of the war. As the quartet captured at Harry's exit were hauled off to the Cooler, the men from 104 were marched to the gate. There, they stood in the cold. Von Lindeiner was so enraged, some thought all would be handed over to the Gestapo. The remaining kriegies were kept in their ranks, shivering, on the Appell ground. All had to stand in place for hours as their belongings were searched and the blocks turned upside down. Eventually, all were dismissed to their blocks.

Within two weeks, all but three of the Stalag Luft 3 escapees had been caught. And Oberst Von Lindeiner had been replaced as the camp's commandant. Relieved of duty by Goering two days after the escape, he would face disciplinary action – but would survive the war and live to the age of eighty-two.

On the morning of 6 April, SBO Massey was summoned to the commandant's office, where he met the acting commandant, Oberstleutnant Erich Cordes, who himself had been a prisoner of the Russians during the First World War. Via an interpreter, Massey was informed by Cordes that forty-one of the men who'd escaped on March 24–25 had been shot while resisting arrest or while attempting to again escape when in custody. Massey couldn't imagine that every one of these escapees had died as a result. To his mind, some must have suffered wounds that weren't life threatening and ended up in hospital. But when Massey asked how many of the forty-one had been wounded, he was stiffly informed that all had been killed. Clearly, they had been executed.[106]

Massey, stunned, called 300 senior officers to a meeting in the compound theatre, and passed on the news. The 300 relayed the information to the rest of the prisoners. Paul Brickhill, like most of his colleagues, didn't believe it at first. He thought the Germans were bluffing, trying to put a scare into inmates to discourage further escape attempts.

Massey left the camp shortly after this, in a group of prisoners repatriated to Britain because of physical or mental infirmities. He was replaced as North Compound's SBO by Group Captain Douglas Wilson, who was transferred over from East Compound. Shot down in June 1943 flying a Halifax, forty-six-year-old Wilson was an Australian, originally from Berowra, New South Wales. In 1942, he'd been RAAF Officer Commanding Northwest Area in Australia when the Japanese repeatedly bombed Darwin. At the time he was downed, Wilson was on exchange duty with the RAF.

Like his predecessor, Wilson was pro-escape, and no coward. Involved in East Compound's wooden-horse escape the previous year, he'd also bravely put his neck on the line to protect Czech prisoners from the Germans, an act for which he would be awarded a medal by the Czechoslovakian Government post-war. But in the wake of the deaths of so many men from North Compound's mass escape, Wilson was now very worried, and ultra-cautious. He was not alone. As news of the executions spread, SBOs and SAOs at British and American POW camps across the Reich ordered all escape planning halted. At Schubin, Oflag 64's Senior American Officer would even order existing tunnels filled in.

On 15 April, Hauptmann Pieber handed SBO Wilson a list containing the names of Stalag Luft 3 escapees who'd been shot. But there weren't forty-one names on the list. There were forty-seven. As Wilson had the list tacked up on the compound noticeboard, the camp's newly appointed commandant, Oberst Franz Braune, had his guards prepare for a possible riot by prisoners.

Paul Brickhill, one of the kriegies who crowded around the noticeboard, saw that the list included Big X Roger Bushell, Wally Valenta the intelligence whizz, first man out Johnny Bull, Aussie supply supremo Willy Williams, George Harsh's two security henchmen McGill and McGarr, and two of Brickhill's closest friends in the camp, chief forger Tim Walenn and the singing Australian compass-maker Al Hake. There was no riot by the kriegies. They were too shocked to muster the anger for that. So shocked, in fact, they kept returning to the noticeboard throughout the day to check that the names of close friends were indeed on the list.

On 25 April, the compound's remaining Australian and New Zealand POWs gathered to commemorate Anzac Day, their joint national remembrance day. The little German camera used to make ID pictures for escapees was put to more traditional use, with the Aussies and Kiwis bunching for a group photo. Brickhill was there, neatly dressed as usual, in battledress, shirt and tie. And, as usual, he was to the forefront yet keeping a low profile, squatting in the front row. Members of the group had one thing in common; all wore slightly shell-shocked expressions. Just two weeks after they'd heard the news of the executions of their comrades, they were still in disbelief.

The news worsened. On 18 May, another, shorter list was pinned to the noticeboard. This contained the names of three more escapees shot by the Gestapo. The total now stood at fifty. From now on, the executed men were referred to collectively by prisoners as the Fifty. The dead men had come from thirteen different nations and included twenty-one Britons, six Canadians, six Poles, five Australians, three South Africans and two New Zealanders. Urns containing the ashes of the Fifty were subsequently returned to the camp and interred at a graveyard nearby, where Oberst Braune permitted kriegies to build a stone monument to the executed men.

Fifteen of the recaptured escapees were returned alive to Stalag Luft 3. Only much later would Brickhill learn the fates of all seventy-six men who'd made it out of Harry. Every one of the recaptured men had been jailed and questioned by the Kripo, Germany's criminal police, but only the Fifty had been handed over to the Gestapo, who shot them. Of the rest, Wings Day, Johnny Dodge, Bertram 'Jimmy' James and Sydney Dowse were lodged in a dungeon at the Sachsenhausen concentration camp, while the others were distributed around various special camps and prisons. All would survive the war.

Three escapees made home runs to Britain. None were Britons. Two of them, Per 'Peter' Bergsland and Jens Muller, were Norwegians who escaped to Sweden by stowing away aboard a ship that sailed from Stettin on the Baltic coast. From there, they flew to England, landing within weeks of the breakout. The third man took four months to get back. That last man 'home' was Bob van der Stock, eighteenth man out of the tunnel. After first reaching his native country of Holland, which was occupied by the Germans, he was hidden for several months by countrymen until he set off to enter Spain via southern France. He reached Spain by walking across the Pyrenees. The British embassy in Madrid sent him to Gibraltar, and from there he was flown to England by the RAF.

Throughout his escape, Van der Stock had worn the RAAF greatcoat, minus military adornment, that Brickhill had likely given him. Like Bergsland and Muller, the majority of escapees had travelled in pairs. The route via France and Spain that Van der Stock took on his own suggests that he and Brickhill, who'd been fervently studying French and Spanish, may have originally intended travelling together, a plan thwarted when Brickhill was pulled from the escape list by Bushell at the last minute.

The three men who succeeded in their escape bids had several things in common. All spoke fluent German, and on the run all traded on their home backgrounds – Van der Stock's cover story, for example, was that he was a Dutch worker travelling for his job. The British and Dominion escapees had no such backgrounds to exploit, and were up against it from the beginning. From England, all three home-runners sent postcards to Stalag Luft 3 using false names, letting the inmates know they'd made it. Just the same, the score was not pretty: three home, twenty-three back behind the wire, fifty dead.

*

In the weeks following the escape, as the grim news of the murder of his colleagues sunk in, Brickhill became determined to document the mass escape, and the sacrifice of the Fifty. As he began talking to survivors of the break, he told fellow Canary transcriber Conrad Norton what he had in mind. Throwing the idea around, they agreed there was plenty of material in the camp for a book about a series of daring escapes. Some stories they'd been told by fellow kriegies about escapes from crashing bombers made the hair stand on end. So, the pair agreed to jointly compile escape stories for a book. As Norton hadn't been involved in the mass escape, Brickhill would focus on that, while Norton collected other individual tales of escape. In the end, Brickhill would also contribute several additional escape stories.

This would be a book they would publish once the Allies were victorious and they were free men again. Brickhill never doubted that victory and freedom lay at the end of the long road ahead. He would later say that the two worst aspects about life as a POW, once he got used to the lack of beer and female company, were the omnipresent feeling of hunger and the indefinite nature of his time in the camp: 'You couldn't say you wouldn't still be there – or worse – in ten years.'[107]

Doug Williams, the new SBO, had no objections to the Brickhill-Norton writing project, and the pair began surreptitiously interviewing colleagues and taking notes. Brickhill made a point of interviewing the returned escapees, West Australian Paul Royle among them, in an attempt to learn what had happened to all the men on the break once they'd left the tunnel.

There were two problems for the chroniclers to overcome. Their captors forbade prisoners from writing anything other than the approved number of letters and postcards every month. The keeping of diaries was *verboten*. No writing materials were dispensed by the Germans apart from a ration of pencils, pre-printed forms for letter writing, and postcards. So, for Brickhill and Norton's notes, in pencil and employing the smallest writing possible, they scrounged every piece of paper they could, including blank pages cut from books with razor blades.

The second difficulty was keeping their notes out of German hands. Anyone found with notes about the camp would be accused by the Germans of being spies, and probably shot. The pair's notes, then, had to be hidden, and with great care. Initially, their growing manuscript was slipped behind a wall panel in 103. But regular searches by the ferrets meant that sooner or later that hiding place could be found. To avoid this, whenever other blocks were searched, Brickhill would wait until the guards had moved on, then relocate the notes to the latest block searched. It never occurred to the methodical Germans to double back and search that block again the next day. With the permission of the reconstituted X Organisation, the writers also resorted to hiding their notes in the dispersal area down Dick.

Ever the good journalist, Brickhill tried to get their guards into conversation to obtain juicy quotes from their perspective. He asked one ferret why, with the war turning against the Germans on all fronts, he would want to continue to be a Nazi.

'You understand not?' said the ferret. 'To be Germans we must be Nazis. I know that the whole country is behind the Fuehrer.'[108]

German radio was routinely broadcast in Stalag Luft 3 over loudspeakers, and, on 6 June, Brickhill and his colleagues heard a German announcement about two massive Allied armadas spotted approaching the French coast off Cap d'Antifer and Calais. This, thought the POWs, must be the much-anticipated Allied invasion of France. 'It gave us great joy,' Brickhill would say, 'but we wondered for months what had happened to those convoys.'[109] Those armadas were radar deceptions, designed to mask the true D-Day landings in Normandy.

Come August, the British, Americans and Canadians had been ashore in France two months. In Italy, the Allies had taken Rome and were pushing north. In the East, the Russians were overrunning German armies and had even established a foothold in eastern Poland. As the Germans retreated on all fronts, life for kriegies became even grimmer than before. Red Cross rations were halved that August, and would remain at that reduced level. At the same time, delivery of clothing from family and friends via the Red Cross, which, up to that time, had occurred every three months, ceased altogether. In North Compound, to keep spirits up, X Organisation began another escape tunnel. Called George, it was dug from beneath a seat in the compound's theatre. There was no specific escape plan in mind, but the project kept minds and muscles active.

By late in the year, outside contacts suggested that Hitler would order the execution of all POWs rather than give them up. George had reached the wire by this time, but the descending winter forced the suspension of tunnelling. Now, SBO Wilson created the Klim Club, a secret army within the compound involving all inmates. Rather than allow themselves to be executed en masse by the Germans, the Klim Club began making weapons, conducting lectures and preparing tactics for a battle of survival inside the camp. George would be used as a bolthole should resistance prove necessary.

Continuing Allied victories and the creeping advance from east, west and south should have been cause for hope and joy for kriegies. In reality, those victories, and the prospect of a cataclysmic end to the Nazi Reich, made Christmas 1944 the gloomiest yuletide yet at Stalag Luft 3.

13.

March or Die

BY THE EVENING of Saturday, 27 January 1945, the advancing Russian Army was getting too close to Stalag Luft 3 for the comfort of German authorities.[110] The Russians had crossed the Oder River at Breslau, just ninety kilometres away, while advance elements of the Red Army were reported to be as close as forty-five kilometres from Sagan. At 9.00 pm, word quickly spread through the camp that all prisoners were to prepare to march in an hour's time. Men in the compound hospital considered too sick to be moved could remain, but close to 11,000 men would be evacuated from Stalag Luft 3 overnight, in one fell swoop.

Sure enough, from 10.00 pm, in darkness, prisoners were progressively herded out onto a road covered with 30 centimetres of snow, and pushed west, away from the Russians. The occupants of West and South Compounds went first, then the men of Centre Compound. The occupants of North

Compound followed. The last to hit the road, at 6.30 am next day, would be the men from East Compound and the inmates from the nearby maximum security camp at Belaria, George Harsh and Wally Floody being among the men marched from the latter. All were part of a forced movement west from Nazi camps of more than 300,000 Allied POWs.

As they left behind the now-abandoned forest camp that had been home for many of them for several years, Brickhill and his colleagues began the march rugged up with as many items of clothing as they could wear, and draped with bedrolls and improvised haversacks. Those haversacks were packed with belongings and as much food and cigarettes as possible from Red Cross parcels stockpiled at the camp. One prisoner was to estimate that 20,000 unopened Red Cross parcels had to be left behind.[111]

Some handy prisoners were the envy of their comrades after ripping out the sides of bunks or pulling down bookshelves to hastily build sleds onto which they piled their loads, complete with improvised tow ropes around their necks. Brickhill wasn't that ambitious; loading his pockets with goodies, he slung a bedroll around his neck, made up of his thin mattress bound up in blankets.

It was 4.00 am before the last men from the last North Compound block departed. The bright moonlight that lit their way was sometimes blotted out by snowstorms, as, preceded by staff cars for Luftwaffe officers and a truck carrying provisions for guards, the prisoners dragged themselves and their loads along in a struggling, slithering column which trailed away for as far as the eye could see. A detachment of Stalag Luft 3's Luftwaffe guards, including the camp's dog handlers with their snapping German shepherds, walked at intervals beside the column. The guards wore greatcoats and gloves, were armed with submachine guns, and carried full packs on their backs. They, too, were being made homeless by this hurried evacuation.

Before long, the prisoners were mixing with retreating German troops and refugees on the road west. Soon, the route was lined with POWs' discarded personal treasures and broken sleds, cast aside in the snow among dead horses and the bodies of refugees who'd perished. There was even a kriegie's saxophone among the flotsam and jetsam. Over seven days, the POWs were marched one hundred kilometres through the snow. En route, their guards gave the prisoners a single meal, of barley soup. The Red Cross packs of raisins, tinned bully beef, chocolate, tea and coffee each man was carrying were supposed to fill the void.

As each day passed and his strength ebbed away, Brickhill progressively offloaded things to lighten his load as he staggered along. He dumped packets of cigarettes, razor blades, even Red Cross food. Through it all, he continued to carry his bedroll. In the centre of that bedroll was a roll of papers – the notes that he and Norton had written in Stalag Luft 3, which they were determined to turn into a book. At night, Brickhill would use that grubby mound of papers as a pillow. Each day, back the notes would go into the bedroll.

Brickhill never seriously considered dumping the papers. Something checked him when the impulse to rid himself of their weight came over him. To Brickhill, that would be like abandoning a child he'd fathered. He could shave his growing beard later, and could scrounge food. But he couldn't recreate, with the needed accuracy, the stories his comrades had shared with him in camp. This was material not even Brickhill, with his excellent memory for detail, could recreate with complete accuracy without the notes. Twice, he fell in the snow, but he didn't abandon the papers as he struggled back to his feet.[112]

Knowing that if he didn't get up he'd be shot by guards, each time he fell a determination to survive and tell his story drove him to find reserves of strength he didn't know he possessed, and he resumed the slow, painful march, still with his precious notes hidden in his bedroll. He would estimate that during the march seventy-five men from Stalag Luft 3 collapsed and died from exhaustion or were shot. He pushed on, huddling with comrades during their night stops in barns, an abandoned cinema, even in a working bottle factory.

Coming down a steep hill to Spremberg, the North Compound column was steered to a railway siding where two trains of boxcars awaited. The column was divided and loaded aboard. One group went north, to Luckenwalde and crowded Stalag 3-A. The train carrying Brickhill's group rattled northwest for two days. Forty men were crammed into each boxcar with their kit, giving Brickhill and his comrades just enough room to sit but not enough to lie down to sleep. During the journey, the men in Brickhill's boxcar were given no food. A sip of water was doled out after thirty-six hours, taken from the locomotive's water tank.

Through Brunswick, Magdeburg and Hanover the train rattled. Brickhill reckoned that he and others around him lost an average of fourteen kilograms in weight during the journey. Most couldn't afford to lose that much, and many haggard, hungry, frozen men looked like skeletons as unloading began at Tarmstedt Ost at 5.30 pm on 2 February. They were north of Bremen, not far from the North Sea coast. Another march lay ahead, of just a kilometre this time, to Westertimke. There, they were halted outside a former naval POW camp, Marlag-Milag Nord, which had been condemned as unfit for habitation.

In teeming rain, lined up in ranks outside the camp, the thousands of prisoners had to wait to be searched before being allowed to enter the camp and take shelter in empty huts. Many men collapsed before their turn came, and had to be carried in once searched. Brickhill stood for seven hours before he was called forward. Others had to wait as long as eight hours. Staggering to the camp gate, Brickhill wearily raised his arms to allow a guard to search his pockets. The guard then pointed to the bedroll slung around his neck.

'What do you have in there?' the German demanded.

A feeling of dread came over Brickhill. Would his precious manuscript be wrenched from him? Summoning up a grin, he replied, in a desperate bid to bluff his way by, 'I've got a tommy-gun in there.'

The German laughed. And waved him through.[113]

In overcrowded huts devoid of furniture or cooking facilities, and with very little food and no medical attention provided by their guards, the Stalag Luft 3 men waited at the Marlag-Milag camp through February and March for the war to end. Sleeping on the floor, Brickhill was grateful for his bedroll. As for food, he and others stretched their Red Cross rations.

On 10 April, with Allied forces crossing the Rhine, the men at Westertimke felt sure that deliverance was at hand. But the Germans were determined not to free them. That day, to the horror of the exhausted prisoners, their guards herded them from the camp to begin another march, north this time, away from advancing friendly forces.

For three weeks, the Germans kept the kriegies on the march, towards the Elbe River. Now they spent the night in fields. The weather had improved. No longer was there snow or ice on the ground. Just the same, the prisoners had to struggle for space on the roads with German troops and refugees. Passing through one town, Brickhill found himself shoved off the pavement by surly local police. Footpaths were reserved for Germans. Other policemen attacked RAF kriegies around Brickhill, bashing them with rifle butts and kicking them when they fell.

'Bandits! Gangsters! Murderers!' raged the policemen.[114]

The Germans weren't the only ones the prisoners had to be wary of. As the weather fined up, Allied aircraft were free to prowl the hazy blue skies. They proved a danger to friend and foe alike. More than once, columns of tramping POWs were strafed by rocket-firing RAF Typhoons which mistook them for German troops. To the disgust of their friends, thirty prisoners were killed by friendly fire. It was a stupid and wasteful end for men who had endured so much and were so close to freedom.[115]

Food was supplemented by bartering. German civilians in areas they passed through traded eggs and bread for Red Cross coffee retained by prisoners – Germans hadn't tasted real coffee in years. On one occasion, POWs plundered a vast quantity of potatoes from a farm. Meanwhile, their guards were still under orders to shoot anyone who fell out of line, and Brickhill saw two RAF men shot and killed when they could go no further. Brickhill only learned later that the guards had orders to shoot *all* prisoners if the column failed to reach the Elbe by a specific date. They were still short of the Elbe by the date in question, but the Luftwaffe men were not SS or Gestapo, and they chose to ignore the shoot-to-kill order.

On the last day of April, Brickhill and his colleagues were sheltering in barns near Lubeck when they heard artillery booming in the distance. The British Army was crossing the Elbe. On trudged the prisoners. On 2 May, they were on the march when, around 11.45 that morning, they heard firing down the road behind them. Presently, two tanks emerged from trees and rumbled towards the column, which had stopped as prisoners and guards alike wondered whether the tanks were British or German. Looking around him, Brickhill could see his colleagues become incredibly tense. Were they about to win their freedom at last, or was this a false alarm? Hatches in the front tank opened, and the heads of two British tank men popped up.

'We ran up to them screaming at the top of our voices,' Brickhill later said.[116]

Free men again, they had to wait another six days before being taken to a landing ground where Lancaster bombers were coming and going. Courtesy of their own service, the RAF, the former POWs were given a one-way ticket, back to England.

14.

A Friendly Interrogation

For its last operation of the war, the RAF's 2nd Tactical Air Force collected and repatriated thousands of POWs from Germany. Packed aboard a Lancaster bomber with other ex-prisoners, Paul Brickhill was one of thousands flown out of Germany by the RAF on 8 May, the day the war ended – Victory in Europe Day, or VE Day, as it became known. Brickhill and other freed RAF kriegies including his Sydney *Sun* colleague John Ulm were flown to RAF Waddington, a bomber base seven kilometres south of Lincoln, in Lincolnshire.

For many returning former aircrew, flying over the white cliffs of Dover for the first time in years proved an emotional experience. Aboard one Lancaster, Ulm was invited up to the cockpit to see the cliffs as his bomber overflew them. The sight filled his heart with joy. Brickhill had no such fond experience. Apparently, this flight, only his second since being shot down – the first being the 1943 flight to Naples from Tunis – proved so nerve-racking for Brickhill that he cringed in terror. This once-fine pilot seems to have vowed then and there to never fly again if he could help it.

At Waddington, the ex-prisoners, unshaven, stinking dirty with long hair and unkempt uniforms, were ushered from their planes towards a line of young WAAFs, members of the Women's Auxiliary Air Force, waiting outside a barrack building. But the women were not there just to welcome them.

'Hang on, you lot!' exclaimed a senior WAAF as the men went to bypass them.[117]

The kriegies stopped in their tracks as the women instructed them to open their shirts, and then their trousers. With giggles from the girls and red faces among returnees, the WAAFs applied generous amounts of delousing powder to each man. Then it was inside the barracks for a steaming hot cup of tea.

Brickhill and his Australian colleagues were ordered to report to the RAAF's 11th Personnel Dispatch and Reception Centre (11PDRC), at Brighton. When they asked how they would get there, they were handed railway 'chits', travel vouchers, and told to make their own way. They set off for Brighton that same day.

From a series of trains, passing down through central England, through London and south to the coast, Brickhill surveyed the outside world feeling oddly detached. London still looked a city at war. Damage from German bombs and indiscriminate V1 and V2 rockets was widespread. Parks and public buildings were bereft of their iron railings, which had been melted down to make munitions. Sandbagged walls

A Friendly Interrogation

stood outside the entrances to stations, government buildings and air-raid shelters. Few private vehicles drove the streets. Uniformed personnel were still everywhere. Long lines of civilians clutching ration coupons still trailed from grocers, bakers, butchers and clothing stores – rationing would continue in Britain for another nine years. As Brickhill would learn, in Australia rationing had never been as severe as in Britain, and would end much sooner.

At Brighton, the Grand and the Metropole, two of the town's premier waterfront hotels, had been taken over by the RAAF and RNZAF. There, the RAAF's 11PDRC prepared Australian airmen for the return to Australia. The Grand, to become notorious for the 1984 IRA bombing aimed at Prime Minister Margaret Thatcher and her cabinet, which killed five, injured many more, and demolished part of the building, was in 1945 set aside for Aussie and Kiwi non-commissioned ranks. The Metropole, which today is used for layovers by aircrew from several airlines, was then reserved for the exclusive use of RAAF and RNZAF officers.

Brickhill joined the crowd of Australian and New Zealand officers at the Metropole, where he was allocated a hotel room and informed that he was to take his time readjusting to life as a free man. Two days later, RAAF Overseas HQ in London would report to RAAF HQ in Melbourne that Brickhill was among scores of RAAF POWs liberated by Allied forces to that point and now being processed at Brighton. Among others on the 10 May list were Jack Donald, the pilot who'd felt he was only in the RAAF to make up the numbers, and Peter Kingsford Smith, one of three nephews of Sir Charles Kingsford Smith who'd become flyers.

As Brickhill arrived in the town that evening of 8 May, the street lights came on in Brighton for the first time since 1939, as they did across Britain. Aussie and Kiwi hospital patients, pulling themselves from their beds, danced in their pyjamas in Brighton's main street with their nurses, celebrating the official end of the war in Europe. Brickhill was in no state to dance in the streets. It was enough just to find a soft bed in a warm, dry room.

The Australian ex-prisoners were informed that the RAAF would eventually want 'a chat' with them about their time as POWs. But not before they reacclimatised to the real world. A medical check-up was first on the agenda. The ex-prisoners were provided with new uniforms and shaving kit, slept in comfortable beds between clean sheets, and were fed the most wholesome meals that rationing would allow. They were also provided with in-house entertainment, with the bar opening most evenings from 5.00, and a band playing in the hotel ballroom. The airmen could wander the town, get a haircut, take in the fresh seaside air and the weak spring sunshine, could see movies at local cinemas and eat out at restaurants and cafes as they spent several weeks reassimilating.

At 3.30 on the afternoon of 12 May, four days into his son's Brighton stay, George Brickhill received a telegram at Greenwich Point in Sydney. With relief, George read wife Dot a message from the RAAF:

PLEASED TO INFORM YOU THAT YOUR SON FLIGHT LIEUTENANT PAUL CHESTER JEROME BRICKHILL HAS BEEN LIBERATED BY THE ALLIED ARMIES AND IS NOW SAFE IN THE UNITED KINGDOM.[118]

A Friendly Interrogation

While, at home, his parents were overjoyed to know that he was safe, at Brighton, Brickhill was struggling with his freedom. He was like a budgerigar freed from its cage: lost, uncertain, easily spooked. Subsequent indications would suggest that Brickhill slept fitfully, if at all, during these early weeks back in England. He would later confess that crowds and confined spaces so terrified him at this time that he couldn't even pluck up the courage to board a bus on his own.[119]

Brickhill's journalist friend Conrad Norton had no such problem. Norton, being non-military, had immediately returned to 'civvy street', and was keen for them to pull their notes together into book form and find a publisher. For the time being, Brickhill avoided revisiting their paperwork, and revisiting his black days as a prisoner. After ten days at Brighton, he was granted twenty-eight days' special leave, unofficially known as POW Leave.

Taking the train to London, and lugging the Stalag Luft 3 notes in his kitbag, Brickhill reported to RAAF Overseas Headquarters at Kodak House in the Kingsway. There, he was given a pile of mail and telegrams that had accumulated for him. Next, he went to Fleet Street, the heart of the London newspaper trade, to visit the UK office of his old Sydney employer, Associated Newspapers. There, he found that the Sydney *Sun* was keen to re-engage him, as a special European correspondent, based in London. Booking into a hotel a comfortable walk from Fleet Street, and with a borrowed typewriter, he tried to apply himself to answering correspondence.

After writing to his family, telling them where he was and what he was doing, he addressed other correspondents. One of the telegrams awaiting him had been from Del Fox, who'd expressed her delight at the news of his release – his name had been published in the Sydney press along with those of other Sydneysiders released from German captivity. Brickhill's feelings towards Del had mellowed while he'd been in the bag, and the letter he typed to her on 27 May lacked the affection of old. He confessed that being back in civilisation again was overwhelming. 'One can't grasp it at first, but can only absorb little bits here and there.' The impact, he said, was a little terrifying. 'However, here I am, and on leave. Believe it or not, also sober.'[120]

He complained to Del that he would have to spend his leave working, trying to finish a book that he and Conrad Norton had begun while prisoners. But he was not looking forward to the task. 'It's a damn nuisance,' he told Del. He added that, as the *Sun* wanted him to work for them in London, he expected to remain in Britain a while longer. He observed that more than four years had passed since he'd left Australia; it seemed longer to him. But he was in no hurry to return. 'One of these days I'll probably land back in Sydney.' Almost dismissively, he signed off: 'So much to do, and so many more letters to write. Bungho – be seeing you.'[121] Del must have been crushed by the lack of warmth and the casual sign-off. But she would not dismiss Paul from her heart.

It seems that Brickhill's off-handedness with Del Fox resulted from the fact that old flame Mary Callanan had re-entered his life. It's likely there had also been a telegram from Mary among the pile waiting for him once he returned to England, expressing pleasure at the news of his release – just as Del had done. Because, when Brickhill wrote home to friends, he asked for news of Mary. One friend would write back urging Brickhill to dismiss Mary Callanan from his mind, suggesting she was not 'a good sort'. She had, he wrote, 'consorted' with American servicemen in Sydney while Brickhill had been a POW. Tens of thousands of Yankee soldiers, sailors and airmen had spent time in Australia during the war, on the way to or from the Pacific theatre and on leave. They had famously been 'overpaid, oversexed and over here'. Although Brickhill was disappointed by this report, he wouldn't soon forget the girl who got away.[122]

As his leave slipped by, Brickhill found excuses not to get to work on the book project, until, with two-and-a-half weeks of free time left, he finally unravelled the grubby notes. He spent all of the next seventeen days working almost without pause, typing up the stories at a frantic pace, editing as he went. By far the longest of the tales was his account of the mass escape from Stalag Luft 3 in 1944. Brickhill would salt the escape's lead-up through early chapters before devoting the last third of the book entirely to the escape. As he pulled these notes together, he found that the fine memory for detail he'd developed at the *Sun* had not deserted him; recollections of his two years in Germany came flooding back.

At the same time, he was approached by RAAF Public Relations. Knowing that he was in London and working on the manuscript with Norton, the RAAF urged him to speak on a BBC program about the mass escape from Stalag Luft 3. That escape had been front-page news in Britain and Australia in 1944. The House of Commons was first advised of it by Foreign Secretary Anthony Eden on 19 May, after the British Government had been informed by the neutral Swiss Government, the 'Protecting Power' in relation to POWs.

SBO Wing Commander Massey, following his repatriation, had been debriefed by MI9, and he'd provided the government with the inside story of the mass break. Standing up in the Commons on 23 June to update the House on the escape, Eden revealed that fifty escapees had been shot by the Germans. 'It was cold-blooded butchery,' Eden added, 'and we are resolved that the foul criminals shall be tracked down.'[123]

Brickhill would have been reluctant to revisit the episode. Apart from the troubling memories that this was likely to conjure, there was the possibility that, in his nervy state, his stutter might re-emerge on air to embarrass him. But his superiors probably put the case that the BBC broadcast would be good for the morale of Australian and New Zealand troops still fighting in the Pacific – it would be aired by the BBC's Pacific Service in a regular program called *Anzacs Calling*. Knowing that his family in Australia would be able to hear his voice for the first time in years, Brickhill agreed, briefly setting aside his writing.

The broadcast would be styled a 'talk', with Brickhill reading from his own prepared notes, which were first cleared by a pair of censors at Britain's Air Ministry. The talk's BBC producer was Elizabeth Davy. Always comfortable in the company of women, Brickhill seemed to be put at relative ease by her involvement, and his stutter did not trouble him unduly.

Just under ten minutes in duration, the talk, entitled 'Tunnel Escape from Stalag Luft 3', was put to air by the BBC on Thursday, 7 June. Brickhill ended the talk by declaring, with an attempt at levity: 'And now I hope we're through with tunnels for good. I'd much rather take a bus.'[124] Ironically, this was the same Paul Brickhill who, so traumatised by his experiences, couldn't pluck up the courage to board any form of public transport.

The BBC announcer who'd introduced Brickhill ended the broadcast by noting that, in collaboration with a South African war correspondent, 'Flight Lieutenant Brickhill is writing a book about the extraordinary escapes from death of some of his fellow prisoners.'[125]

An article about the broadcast would appear in the Australian press, accompanied by a photograph of Brickhill in uniform chatting animatedly to the producer while sitting in a leather armchair. Del Fox would cut the report from a Sydney paper and lodge it in a scrapbook she was keeping about Brickhill.

With the radio broadcast out of the way, Brickhill returned to putting the book together. As his leave ended on 19 June, he passed the completed manuscript to Conrad Norton to review, and set off for Brighton. Ordered to report back to 11PDRC, he was to be debriefed on his experiences in captivity.

Three days after he returned to Brighton, on the morning of 22 June, Brickhill was called into a Metropole Hotel room serving as an office for an RAAF debriefing officer of 11PDRC's Special Administrative Section. Behind a desk waited Flight Lieutenant William Wadery. On the desk sat a typewriter and piles of forms. Inviting Brickhill to take a seat, Wadery explained the purpose of the debrief – to collect information about the fate of missing airmen and the treatment received by prisoners while in enemy hands. Any information that might be used as evidence in war-crimes trials against the enemy was to be promptly passed along to a mysterious Room 255, in documents marked 'SECRET'.

As the pair chatted, Wadery sought to put Brickhill at ease while determining the extent of information he could provide. When Brickhill informed him that he'd been at Stalag Luft 3, had participated in the mass escape of March 1944 and the 1945 marches through Germany, his inquisitor's level of interest went up several notches. For it soon became clear that Brickhill was one of few Australians to have been intimately involved in the escape attempt and survived to tell the story. And Brickhill was able to confirm that five Australians, including his friend Al Hake, were among the fifty recaptured escapees executed by the Gestapo.

Slipping several copies of a form separated by carbon paper into his typewriter, Wadery began asking Brickhill a series of questions from the form, a War Crimes Questionnaire. Most questions only required affirmative or negative answers. With each response, Wadery typed 'YES' or 'NO'. Brickhill affirmed that he'd experienced or been witness to: atrocities committed against POWs and civilians; killings and executions; torture, beatings and other cruelties; imprisonment under improper conditions; exposure of prisoners of war to danger of gunfire, bombing and other hazards of war; transportation of POWs under improper conditions; failure to provide POWs with proper medical care, food or quarters; and collective punishment for offences of others.

Brickhill's friendly inquisitor then handed the form and a fountain pen to Brickhill and asked him to spell out occasions on which he was aware his captors had murdered prisoners.

A Friendly Interrogation

Brickhill wrote down the executions of the Fifty, the shooting of an American sergeant on the wire at Sagan, as well as the shooting of a Flight Lieutenant Bryson at Westertimke and of two other officers on the march from Stalag Luft 3. He also completed a section describing the manner of his capture. He recalled being shot down over the Mareth Line, and wrote of being trapped half in, half out of his falling Spitfire. He described the wounds to back and head, and the feeling of helplessness as his parachute dragged him through the minefield to Italian lines. Quickly, he rounded out the account by saying that he had spent a week in Italian hospitals before being flown to Naples then sent to Dulag Luft by train.

Turning the form over, Brickhill found an entire page which provided for more detailed information about potential war crimes by his captors. Brickhill didn't want to linger in the painful past. Leaving the page blank, he put the cap back on the pen and pushed the form across the desk to Wadery. He wanted no more reminders of the dark days.

Impatiently, short, stocky Pilot Officer John Ulm looked at his watch. For what seemed hours he'd been sitting in the Metropole Hotel corridor, awaiting his turn to be debriefed. It occurred to him that the man ahead of him must have had a lot more to tell the debriefing officer than he did. Ulm, the former Sydney *Sun* journalist, had been shot down in Northern Italy in early 1945, flying a Mark VIII Spitfire with the RAF's Number 145 Squadron. He'd been strafing a German train at low level at the time, meeting determined flak that came spitting up from railway cars and burst with flaming red ferocity all around him. Ulm felt shrapnel hit his Spit, but had managed to get the fighter back up to 3000 feet, where the engine died. Turning his silent, crippled machine into a glider, he'd succeeded in putting it down in a field in a slithering belly landing. He was proud of his crashlanding; pretty perfect, as crashes go, he reckoned.

Ulm had walked away unscathed, but was quickly made a prisoner by German troops. He'd been escorted to Germany by three Luftwaffe men toting MP40s. 'They were alright,' he would say of his escort. But things became a lot tougher once he joined fellow prisoners in a POW camp, and on the road during the gruelling marches in the last weeks of the war. Not that Ulm was one to complain. He felt his plight was nothing compared to that of comrades who'd been prisoners for years.[126]

The door to the interview room opened, and out walked a moustachioed flight lieutenant. Ulm looked at the man with a mixture of surprise and disbelief.

'Paul Brickhill?' said Ulm, coming to his feet.

A smile lit up Brickhill's face, as his eyes sparkled with recognition. 'John Ulm?'[127]

They had not seen each other since Brickhill left the *Sun* at the end of 1940. After that, Ulm had unwittingly followed in Brickhill's footsteps, getting a little closer to him with each step, first joining the RAAF, training as a pilot in New South Wales and Canada, being transferred to the RAF in Britain to become a Spitfire pilot, following Brickhill to 145 Squadron, then being shot down and becoming a POW in Germany. Now, their paths were joining, here in the Brighton hotel. They had not known each other well, yet the sight of a friendly face from the carefree days back at the *Sun* in Sydney was enough to make both men emotional. 'We fell into each other's arms,' Ulm would say.[128]

After briefly catching up, exchanging details of how they came to be there that day, the pair parted. They would not see each other again in England. Before long, Ulm would be on the P&O liner *Stratheden* heading back to Australia with other Australian servicemen. But the paths of the pair were destined to cross again.

Most of Brickhill's RAAF POW colleagues were going home to Australia by sea, but Brickhill had made it clear that he was in no hurry to return to Australia. The Air Force was sticking to his enlistment requirement that he continue to serve for twelve months after the cessation of hostilities. And as the war against Japan was still being waged in the Pacific, there was the possibility he would be sent there and put back in a cockpit. That possibility did not appeal to him at all. Brickhill had had his fill of the war.

Besides, the *Sun* wanted to put him to work here in England, at the centre of the post-war European action. And he had a book that needed a publisher. So, he applied to the RAAF for six months leave without pay, with his erstwhile employers Associated Newspapers supporting his application. While that application was being assessed, he was granted a further fourteen days of POW leave from 5 July.

Brickhill's six months leave without pay was duly authorised.

From the third week of July he was, in theory, a free man until January 1946. He would continue to be considered a serving airman, but that suited him fine, for a flight lieutenant might go where a civilian could not in Europe in these days immediately following the war. Returning to London, he took a small flat in Westminster and reported for duty at the Associated Newspapers office at 85 Fleet Street. Avoiding buses, the claustrophobic London Underground railway, and any other confined space that would feed his anxieties, Brickhill walked everywhere in London. As soon as he could find the time, he went looking for a literary agent who could sell his and Norton's manuscript to a publishing house.

Financially, Brickhill was in a good place for the moment, with two years' RAAF back pay in a new English bank account and a wage coming in from Associated Newspapers. But his parents' financial devastation by the Depression had left them and him so insecure that he would always take a very careful and calculated approach to his spending. Not that he would be a cheapskate. Appreciating quality in all things, such as the clothes he wore, he would aim for the best. But only when he felt assured he could afford it, and could avoid debt.

He found his literary agent a short stroll from Fleet Street, and not far from the RAAF's Kingsway offices and Australia House in the Strand. This was at decade-old agency Pearn, Pollinger and Higham. In 1935, Nancy Pearn, Laurence Pollinger and David Higham had split from established literary agency Curtis Brown to go out on their own, initially working from Higham's Fitzroy Square flat before flourishing and taking their own premises. Fifty-year-old Higham liked the potential of Brickhill's manuscript and liked young

A Friendly Interrogation

Brickhill. Most importantly, Higham was confident he could sell this collection of war stories to a good publisher, once it had been polished. So began a relationship that would last the rest of Brickhill's life. Brickhill would stick with Higham when remaining agency partner Laurence Pollinger set up on his own in 1958 – Nancy Pearn died in 1950. As David Higham Associates, the agency still manages Brickhill's literary estate to this day.

Over the succeeding months, after working for Associated Newspapers by day, Brickhill polished and expanded the book at night and over weekends. The manuscript he'd delivered to Higham was rushed and rough, and there was plenty of work to do to bring it up to the standard required by a publishing house. For one thing, introductions and explanations giving context to the stories were required.

The authors also needed permission to use the names of men still living who appeared in the book. Brickhill had to try to track them down, via the RAF, then type letters to them in Britain, Australia, New Zealand, Canada, South Africa and the United States. This involved months of work, and even then Brickhill would not be able to locate all the men involved. Where he didn't have permission to use a name, he would use an initial for the surname – Jeff B, Ginge C, Lieutenant R, etc. Many of Brickhill's former colleagues did respond favourably to his approaches, often volunteering more information about themselves and others.

One aspect that became clear as Brickhill toiled on manuscript revisions was the fact that the stories were predominantly about 'bomber types'. With the book crying out for the inclusion of another interesting story about an escape by a fighter pilot, he weighed up whether or not he should also include his own story – of his two chance meetings with brother Russ in Halifax and Alexandria followed by his near-miraculous escape from the plummeting Spitfire over the Tunisian desert. The journalist's tenet was that the reporter was not the story, and should remain anonymous. Yet if anyone else had told him that tale, Brickhill would have included it in a heartbeat.

Just the same, he didn't want to be accused of setting himself up as some sort of hero. In fact, he had an aversion to using the word 'I' in his writing. That seemed pompous and egotistical. It was fine to identify Norton and himself as the authors of the collection, but that was where he drew the line. Still, his journalist's nose told him that his personal escape story was worthy of inclusion. In the end he decided to use it, but disguising his identity. It occurred to him that the need to identify some of the men in the book with just an initial for their last name offered the perfect device for disguise. In including his own story, he could preserve his anonymity by identifying his surname with just the letter B.

On reflection, Paul B still seemed too close, too easy to connect with him. For the purposes of his story, he opted to call himself Ted B. He changed nothing else, even leaving the name of his brother Russ unaltered. Those who knew him, knew his background and the fact that he had a brother named Russ, would recognise that he was writing about himself. But the rest of the world would never know. He would keep this harmless little secret for the rest of his days.[129]

The last dozen of the book's thirty-seven chapters would be devoted to Brickhill's account of the mass escape from

A Friendly Interrogation

Stalag Luft 3. He separated them from the earlier chapters by calling this Part 2, and would precede his chronicle of the escape with an 'In Memoriam' page dedicated to the Fifty, listing the names of the executed men in alphabetical order.

As he toiled his way through the escape story, he made another editorial decision. Wings Day and Roger Bushell had told him, and he'd noted down, 'We began planning the big break about Christmas 1942.'[130] This was a phrase Brickhill had used in his BBC talk, word for word. Yet Brickhill wasn't one of those who had begun planning the break in December 1942; he would not arrive at the camp until the following April. As Brickhill put together these chapters, he wrote, 'A few days after we moved into North Compound on April Fool's Day, 1943, the "X" Organisation, so long planned in detail, had taken material form.' He went on to talk about what 'we' did that day of the relocation to North Compound.[131] Brickhill, though, had not been one of the 700 prisoners who were transferred to North Compound on 1 April. He hadn't arrived from Dulag Luft until three days later.

Twice placing himself in the camp earlier than he was in fact there may not have been deliberate. He was working from his notes. And, by no means physically or mentally recovered from his ordeal as a POW, he was working at a forced, frantic pace to pull the book together in a ridiculously short time. Yet the decision to give himself a false name in the story he included about himself was quite deliberate. This leads to the conclusion that, to lend authority to his role of the escape's narrator, he was prepared to bend the truth a little, for the sake of a flowing narrative, putting himself in the camp earlier than he was. What harm, he might have asked himself, would that do?

Higham also pointed out that the book would need maps and illustrations. A publisher could organise maps, guided by the authors. But illustrations would not be so easy. At that time, just after the war, Brickhill had no access to photographs of the camp, but he knew that one of the forgers, artist Ley Kenyon, had, at Roger Bushell's request, sketched the workings of Harry. Kenyon had been one of the seventy-six men to break out in the Great Escape. Recaptured within a mile of the camp, he'd been among the lucky few returned alive to Stalag Luft 3. On the 1945 marches he'd been in Brickhill's group, the one sent to Marlag-Milag. Tracking Kenyon down in England, Brickhill asked what had happened to his sketches.

Kenyon responded that, in the rush of evacuating Stalag Luft 3 on 27–28 January, he'd been forced to leave those drawings down Dick. Worse, Kenyon had learned that the occupants of 123 block had deliberately flooded Dick as they departed, to destroy incriminating evidence which might have resulted in reprisals levied by the Germans on the men on the march. Kenyon's drawings should have been lost, but now Brickhill had a little luck. The drawings had been located, intact, and returned to Kenyon in Britain.

As Kenyon had learned, the Wehrmacht had moved into Stalag Luft 3 once the prisoners were marched away, using it as a forward base for several weeks until it was overrun by advancing Soviet troops. Right through this period, a number of sick RAF prisoners had remained in camp hospital. With the arrival of the Russians, those prisoners were freed. One

British officer among these men knew about Dick, and took others down the abandoned tunnel for a look-see, to find that the water had seeped away. In any event, the tin containing Kenyon's drawings had remained above the water, high and dry. Its contents were pristine. The officer had taken possession of the drawings and brought them back to England. Knowing that Kenyon had been their creator, he located him and passed them over.

Not only did Kenyon offer these drawings to Brickhill for the book, he provided a number of new ones as well. He sent sketches of the wretched Stalag Luft 3 column on the march in January, of kriegies packed in a cattle car on February's rail journey, and of the group's arrival at Westertimke. Kenyon also produced perspective drawings of Stalag Luft 3, plus a cutaway cross-section sketch of Harry, showing the tunnel slicing beneath the camp from 104 to the forest outside, complete with diggers and air pumpers hard at work inside.

Brickhill selected the best of Kenyon's illustrations, bashed out thousands of original words, and compiled and edited Norton's contribution. It would not be until later in the year that literary agent Higham found a home for Brickhill and Norton's untitled manuscript, with leading British publishers Faber & Faber. The authors would be named as Flight Lieutenant Paul Brickhill and Conrad Norton, in that order. Faber & Faber would come up with the title *Escape to Danger*. 'I've never thought of a title in my life,' Brickhill would confess fourteen years later.[132]

Higham also secured a modest publishers' advance for his two new authors, and publication was set down for August 1946, a year away. This delay was dictated in part by the shortage of paper immediately after the war. It was hoped that, by the summer of 1946, sufficient paper stocks would be available for a sizable print run. Part of that print run would be shipped to the Dominions – Australia, New Zealand, Canada and South Africa – where the book should be available within a month of the UK release.

This long delay in publication frustrated Brickhill. He and Norton had agreed that each would retain the copyright to the stories they had individually written. So he now condensed his Stalag Luft 3 mass escape story into a long newspaper article and tried to sell it to his employers, Associated Newspapers, for immediate serialisation across Australia. He saw this as good pre-release marketing for the book. There was also the fear that as the war slipped from top of mind, people would lose interest in war stories.

When, to his annoyance and frustration, Associated Newspapers turned his article down, Brickhill decided to try other Australian publications. From London, he wrote to leading papers across the nation. His first success was in Port Pirie with the *Recorder*, which his father had once run. It's probable that George Brickhill used his contacts there to recommend his son's article – four of the senior editorial staff who'd been working at the paper when George left in 1927 would still be there as late as 1953.

The *Recorder* ran the story as a feature article that August of 1945. The *Sydney Morning Herald*, from a rival stable to that of Brickhill's own paper the Sydney *Sun*, published the article in September, under the headline 'Thrilling Story of the Stalag III Tunnel Escape, by Flight-Lieut P C J Brickhill, RAAF', no doubt causing gnashing of teeth among Brickhill's bosses across town. The *Herald* also used several Ley Kenyon drawings with the article. In Darwin that same month, the *Army News* ran the article. Brisbane's *Courier-Mail* and Adelaide's *News* would serialise it in December. The *News* would also publish another of Brickhill's *Escape to Danger* stories in December, the tale of how Joe Herman was blown out of a Halifax bomber at 17,000 feet without a parachute, and survived to tell Brickhill the story.

Once he'd put his signature to the Faber & Faber contract, and received a cheque with his share of the advance, Brickhill was keen to find expert advice on how to preserve as much of his book royalties as possible, avoiding Britain's punishingly high rates of personal income tax – the top marginal rate was then 97.5 per cent. He found his accountant, Arthur D. Fincham, of chartered accountancy firm Fincham, Vallance and Co, at Clements Inn in the Strand, just a few minutes' walk from both his Fleet Street office and David Higham's office in Bedford Street.

Fincham advised Brickhill to set up a private company and direct all his writing income into that. To offset tax, the company could make claims for substantial expenses incurred in the earning of that income. Plus, if Brickhill generated large sums from his writing, his company would also be able to buy property, even purchase him a car, avoiding personal tax. Brickhill would indeed set up a private company, Brickhill Publications Limited, into which he would divert his book income. After the publication of *Escape to Danger*, he would send Arthur Fincham an autographed first edition, accompanied by a note: 'With enormous thanks for advice that was literally worth its weight in gold.'[133]

Brickhill would also team up with *Life* magazine correspondent and regular *Reader's Digest* contributor Allan Michie to write an article about the Stalag Luft 3 mass escape, 'Tunnel to Freedom', which would be published by the *Digest* under both their names in 1946. Meanwhile, knuckling down to the journalistic grind for Associated Newspapers, Brickhill fought with his anxieties and reaccustomed himself to confined spaces as his first assignments kept him in London.

By late 1945, his Sydney editor was keen for him to go to Germany and report on the situation there. And the RAF was happy to find him a place on a transport flight going to Berlin. This would entail going back to the country where he had been a prisoner. And to get there, he would have to fly again. Both prospects must have sent shivers down Brickhill's spine. Somehow, he would have to conquer his fears.

15.

The Man Who Came Back

The C-47 Dakota transport aircraft eased down out of the clouds and began its landing approach. Below, Brickhill could see green fields sliding beneath the Dakota's wing. Those German fields were pockmarked with ugly black bomb craters. It was Saturday, 15 December 1945, and Christmas was just ten days away. The war had only been over for seven months, and in Germany its scars had barely begun to heal. With his official ID papers as a correspondent for Australia's Associated Newspapers in his pocket, Flight Lieutenant Brickhill was returning to Germany for the first time since his flight out in May.

Describing himself as 'The man who came back', he would soon write, in an article for the Australian press: 'Once I hungrily dreamed, "If only I weren't a wretched prisoner of the Nazis; if only the positions were reversed." My dream has come true.'[134] It was a weird feeling, coming back like this, so soon after all that had occurred while he was a prisoner. It was not at all what he had expected, or imagined.

Before they'd lifted off from a London airfield, Brickhill had told the Dakota's balding Canadian navigator that he'd been a prisoner at Stalag Luft 3. Now the Canadian leaned over, nudged him and pointed down. 'There you are,' he said with a grin. 'You're back here, in Sausage Land.'[135]

Brickhill nodded. 'Heaven knows I never intended to return among the Germans,' he yelled in reply over the noise of the aircraft's engines. 'They shot fifty of my friends for escaping, and would have shot me too, if I'd drawn an early ticket for the escape tunnel. So I didn't exactly acquire a love for them.'[136]

Brickhill had kept up a front for the crew of the Dakota, pretending nonchalance as he fought his flying demons. Only the white knuckles as he gripped his seat betrayed the newfound terror of flying that rose in the breast of this once-confident fighter pilot. Meanwhile, part of Brickhill's statement to the Canadian was an exaggeration; in fact, an outright fib. Brickhill knew that even if he had drawn one of the first seventy-six escape 'tickets' he could not have been among the recaptured escapees who were executed, after Roger Bushell had taken him off the list as a result of his claustrophobia. Brickhill's pride had been savaged by that decision. In these early months following the war, his pride, and his ego, would not permit him to reveal that he had been sidelined because of a weakness, because of a flaw in his character.

There was also another factor in play. In banishing him from the escape list, Bushell had saved him from the executioners. Brickhill was feeling guilty, for surviving when his friends did not. It was the same sort of guilt suffered by countless survivors of the war, men and women who'd seen friends and family die beside them and lived to wonder, to the point of distraction, why Fate had spared them.

The Dakota was soon touching down at RAF Gatow, a British airfield in western Berlin that had formerly been a Luftwaffe base. Between 1936 and October 1944 it had been home to a German aircrew training school. Then, with the transfer of all flying instructors to front-line units in a final and ultimately futile attempt to keep Germany's depleted air force in the air, the Gatow airfield had served as a paratroop training facility. After Berlin's main airport, Tempelhof, had fallen to the advancing Russians on 26 April, Gatow had held out as the Nazi capital's last remaining airfield for another three days. The centre of Berlin had fallen to the Russian Army on 2 May. With the city's carve-up by the conquering Allied powers following war's end, Gatow had come within the British zone, and the Royal Air Force had turned it into an operational RAF airfield.

Taxiing towards the Nazi-era brick administration buildings, the Dakota came to a stop and its two engines died. The door opened. Brickhill jumped down, then took his bags from a Dakota crewman. Hardly had he set the bags on the tarmac than a young German wearing a Wehrmacht forage cap, minus its Nazi insignia, came dashing towards him. The former German soldier picked up Brickhill's bags, bowed to him, then trotted along beside him, guiding him to the airfield's control tower, seeming almost frantic in his desire to please the Australian officer. Inside the building, Brickhill found what he described as 'a bevy of attractive frauleins in diaphanous dresses and silk stockings', all offering him welcoming teacakes. This was certainly a surprise. He hadn't seen silk stockings or diaphanous dresses on waitresses in London.[137]

An RAF car and driver were provided, and Brickhill was driven towards the city centre over frosty roads. Ahead lay the ravaged skyline of one of World War Two's most bombed cities. Close to 6500 acres of Berlin had been levelled by Allied bombing, with most of the damage done in 1944 and early 1945. This compared to 600 acres of London destroyed by German bombing during the war. Forty-three of the seventy German cities attacked by RAF Bomber Command had more than half their surface area devastated.[138] Nazi Germany had certainly reaped the whirlwind. One quarter of Berlin's population had been either killed or relocated, but three million people still lived in the ruins. Brickhill had tramped to within seventy-five kilometres of Berlin on the first of the horror marches earlier in the year, but had never visited the city before now.

It was late afternoon when his driver took him down the broad Kurfürstendamm, or Ku'damm as Germans nicknamed the avenue. The driver explained that before the war this boulevard had been filled with upmarket stores and cafes and lined with plane trees. Back then, the Ku'damm had been Berlin's most fashionable street for shopping and meeting for coffee, the Champs Élysées of the German capital. Now, Brickhill reckoned, the bombed-out thoroughfare 'resembled the ugly smile of an old beggar showing a mouthful of broken and blackened teeth'.[139]

He was deposited at the pressmen's hotel, a largely intact downtown hotel frequented by visiting journalists. After Brickhill had checked in, a bowing, pink-faced German porter took charge of his bags. In the space of four minutes the porter called him 'Sir' almost as many times as he'd been called 'Sir' during four years in the Air Force. Whenever Brickhill later passed the porter, the man would produce his jerky bow, and the 'Sir' would pop out, 'like a chronic hiccup', as Brickhill described it.[140]

At the hotel, Brickhill was met by a British Army officer delegated to look after him, and together they adjourned to the hotel's dining room for dinner. Brickhill, who had resumed his heavy smoking habit since returning to Britain, noticed that, as soon as he or another diner stubbed out a cigarette in an ashtray, a hawkeyed waiter would swoop, removing the ashtray and returning it shiny clean. This happened so frequently that Brickhill asked his companion why the waiters were so intent on emptying the ashtrays.

The Briton laughed gently at the question. 'So would you, too,' he replied. 'For each table that a waiter serves he is paid a retainer of about 200 marks (£5) a week by a black marketeer to hand over all the cigarette butts diners leave.'

Only now did it dawn on Brickhill that the remaining shreds of tobacco were removed from the butts to go into the making of new cigarettes, on an industrial scale.

'The black marketeer sells the tobacco at a fat profit,' Brickhill's host continued, 'as cigarettes cost seven marks each.' This was more than an entire pack of cigarettes cost in Britain.[141]

Following dinner, Brickhill was to see some of the German black marketeers enriched by such dealings. The British officer took him back to the Kurfürstendamm and one of the few undamaged buildings on the once-grand avenue. This was the Royal Club, a nightclub. Outside, it was austere. Inside, it was a revelation of pink and pale blue rooms resplendent in rococo gilt. After depositing their greatcoats at the cloakroom, the pair toured the premises. Power restrictions meant that lighting was provided by candles. The low yellow light from candelabra added to the atmosphere, at once both sordid and seductive.

In the main room there was a small dance floor, and a large bar being propped up by Berlin's new elite, the black-market barons – 'rolling in money, plump, impeccably dressed,' Brickhill was to observe.[142] One drink cost the equivalent of fifteen shillings – outrageous by British standards. But the black marketeers were happily paying. At tables, smartly dressed German women were dining on sardines, from tins, garnished with dry bread. One wall was decorated with lurid murals of naked women. Lounging in front of the murals was a shapely blonde. Going up to her, Brickhill asked if she spoke English.

'Yes, I speak English,' she replied in a deep, throaty voice. Telling him her name was Gertrude, she asked what he was doing in Berlin.

He told her he was writing about Germany for the foreign press.

'I hope you will grow to like us and our country,' she responded. 'We are not bad people.'

Brickhill's eyebrows raised.

'You think I am a Nazi?' she said defensively. 'I am not! No! No!' She sounded almost persuasive. 'Few of us Germans were Nazis, but we couldn't fight them. They held power. The cruel brutes murdered anyone who would not bow to them.'

Brickhill's mind went back to 1944, and the guard at Stalag Luft 3 who had said to him, 'To be Germans we must be Nazis.'

Gertrude's conversation had moved on. 'I am always hungry. I live for the day I can get a real meal again. Life is still very bad.'[143]

Brickhill half-smiled to himself. Gertrude didn't look too starved to him. Pasty-faced, perhaps, but she was, if anything, a little plump. He could tell her about always being hungry. Food had been all he'd thought about for much of his time as a prisoner of Gertude's countrymen. Changing the subject, Brickhill asked Gertrude for her opinion of the war trials of German leaders beginning that month at Nuremberg. To his amazement, she professed never to have heard about them. Nor could she comprehend why there would be such a thing as war trials. Disconcerted by her reaction, Brickhill went to bid her goodnight.

Reaching out and taking his arm, Gertrude lowered her voice. In Brickhill's words, she then let him know 'the considerable extent of her immoral amenability'. For a packet of twenty cigarettes, she would go to bed with him. Reckoning her price distinctly ambitious, he declined the proposition.

As Brickhill and his British companion took their leave of the Royal Club, staff smiled and bowed, and again Brickhill found himself being addressed as 'Sir'. But as he waited at the cloakroom for his coat, his eyes flicked to a mirror by the door. In it he saw the same German staff who, moments before, had been bowing and scraping to him. Now, behind his back, they were scowling sourly at him.[144]

That night he slept in a luxurious hotel bed, in sharp contrast to the uncomfortable places he'd slept when last in Germany. And before he dropped off to sleep, Brickhill mused that, quite probably, his former prison camp guards were now enduring hard beds on the wrong side of POW camp wire. He was a little surprised by his reaction to the thought of their plights being reversed. He would write: 'I am not so maliciously glad as I thought I might be. But I'm not sorry, either.'[145]

Over the coming weeks, Brickhill would rattle off a succession of articles for Associated Newspapers in Australia, using his shiny new portable typewriter. In one, written under the headline 'How the Germans Have Changed', he would write of his return to Germany, of the ex-soldier at Gatow who'd been so frantic to please him, of the ever-bowing, pink-faced porter, and of his encounter with prostitute Gertrude at the Royal Club.

In the days immediately following his return, he went back out into the shattered streets, scouring the British, French and American sectors of Berlin for more stories, and in search of Nazi documents that would tell him more about the fates of Roger Bushell and the other forty-nine Stalag Luft 3 escapees shot by their captors. For Brickhill was more convinced than ever that all fifty could not have been shot while trying to escape. At least some should have been wounded, surviving to be returned to captivity. And he could not imagine all fifty attempting to flee anew once they were caught. Some, he knew, had been half-hearted about their chances of escaping back to Britain. They had taken part in the escape merely to cause the Germans headaches, and would surely have settled for being sent back to Stalag Luft 3 once caught, would never have tried to make a fresh run for it. The whole story was all too fishy for Brickhill. The journalist in him, and the suspicious ex-kriegie in him, both wanted to know the truth.

He reasoned that there should be a wealth of documents in the city's Soviet Zone, which encompassed the Reich Chancellery, the Reich Air Ministry and other important former Nazi government buildings. Unfortunately, the Soviet Zone was off limits to foreign servicemen and journalists. Learning that the British were lobbying the Soviets to permit a party of British journalists to enter the Soviet sector, Brickhill put his name down to join the party, representing Associated Newspapers, and continued the quest for news material.

On 22 December, having heard that medical authorities in Berlin feared devastating health problems for the city that winter, he found his way to the office of a senior British Army medical officer. That officer was not very sanguine about the chances of Berlin's population surviving the winter without massive fatalities.

'So far, the battle is going better than we feared,' said the medical officer solemnly. 'The people will not starve to death this winter. Enough food has been assured to keep them alive, though not much more than that. They will be wretchedly hungry and cold, but not beyond human endurance, unless they are old and weak.' Gazing out the window of his office to a blackened, ravaged city landscape, he added, 'The great enemy is an influenza epidemic.'[146]

The medical authorities feared an outbreak similar to the Spanish influenza epidemic that had killed millions across the globe in the wake of the end of the First World War. Berlin had already suffered outbreaks of dysentery and typhoid fever, without overwhelming numbers of fatalities. Yet many among the population were living in highly unhygienic situations, crammed into cellars and bombed-out houses, with little or no running water or heat. The doctor told Brickhill that Berlin could become pivotal to a global influenza epidemic. If Spanish flu reached the city from the east, it could not be contained there, would spread fast and sweep the world.

'Give us a good hard frost and we will get them through,' said the medico. 'A few might die of cold, but that is better than a million dying in an epidemic. We have our fingers crossed.'[147]

Feeling heartily depressed, and not a little alarmed, Brickhill left the doctor and went in search of a typical Berlin family, one likely to take the brunt of the doctor's feared epidemic. He was interested to see what sort of Christmas they, and most Berliners, could expect. In a crumbling back-alley hovel he found a Frau Gades and her six young children living in two miserable rooms without power. The children were bright, a little grubby, and clad in understandably shabby clothes. Herr Gades had been missing since April, and was presumed dead. Since then, Frau Gades had been keeping her brood alive with whatever food she could scrounge.

When Brickhill asked what sort of Christmas the Gades children could expect, their mother told him that she would be digging into her supply of potatoes to make the children potato and barley soup, plus bread spread with the luxury of a little ersatz honey or jam. Normally the family's daily ration was a few potatoes, some dry bread with a hint of margarine, and for ten days a month, a little meat. Vegetables were unheard of. On being asked by Brickhill if the children would be receiving Christmas gifts, Frau Gades showed him two pathetic rag dolls she'd made for her daughters, three-year-old Brigide and seven-year-old Lise. Her four sons would not be receiving presents. The boys were stoically resigned to the fact.

When Brickhill asked the children whether they believed in Father Christmas, all shook their heads. Frau Gades said that Christmas Day would, for her family, be much like any other winter's day in 1945. After their meal, the children would play in their rubble-strewn street until around 4.30, when the sun went down, and then clamber into their beds to keep warm. With luck, the authorities might give the family a hoped-for gift of candles. Otherwise, Christmas night would be long and dark for Frau Gades and her children.[148]

Returning to his warm hotel, and after a good dinner, Brickhill sat down at his typewriter to write about the Gades family, feeling a little less embittered towards all Germans than he had a few days before.

Christmas Day, 1945. A Tuesday. Before Brickhill enjoyed a relatively lavish Christmas dinner at his hotel, he had a driver take him around the city to see how Berliners were celebrating their first Christmas after twelve years of Nazi rule.

Few people ventured into the streets. Those who did seemed to Brickhill to be in a daze. A number walked lethargically into the path of his car, jumping back as if in slow motion when the driver tooted them.

As he was being driven through the poorer districts, Brickhill opened his window. Eerily, he didn't hear a thing. No traffic noise, no singing, no laughing children. Millions of Berliners were cloistered indoors, huddled, shivering in the winter cold and downing their meagre Christmas fare. In wealthier suburbs, he did hear the occasional sounds of revelry. Black-market food and booze had obviously found their way here. At one point he got out to walk, hoping to find an English speaker among these Berliners who could afford contraband luxuries. A woman walking along the broken pavement told him her name was Dolly Angels, and that she was a doctor of philosophy. He asked her if she was fearful of the threat of a major epidemic striking the city.

'I think such fears are exaggerated,' said Dr Dolly, nonplussed.

He asked her what she thought of the Nazis.

'They were not too bad,' she said, betraying lingering National Socialist sympathies.

What were her thoughts on the Nuremburg trials?

'Grossly exaggerated,' she said dismissively. At least she was aware of the trials, unlike Gertrude the nightclub girl and other Berliners Brickhill had spoken to. But the doctor of philosophy seemed to have ceased to care about anything other than the exacting business of maintaining life from one day to the next.[149]

Dr Dolly went on her way, and Brickhill returned to the car, resuming his trawl of the city. In the Bülowstrasse, he saw an old man slip and fall to the frosty pavement. Too weak to regain his feet, the old man lay there, working his arms and legs uselessly, reminding Brickhill of an overturned beetle. Other pedestrians walked on by as if he didn't exist. Instructing his driver to stop, Brickhill jumped out and went to the old man's aid. Helping the German to his feet, he steadied him as he wiped blood from his nose.

What had the old boy done during the war? Been an air-raid warden, perhaps? He was too old to have served in the military. In all probability he had fought in the First World War. Pulling a chocolate bar from his greatcoat pocket, Brickhill broke off a large chunk. The old man accepted the chocolate, stuffing it all into his mouth at once. Brickhill looked at passers-by. They were glassy-eyed, indifferent. Feasting on the Australian's chocolate, the old man stumbled away.[150]

Continuing to cable articles to Sydney, Brickhill lingered in Berlin, hopeful of receiving permission to enter the Soviet Zone. He knew that people enjoyed reading about other people, and was always looking for what the American press called 'human interest' stories. Once 1946 rolled around, in the first week of January he stumbled on a rich source of stories, an office in Military Government House in Berlin's British Zone with an intriguing role and a very interesting female operative. To this office came applications from Berliners claiming British citizenship and seeking to escape war-ravaged Germany. With Australians then still officially

British citizens, Brickhill was intent on documenting the stories of applicants hoping to settle in Australia.

Assessing these applications was the British Army's Paddy Rose, a Suffolk girl of mixed Anglo-Irish parentage. 'She is one of the most ruthlessly efficient, likeable characters I've ever met,' Brickhill would write. Pert, pragmatic Paddy showed a typical application to Brickhill, from seventy-three-year-old Rudolph Laver. After migrating to Australia as a young man, Laver had returned to Germany in 1899. During both world wars he'd produced electrical equipment for Germany. In his application he wrote that 'my constitution is weak', and that his wife suffered from 'child failure' and 'overdosisses of morphium' (sic). Paddy had turned down his application.[151]

At least Herr Laver could speak English, if imperfectly. Many applicants could no longer speak or write English, and frequently they were consigned to the 'Rejected' pile, along with those whose names appeared on what was called the 'Renegades list' – British citizens living in Germany or occupied Europe known to have supported the Nazis.

'I get the same stories every day,' Paddy told Brickhill, 'and they're nearly all lies. I'm getting so I can smell this pure Aryan blood a mile away. They all claim to be of such loyal British stock, but most of them have been sitting on the fence during the war and are sorry that the Nazis lost. Had the Germans won they'd have been rabid Germans. They thought they had it all lined up so they couldn't lose.'[152]

But Paddy had been briefly shaken a few days earlier when a woman claiming to be a duchess appeared in her office. Aged around fifty, she had given her name as Lilli von Kent. She'd demanded special and immediate treatment, failing which her husband the duke would not be pleased. But she astonished Paddy by proceeding to list the names of thirty illegitimate children she'd borne all over Europe. Deciding that Lilli was more prostitute than aristocrat, Paddy sent her for immediate attention – from a doctor.

Those applicants who seemed to have a genuine right to repatriation to Australia were invited in for personal interviews with Paddy. Among them was Mrs A. Pianos, who'd been born in Sydney to Australian parents and in the 1930s married an Englishman. In September 1939, when war was declared, she was visiting Germany, and found herself trapped there. Paddy was likely to give her favourable consideration. A number of other Australian-born women who'd married German men and survived the war in Germany would also receive the nod.

Brickhill used his charm to wheedle the address from Paddy of a woman who'd passed muster and received approval to return to Australia. Vera Hoffman had been born in Tanunda, South Australia to a German immigrant family involved in grape growing. She had married and had a son, Dirk, but lost her first husband when Dirk was very young. In 1930 she'd married a German, Herr Boeckmann, and Vera and Dirk had moved with him to Germany. Herr Boeckmann had survived the war and was still living with his wife and stepson in Berlin. While mother and son would soon be leaving for Australia, Vera's husband hadn't received permission to migrate, and would be remaining in Berlin. When Brickhill tracked down Vera, he found a woman who was painfully thin and weak as a result of the food shortage. She was only now recovering from illness with the help of fortnightly Red Cross food parcels from England.

'Recently, after a couple of weeks in bed,' Vera told Brickhill, 'I fainted at suddenly seeing in my mirror how thin I had become.' She assured Brickhill that she'd had nothing to do with Nazis. 'Throughout the war I dropped all friends showing Nazi tendencies and lived very quietly.' Since the German capitulation eight months before, Vera had been teaching English to eager Germans, and had more prospective students than she could handle. She had also written an English textbook for German readers, which would soon be published in Berlin.[153]

Brickhill was able to meet Vera's son, seventeen-year-old Dirk, an intelligent blond-haired youth who spoke good English and was looking forward to going to Australia.

'For democratic freedom?' Brickhill asked.

'Not so much,' Dirk confessed. 'For eating grapes, which I have tasted only once.'[154]

Vera told Brickhill that she had kept up her morale during the war with a chain letter that had circulated since 1942 around Australian-born women living in Hamburg, Coblenz, Danzig, Vienna, Paris and Berlin. Her correspondents were Leonie Miller, Muriel Mudge, noted Kalgoorlie-born contralto Lorna Sydney, who had married an Austrian baron, and, most surprising of all, Margaret Murdoch, niece of Sir Keith Murdoch and cousin of Rupert Murdoch. The Australian women had called this chain letter hopping around Nazi Europe their 'kangaroo'.

Wishing Vera and Dirk every success with their new life in Australia, Brickhill retired to his hotel to write up several articles. He had completed one about Paddy Rose and her work when he received a message to say that a party of

British journalists had been approved by the Russian military to shortly enter their sector, and he had been included. Generously handing his notes about Vera and Dirk to fellow Australian journalist Keith Bean, who would file an article about the pair under his own name but with an acknowledgement to Brickhill as his source, Brickhill prepared to be in that first British press party to enter the Soviet Zone. At last he might have the chance to view Nazi documents which could reveal the true fate of the Fifty.

Beyond the bullet-scarred pillars of the Brandenburg Gate, the Soviet Zone in eastern Berlin was just as bleak and war-torn as the sectors controlled by other Allied powers. The first thing that Brickhill noticed as he and other journalists in the press party were taken into the Soviet Zone was that the Russian military drove much more quickly than the British, French or Americans did in their sectors. Heaven help any Berliner who walked into the path of a Russian vehicle. The driver would happily run him or her down, or so it seemed.

One of the first places the journalists were taken to in the Soviet Zone was the Jewish Relief Committee's transit camp, which was occupied by 1700 Jewish refugees from Poland. Jews had been arriving in the British Zone with stories of intimidation by Polish partisans, who'd allegedly given Jews two options: pay up and leave the country within twenty-four hours, or be shot on the spot. Speaking with Jewish refugees, Brickhill found no one who could corroborate that rumour. While the British journalists were in the Russian sector, the Jewish camp emptied overnight. It turned out that the Russian military had suddenly warned Jewish refugees that within two days they would be taken to camps close to the Polish border. Some fleeing Jews turned up in the British and French sectors. Others evaded Russian troops to reach the Americans in southern Germany.[155]

Meanwhile, Brickhill's quest for information about the fates of the Fifty hit a brick wall. The Russians were keeping a firm grip on captured German records and weren't sharing them with anyone.

Across the room from Brickhill sat Hermann Goering. What an odd feeling, seeing the infamous Reich Marshal in the flesh. It was early February, and Brickhill was in Nuremberg, Bavaria, to cover the war trials being held at the Palace of Justice by the International Military Tribunal. Here, the Australian would apply his forensic eye for detail, mood and character to the men in the dock, and their judges.

In January, Brickhill's six-month leave without pay had ended, and he'd reported back to 11PDRC. Brickhill was enjoying his press work, and was coming to terms with the demons that had gripped him when first he'd been released from captivity. He was in no hurry to return to Australia. With his leave without pay extended as 'emergency leave' until his discharge from the RAAF in April, he preferred to remain in England for the publication of *Escape to Danger*, and to cover the big stories of the day. And the Nuremburg trials were the world's biggest news story at that time.

Nuremberg had been deliberately chosen by the victorious Allies for the trials of surviving National Socialist leaders because the city had been the spiritual home of the Nazis in the 1920s and 1930s, the place where they'd held their massive party rallies. Now, Nazi political and military leaders were in the large, two-level dock, being called to account for their crimes, and Brickhill was in the press gallery alongside the world's leading newspaper correspondents, to observe and report.

Hitler, Himmler and Goebbels had all suicided. But Goering, Hitler's former number two, was alive and well and taking pride of place among the defendants in the crowded courtroom. For the first time, Brickhill laid eyes on the man whose air force he'd fought, whose Luftwaffe men had held him captive, and who'd personally played a leading role in the fates of the seventy-three Stalag Luft 3 escapees in 1944. The once-ostentatious Goering still wore the pearl grey Reich Marshal's uniform he'd designed for himself. The brass buttons remained, but not the once-numerous decorations or eagle and swastika emblem. Brickhill noted a red scarf around Goering's neck. And, in the winter chill that gripped the vast barn of a courtroom, he had an American army blanket wrapped around his 'Falstaffian' middle.

'Goering still has an aura of cruel strength as he continually gestures and poses,' Brickhill wrote.[156] Yet the Reich Marshal didn't come across as a politician, or a military leader. There was something 'rascally' about Goering. He put Brickhill in mind of a pirate.[157] Goering had been a key figure in the rise of the Nazi Party, creating the SS, overseeing the murder of political opponents, even administering the German economy at one point. The fact that an increasingly insane Hitler had ordered Goering's arrest by the SS in the dying days of the war in no way mitigated the war-crimes charges the Reich Marshal faced.

Another man in the dock, former German foreign minister Joachim von Ribbentrop, had also fallen out of favour with Hitler towards the end of the war, but that would not save him from Allied retribution either. 'The bags under Von Ribbentrop's eyes seem to be getting heavier,' Brickhill observed. 'He is a very worried and frightened man as he follows the trial closely and constantly scribbles notes to his lawyer.'[158]

For the previous few days, Brickhill had been closely watching two of the accused in particular. Red-faced Hjalmar Schacht, one-time finance minister under Hitler, a man Brickhill described as possessing a face like 'an over-ripe tomato with an expression of wounded dignity'. And handsome forty-year-old Albert Speer, the former Nazi armaments minister, who, in Brickhill's opinion, was looking heavy and gloomy. Schacht and Speer had been in a huddle for two days, and none of the other defendants had spoken a word to them in that time.

'They're getting ready to spill the beans,' another journalist assured Brickhill. The Australian's next report for readers Down Under would be headlined: 'Nazi Leaders Plotting To Rat on Mates.'

Once the trial wrapped up for the day and Brickhill was leaving the massive court building, he noticed that machine-guns had been installed along hundreds of metres of rambling corridors. Out front, a Sherman tank stood by the wrought-iron gates. For the past few days, a rumour had been circulating that Nazi sympathisers were planning to raid the Palace of Justice and free Goering and his co-defendants. The American military, who had charge of the security of the building and the trials, weren't taking any chances.

Yet in the street, something resembling normal city life was playing out, with vehicles and pedestrians passing without anyone giving a second glance to the court building. 'From the outside,' Brickhill would comment, 'you wouldn't think that a trial – the greatest in the world – was in progress, has been for three months. Even inside the court the proceedings go their quiet and almost prosaic way.'[159]

The rumoured bid to rescue the Nazi leaders failed to eventuate. Apart from Goering, none of the men in the dock was widely popular with Germans, and most friends of the military men on trial were now either dead or themselves under indictment.

In March, Brickhill was on assignment in Austria and Hungary for Associated Newspapers. From Budapest, he reported on the political and economic situation in former Nazi ally Hungary. Tongue-in-cheek, he told readers back home, 'Budapest shows you can survive on £40,000 a week,' as he described out-of-control inflation and widespread starvation in a country where 'Millionaires go hungry'.[160]

He also saw the political writing on the wall. 'They whisper in Central and Eastern Europe that Stalin made two mistakes – he showed the Red Army to Europe, and Europe to the Red Army.' Despite obvious dislike of communism among the majority of Hungarians he encountered, Brickhill perceived that the Red minority held sway, and predicted, presciently, that under the threat of the Red Army the entire Eastern Bloc would before long become governed by the communists.[161]

Returning to England for his official discharge from the RAAF on 8 April, Brickhill prepared for a new posting – US correspondent for Associated Newspapers, based in New York City. His parents were keen for him to return home, but the temptation of a new adventure was too great. On 7 May, he boarded the *Ile de France* at Southampton to sail to New York via Halifax, Nova Scotia, revisiting that Canadian port city for the first time since his departure from there in 1941.

Manhattan proved a revelation, but putting together general news stories and features about American life became humdrum. While Brickhill professed to be totally disinterested in politics, the power that came with money proved a recurring theme in his articles, and one of his American features was about corrupt American politicians. Influenced by writers around him, Brickhill displayed the breezy, unfettered and insightful writing style that would later make his books so readable. About Huey Long, Governor of Louisiana in the 1930s, he wrote: 'Huey started as a poor farmer's boy, began to peddle books, gulped down a law course in seven months, and climbed on the political bandwagon. Before you could say "Chiseller", he was a bread and circuses demagogue, sitting in the Governor's chair and proclaiming, "I am the Constitution in Louisiana."[162]

Brickhill quickly made several female friends in Associated Newspapers' New York office, including Pat Dunne, a married woman. Very early on, too, he found himself a New York literary agent to hawk *Escape to Danger* to American publishers. Mike Watkins at the Ann Watkins Agency on Park Avenue became his agent. The Watkins agency handled several British authors, among them Roald Dahl. Like Brickhill, Dahl had been shot down and wounded in North Africa, but unlike Brickhill he hadn't fallen into enemy hands. From 1942, Dahl had been based in Washington DC as assistant British air attaché and an intelligence officer, ending the war a wing commander. Watkins would fail to interest American publishers in *Escape to Danger*, but he would become a valuable future ally.

Late in the year, Brickhill received a despairing letter from his parents in Sydney. Their rented house at 41 George Street at Greenwich Point was being sold from under them. George, who was still working as Sydney correspondent for the *Newcastle Sun*, was approaching retirement age, and he and Dot couldn't bear the thought of upping and moving yet again, leaving the little house by the water they loved. Paul made a momentous decision. From New York, he put in a bid for the George Street house. That bid was accepted. Pooling his advance for *Escape to Danger* and his saved RAAF back pay, Brickhill put down a deposit, and via the Manhattan branch of an Australian bank, arranged a mortgage.

By early 1947, the sale was settled, and Paul Brickhill was the proud owner of 41 George Street. He would always be responsible for the mortgage payments, ensuring there was never again financial pressure on George and Dot. To make his parents' occupancy official, he charged them an annual peppercorn rent of a pound or two, and he vowed that never again would they have to worry about losing the roof over their heads. It was a promise he would not break.

By this time, too, *Escape to Danger* had been published in England in hardback. Receiving encouraging if restrained reviews, even making it into the *London Review of Books*, it sold out the modest first print run. To cash in on Christmas book sales, Faber & Faber released a new edition on 1 December. But the book wasn't a runaway bestseller by any means. Brickhill would have to keep his day job. The lack of spectacular success as an author, the paucity of friends in the US and the drudgery of his reporting work all combined to sap his spirits. In the second half of 1947, Brickhill succumbed to homesickness. He hadn't seen his parents in more than six years, and had yet to see the house he'd bought for them. After he asked Associated Newspapers for a transfer back to Australia, he was offered a subeditor's position with his old paper, the Sydney *Sun*.

Come December, Brickhill had arrived back in Australia for a tearful reunion with parents and siblings, and his first Christmas at home since 1940. All his brothers had survived the war. Russell had married, returned to the University of Sydney to become officer of works, a post he would hold for decades, and had bought a house in Greenwich Point not far from their parents. Geoff had also married. Lloyd was flying for Australian National Airways. Clive had settled in Toowoomba, Queensland and was working as a laboratory assistant. Brickhill moved in with his parents in his Greenwich Point house, and in the first week of January 1948 began work once more at the Elizabeth Street offices of the *Sun*. One of the first people he passed in the corridor was John Ulm, who was back at the paper as a reporter. The pair's paths had come full circle. Their tale of coincidence had one more chapter to play out – Ulm would end up living at Greenwich Point.

Prowling Sydney's bookshops in his spare time, Brickhill was soon broken-hearted. Nowhere could he find a copy of *Escape to Danger* on sale. When he asked Faber & Faber's local agents the reason, they responded that paper shortages meant that very few copies had been shipped to Australia. Determined that his work, and the story of the mass escape from Stalag Luft 3, would not go unrecognised, Brickhill contacted former *Sun* journalist and Department of Information executive Lionel 'Wiggy' Wigmore. He'd heard that Wigmore would be putting together a history of Australia's involvement in World War Two, and wanted to bring to his attention the important information his book contained. Wigmore put him in touch with his editor, and *Escape to Danger* would be duly added to the masses of source material for that work.

Brickhill was now back in the Australian sunshine, and back with his family. But he found the work as a subeditor stultifying. It was 'a bloody misery' of a job, he would later say.[163] He'd known, when he'd enlisted in the RAAF seven years before, that slogging away as a press hack was not what he wanted to do for the rest of his days. And, from across the world, England, and one particular Englishman, began tugging at him. During 1948, David Higham wrote to tell Brickhill that he'd been contacted by John Pudney.

Pudney, an erudite man who'd gone to school with W. H. Auden and Benjamin Britten, was an editor, short-story writer, novelist and noted poet – his wartime ode to British airmen, 'For Johnny', became celebrated. At this time Pudney was an editor with London's *News Review*, but he'd worked for the BBC as a writer-producer before the war and was trying to get into the fledgling television business as a producer. As Pudney told Higham, he was a fan of Brickhill and Norton's *Escape to Danger*, and was keen to turn its content into a series for BBC TV.

Conrad Norton was back in South Africa, where, this same year, he had a new nonfiction book published, *Opportunity in South Africa*. From the southern corners of the globe, both he and Brickhill enthusiastically told Higham to give Pudney permission to pursue the televising of their book, in their minds picturing their work on the revolutionary small screen. Pudney's concept was, however, an ambitious idea for the time. BBC TV was then only broadcasting to the London metropolitan area, and the budget for the sort of program Pudney had in mind was well in excess of what the 'Beeb' could afford. Yet unbeknownst to Brickhill, the Pudney association would before long change his life.

In February 1949, Brickhill received an approach from John Nerney, head of the Air Historical Branch at Britain's Air

George Brickhill, Paul's father, co-founder of the Australian Journalists Association.

Future Hollywood star Peter Finch at Mosman, just months before Paul Brickhill befriended him in 1927.

Paul Brickhill (sitting on the ground, front row, second from the left) with RAF Spitfire fighter pilot training course No. 10 members, Llandow, Wales, 1942.

Paul Brickhill (front row, second from the right, squatting) and other Australian and New Zealand prisoners of war commemorating Anzac Day in Stalag Luft 3 in 1944, two weeks after learning that fifty comrades had been shot by the Gestapo following the Great Escape. The photo was taken on the secret camera smuggled into the camp to take ID photos for Great Escapers' forged papers.

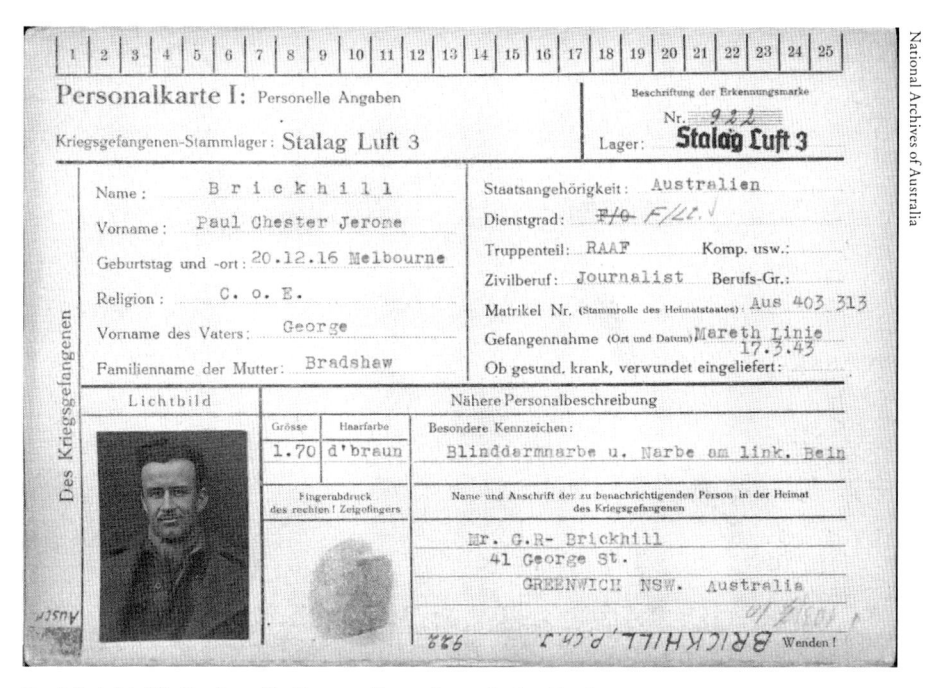

Paul Brickhill's Luftwaffe *Personalkarte* from Stalag Luft 3.

The house at 41 George Street, Greenwich Point, Sydney, purchased in 1947 by Brickhill for his parents, and where he lived with them briefly on several occasions between 1948 and 1964.

ABOVE LEFT: Brickhill and new wife Margot in London, at a 1950 Australia House function of the Society of Australian Writers, which Brickhill co-founded, just as *The Great Escape* was becoming a bestseller.

ABOVE RIGHT: Paul and Margot arrive in Sydney in 1953 on their first return to Australia as a married couple. Paul was unaware at the time that Margot was pregnant with their first child.

BELOW: Paul and Margot aboard the *Fairsky* at Fremantle on their 1959 return to Australia with their children, Timothy and Tempe.

The RAF's 617 Squadron commander and Dam Busters hero Guy Gibson with wife Eve at Buckingham Palace in 1943, after King George VI presented Gibson with the Victoria Cross. Eve would later cause Brickhill major headaches, delaying the release of the *Dam Busters* movie.

A still from the *Dam Busters* film, with, centre, Richard Todd playing Guy Gibson, and beside him, with the moustache, Bill Kerr, playing Australian pilot Micky Martin.

Legless RAF fighter pilot and POW Douglas Bader with wife Thelma (right) and his sister-in-law, Jill Addison.

John Sturges, producer and director of the Hollywood adaptation of Brickhill's *The Great Escape*, on location in Bavaria in 1962 with his temperamental star Steve McQueen, during the shooting of motorcycle chase scenes that never occurred in the original true story.

Brickhill at 'Little Barr', his house outside London, with his Jaguar, 1962.

Brickhill's close friend and fellow author Jon Cleary, who, at one point, loaned Brickhill, his wife and children his house and car on Sydney's North Shore.

Brickhill at his Balmoral, Sydney apartment in the early 1980s, when he was planning a new book, which he never completed.

The exterior of Brickhill's Balmoral apartment building, overlooking Middle Harbour. Brickhill spent the last twenty-five reclusive years of his life in a small top-floor apartment here.

Ministry. Nerney wondered whether Brickhill would be interested in writing the history of the RAF's 617 Squadron, which gained wartime fame for Operation Chastise, a raid against the Ruhr Valley dams, after which the unit had garnered the swashbuckling title of 'the Dam Busters'.

Nerney had initially approached Leonard Cheshire VC, commanding officer of 617 Squadron following the dams raid, to write the squadron's history. But Cheshire had turned him down, citing other work commitments and health issues – he was running a hospice for the dying which he'd set up in an old Hampshire house left him by an aunt. In declining the offer, Cheshire had recommended former 617 Squadron intelligence officer McGowan Cradon in his place. Cradon's commitment to such a task was questioned by the RAF; he'd been considered too interested in buzzing about in Lancasters during the war and unfocused on his desk role.

As Brickhill would only learn several years later, Nerney had then spoken with John Pudney, who'd promptly recommended Brickhill. Although an Australian, Brickhill had been an officer and pilot with the RAF, and was a well credentialled writer, having worked as a journalist in London and New York. The Air Ministry would do all it could to facilitate his research, but Nerney's offer entailed only a small honorarium, and there was no guarantee of publication beyond a government-produced edition. There was also a significant hurdle – to research the squadron, its men and its missions, Brickhill would have to base himself in the UK.

Despite the drawbacks, Brickhill jumped at the offer, seeing this as an opportunity to dump his boring day job and set the foundations for becoming a full-time author – if he could interest a publisher in the book. And it would get him back to England. To satisfy British Air Ministry requirements, he applied to the RAAF for written confirmation that he'd been a serving officer attached to the RAF. But how, he wondered, could he afford to get back to England, especially as he had to keep up mortgage payments on his parents' home?

It occurred to him that if he could interest an Australian publisher in a commercial Australasian edition of the book, he could generate an advance that would pay his fare, while retaining the potentially much more lucrative UK rights. Touting a Dam Busters book proposal around Australian publishing houses, he pointed out that a number of Australians had served with 617 Squadron and taken part in the dams raid. To his disgust, not a single Sydney publisher saw any merit in the idea. As Brickhill told Brisbane *Courier-Mail* journalist Roy Connolly, they all turned down his proposal, advising that it was 'unsuitable for publication'. Unable to see how he could afford to get to England, Brickhill unhappily declined Nerney's offer.[164]

Then, in March, just as Brickhill received the paperwork he'd requested from the RAAF confirming his commission, war service and service medals, agent David Higham again made contact. John Pudney was proving to be Brickhill's guardian angel. Having just joined London publishers Evans Brothers as an editor, he was looking for new books, and had approached Higham with a proposal that Brickhill write an extended version of the Stalag Luft 3 mass escape covered in *Escape to Danger*, to be entitled *The Great Escape*. The commercially canny Pudney knew that Eric Williams' novelised Stalag Luft 3 escape adventure *The Wooden Horse* had sold very well for William Collins and Sons, and he also knew that a film version was in the works, for release in 1950. To Pudney's mind, *The Great Escape* book could ride on the back of the success of the *Wooden Horse* movie.

Brickhill was thrilled. He hadn't been happy with the job he'd done on *Escape to Danger*. Years later, he would confess, 'It bore all the marks of haste.'[165] Not only would Pudney's offer allow him to do justice to the mass escape story and its participants, it could give him the wherewithal to get back to England and get down to work as an author. Cabling Higham with his agreement to write *The Great Escape*, he pushed for a swift contract and a publisher's advance large enough to get him to England. If need be, once in London, he could turn to freelance journalism to boost his income.

In April, once Higham had agreed contract terms with Evans Brothers, Brickhill threw in his job at the *Sun* and prepared to sail to the UK. In the end, it wasn't until May that all was finalised. Brickhill was the second-last passenger to book a tourist-class passage to Southampton aboard the next sailing of the SS *Largs Bay*. Brickhill was on his way, to England, and to the top of the writing profession. Years later, when he sailed back into Sydney Harbour, he would return as one of the most successful authors in the world.

16.

Back in England

PAUL BRICKHILL SAILED out of Sydney's heads to return to England on 14 May 1949 aboard the 14,000-tonne SS *Largs Bay*. Launched in 1921, she had been a troopship during the war. Returned to her owners, the ship had been refitted during 1948–49 and was once again sailing the Sydney–Southampton route via the Suez Canal as a combined passenger and cargo vessel. Half the size of handsome liners such as the *Orontes* and *Strathaird*, which had sailed out of Sydney Harbour in April, England-bound, the *Largs Bay*'s attraction was the economy of its fares. The day would come when Brickhill would deeply regret choosing this ship and this sailing.

Unlike larger liners on the England route, which routinely carried a thousand-plus passengers each, the *Largs Bay* had just 164 passengers aboard. It made for a more intimate voyage, with passengers soon mixing as if the ship were a private club.

Among the tourist-class passengers strutted a striking, pencil-slim twenty-year-old girl with boyishly short dark hair and hazel eyes. Margaret Olive Slater hailed from Richmond on the Hawkesbury River, to the near west of Sydney. When younger, she had given herself the French-sounding name of Margot. Now, Margot Slater was travelling to England on holiday with her sister Jeanette, two years her junior.

Within hours of the ship clearing Sydney Heads, Paul Brickhill had spotted Margot and made her acquaintance. They were soon deep in conversation. Margot told Brickhill that she had been born at Narrabri in northern New South Wales, growing up in Richmond. Her mother, Olive, was a country girl, her father, Edric, an importer, making a name for himself in his spare time as a nature photographer. After attending Parramatta High and Homebush High, Margot had been an art student at East Sydney Technical College for two years, and enjoyed painting. Margot was two inches taller than Brickhill, taller still in high heels. Despite this, and the fact that Brickhill was twelve years her senior, she was attracted to the cheeky yet worldly journalist who'd worked in London and New York and told her he was going to London to become a successful author. Brickhill's nervous stutter dissolved away in her company. Affectionately, he was soon calling her Maggie.

Margot told Brickhill that she had sailed to England two years earlier, on a trip with her mother, also visiting Germany's British zone to see elder sister Beth, who lived there with her husband, British Army chaplain Thomas Yates. Brickhill told Margot about his writing projects, mentioning that he'd turned down the 617 Squadron history after receiving a negative reaction from Australian publishers. Margot suggested he not be so hasty, feeling that British publishers must surely be interested in the subject. She urged him to approach the RAF when he reached the UK and tell them he had reconsidered. Brickhill would later credit Margot with convincing him to revisit the book that was to become *The Dam Busters*.[166]

Brickhill was impressed by Margot's interest in him, and his work. In the past, his stammer and shyness had meant he'd rarely shared his dreams and aspirations with anyone other than boyhood friend Peter Finch. Margot was a great sounding board, and he looked forward to relaxing in the young woman's company each evening. By day, he worked. Having brought his trusty typewriter along, he used the four weeks at sea to commence rewriting his mass escape chapters from *Escape to Danger* to create the beginnings of *The Great Escape*. By the time the *Largs Bay* docked at Southampton on 14 June, Brickhill had the foundations of an 80,000-word book. Meanwhile, the chemistry between writer and art student was obvious. As they departed the ship, Brickhill and Margot agreed to keep in touch.

While Margot and her sister set off on a trip around Britain, Brickhill immediately resumed work. Staying at a cheap London hotel, he met with David Higham and John Pudney to plan the course necessary to bring *The Great Escape* to fruition. Pudney made several recommendations. This book should have the feel of a novel. Eric Williams had novelised his *Wooden Horse* escape, even changing his name and those of his fellow escapees, which helped boost readership. Brickhill was determined to stick to the facts and to retain the real names of the men involved; anything less would be an insult to the memory of his mates the Fifty, to whom he would dedicate the book. Nonetheless, he was open to making the book read like a novel.

Brickhill would write the book in newspaper style, using short sentences, short paragraphs and short chapters. He and Pudney agreed the book could do without an index, a stamp of nonfiction likely to discourage fiction readers. *Escape to Danger* had been almost devoid of conversation, but, with snappy dialogue a staple of popular fiction, in *The Great Escape* Brickhill would include conversations as they'd occurred, taken from his memory and the memories of other participants. And he would use his writer's licence to insert occasional witty asides.

Pudney talked him into discarding unfamiliar terms and abbreviations that would be a barrier to readership. In *Escape to Danger*, Brickhill had frequently referred to POWs as kriegies. This term was now obliterated from the narrative. So influential would Brickhill's book become, 'kriegies' would disappear from the popular POW escape lexicon despite being commonly used by prisoners. Brickhill also omitted reference to the depressed NI individuals he'd mentioned in *Escape to Danger*, and the many men who didn't cooperate in escape activities. He likewise failed to mention homosexuality. Fellow Stalag Luft 3 inmate and author Robert Kee, in his 1947 book *A Crowd Is Not Company*, had said there were known homosexual couples in camp, while one or two homosexuals preyed on handsome young new arrivals. None of this, Brickhill decided, contributed to the heroic escape narrative.

Two other important editorial decisions were made by Brickhill, one prompted by insecurity, the other by modesty. As in *Escape to Danger*, he wouldn't mention that he was Australian, fearing that British critics would not take his tale of RAF prisoners seriously if perceived to be coming from the pen of a 'colonial'. Rather than irritate that sore, Brickhill stepped over the matter of nationality, and let it be assumed by Brits that, as a former RAF fighter pilot, he was 'one of them'.

Then there was the matter of his modesty. Like his grandfather James Brickhill, he was 'unobtrusive and retiring'. Like his father, George, he was 'quiet' and 'unostentatious'. While, in the years to come, Brickhill would use the press to advantage, his self-publicising would invariably be about selling books, not selling himself. As he had in *Escape to Danger*, he would refrain from making all but the most passing reference to his own part in *The Great Escape*. Only a dozen years on would he add a foreword to the American edition in which he mentioned his role: 'Of my part in the show – little enough to say. I am a sort of Boswell, not a hero. I was a cog in the machine, boss of the gang of "stooges" guarding the forgers.'[167]

On the ship coming over from Australia he'd had time to think about the focus of the book. The journalist in him told him to go for 'the guts' of the story, the inherent drama he'd always sought when reporting for the *Sun*. His story needed a central figure, a hub around which all the other characters and events revolved. It was obvious to Brickhill that this central figure was Big X, Roger Bushell. Without Bushell's relentless drive, autocratic control and fiendish creativity, the mass escape would probably not have happened.

Brickhill would open his book with Bushell, and thereafter use him as the glue that held the story together. He would be honest about Bushell's off-putting qualities, but would inevitably, if unconsciously, paint Bushell as the epic hero: one man against a murderous regime, the underdog struggling against impossible odds. Inevitably, too, the other escapees would bask in Bushell's Herculean glow and take on heroic qualities of their own.

Then there was the structure of the book. The long, detailed preparations for the mass escape and its tragic culmination formed two parts of a gripping three-act drama. The third act remained unwritten. Precisely what had happened to each of the Fifty? And what had happened to those responsible for their deaths, from the Nazi hierarchy who ordered the executions down to the grubby Gestapo gunmen who'd carried them out? Brickhill learned that the RAF's Special Investigations Branch had conducted an extensive hunt for the murderers in 1945–46. That criminal investigation had been carried out by a team of fifteen investigators led by Wing Commander Wilfred 'Freddie' Bowes, a Scotland Yard detective before the war. For a resonating denouement, Brickhill knew he would have to delve deep into official records released in 1948 and pick through that SIB investigation.

Despite his focus on *The Great Escape*, he hadn't forgotten about the 617 Squadron history. As soon as he'd arrived in London, with Margot Slater's advice fresh in his mind he'd written to the RAF's Air Chief Marshal Sir Ralph Cochrane, who'd been responsible for 617 Squadron during the war, to say he was prepared to 'have a go' at the squadron history after all.[168] The response was immediate. To Brickhill's relief,

John Nerney had yet to find a writer for the project, and the Australian received the blessing of Her Majesty's Government to tackle it.

Plus, John Pudney was keen to secure the book for Evans Brothers, having recommended Brickhill for the project in the first place. To Pudney's mind, it was the ideal title to follow *The Great Escape* and capitalise on its success. But Brickhill would have to produce a draft manuscript; Pudney's superiors wouldn't buy the 617 Squadron book on the basis of a proposal. And first, Brickhill had to write *The Great Escape*. He would end up working on both books at once.

Brickhill embarked on a tried and true journalistic approach to each book, interviewing as many surviving witnesses as possible to get their perspective on the people and events involved. For *The Great Escape*, tunnel king Wally Floody and security chief George Harsh topped his list for interview. Floody was back in Canada, and Harsh was living in New York City. Making contact with the pair, Brickhill arranged to go to North America to meet with them. Knowing that the *Largs Bay* was sailing on from Southampton to Halifax, Nova Scotia on 27 June, he hurriedly booked a ticket.

Before he left London, he put his head in the door of his old employers. Upon landing in North America, because he had no fixed address in England, he would give his address as the Associated Newspapers office at 85 Fleet Street. Thirteen rushed days after arriving in England, he set sail for Canada aboard the same ship that had brought him from Australia. He received a warm welcome from Floody, who Brickhill thought still looked like a consumptive. There was an equally effusive welcome from Harsh. Both men were able to fill him in on conversations they'd had with Roger Bushell and other key players in the real-life drama they'd all shared leading up to the breakout.

While Brickhill was in New York, he caught up with his US agent Mike Watkins, giving him as much material as he could on *The Great Escape*. Based on this, Watkins was able to interest US publishers Norton & Co, and a contract was soon forthcoming. Now Brickhill would be a published author in the massive and influential United States market, a dream come true for any non-American author. The book would be released in the summer of 1950 in Britain and as part of Norton's 'fall' catalogue in North America. Brimming with confidence, and with a suitcase full of notes from his conversations with Floody and Harsh, Brickhill returned to London to get to work.

Renting a small flat in Westminster, he set his typewriter on a table and wrote day and night. But something was nagging at him. He needed to go back to Germany again, to revisit the site of Stalag Luft 3. While in Germany, he could make the trip doubly worthwhile by also going to the Ruhr Valley, to visit the dams attacked by 617 Squadron.

The Moehne and Sorpe dams, breached by the RAF in 1943, had been fully repaired within five months of the raid. Their lakes were again full, and there were few signs of the anti-aircraft gun installations that had topped and flanked the Moehne dam – the smaller Sorpe dam had been undefended. Looking down from the top of Moehne dam's massive, gently curving structure, Brickhill could see that the valley below was littered with twisted, rusting girders and lumps of concrete that had once formed part of the dam's wall. Formerly picturesque and productive fields flanking the river lay churned and ugly. 'The earth still looks as though a giant's rake had scoured it,' he noted.[169]

Going three kilometres downriver, he arrived at the ruined village of Himmelpforten. Ironically, Brickhill would discover, the village's name meant 'Gates of Heaven'. Locals told him that, after the dam had been ruptured by the RAF in the early hours of 17 May 1943, the village was engulfed by floodwaters. Himmelpforten's pastor, sixty-two-year-old Joseph Berkenkopf, had long predicted that the British would one day bomb the dam, and told his parishioners that in that event he would ring the bell of his church, the Porta Coeli, a former thirteenth-century monastery, to warn villagers to escape to higher ground.

On the night of the raid, Berkenkopf had done just that. Awakened after midnight by the detonation of the first of four 'bouncing bombs' lobbed against the dam by the Lancasters of 617 Squadron, the pastor had dashed to his belltower. The villagers, mostly women and children, were warned by the tolling bell and had fled to the hilltops. But Pastor Berkenkopf was still ringing his bell when a wall of water twelve metres high swept him and his historic church away.

Locals told Brickhill that the pastor's body had never been found. They had located the church's chalice, christening font, crucifix, and a few of its stones strewn as far as ninety kilometres down the valley. When Brickhill visited, the people of Himmelpforten had just finished building a new church, the St Bernardus, using remnants from the destroyed monastery, a kilometre from the site of the original. Inside, Brickhill found an inscription in Latin on the newly raised altar: *The wreckage of the church of Himmelpforten, destroyed by flood in 1943, served six years later to build this new altar and this new church.* Brickhill was struck by the 'restrained and unmalicious' nature of the inscription; no mention of war or the bombing raid, no blame cast the way of Britain, its air force or its airmen.[170] To this day, locals simply refer to the raid as the 'Moehne Catastrophe'.

Leaving behind the sad little German village, Brickhill travelled on to Berlin, still a city in ruins. This was just several months after the end of the Berlin Airlift, an eleven-month operation by the British, American, Canadian and Australian air forces to supply West Berlin by air after the Soviets closed off all land access. Although the communists had backed down, tensions were still high between Moscow and the West. Yet Brickhill succeeded in travelling to Sagan and visiting the site of Stalag Luft 3. Brickhill would say he was able to 'fossick once more around the scene of the crime'.[171] The bones of the camp remained. Otherwise, there was now little to see in Sagan Forest, but much to remember.

From his cramped London flat, Brickhill continued to track down and interview escape survivors he'd previously been unable to talk to – men like Wings Day, Johnny Dodge and Dutch home-runner Bob van der Stock. Throwing them probing questions, he pieced together the internal narrative of

The Great Escape from his recollections and theirs. He received copies of letters that Roger Bushell had sent from Stalag Luft 3, provided by Bushell's mother in South Africa and Mac McGowan, adjutant of his own 92 Squadron when Bushell was CO. With relish, Brickhill waded through the thousand pages of documents released by the British Government the previous year which covered the doggedly thorough and grimly elucidating British investigation into the murders of the Fifty.

He discovered that, on the morning of Sunday, 26 March 1944, twenty-six hours after the break had been discovered at Stalag Luft 3, the first report of the mass escape had reached Adolf Hitler, who was then at his mountain retreat at Berchtesgaden in Bavaria. Luftwaffe chief Hermann Goering, SS chief Heinrich Himmler and General Wilhelm Keitel, Chief of Staff of the OKW, Germany's Army High Command, were also at Berchtesgaden that weekend. Flying into a rage, Hitler had summoned the trio to an immediate conference, ordering that no record be kept of what was said at the meeting. From later testimony at the Nuremburg war trials, it had become clear that Hitler ordered every single escapee shot when they were recaptured.

As tactfully as he could, Goering had argued against this, suggesting that shooting all escapees could not be disguised as anything but murder. Besides, he said, the Allies might reciprocate with harsh reprisals against German prisoners in their hands. Hitler had relented; but only marginally. More than half the escapees were to be shot on recapture, he ordered, with the excuse to the Swiss Government, the 'Protecting Power', that they had been shot while attempting to escape from custody after recapture. The documents also revealed that General Arthur Nebe was the one who'd physically chosen the names of the fifty men to be shot. As Brickhill now knew, Nebe had not lived long after this. Implicated in the July 1944 plot to assassinate Hitler, he'd been executed by his own side.

And, as Brickhill discovered with some satisfaction, as a result of the British investigations, a number of former Gestapo officers had been arrested, tried and convicted for their parts in murders of the Fifty. Thirteen Germans had been hanged. Even Gestapo men who'd driven the vehicles carrying the men to their deaths had received ten years imprisonment. A number of culprits would continue to be sought; the last trial in Germany involving the murder of the Fifty would take place in 1968.

As he read the file, Brickhill learned how, where and when Bushell and the others were caught, interrogated by the Kripo, and handed over to the Gestapo. They hadn't been executed en masse. Often in groups of two, all were being driven back towards Sagan and Stalag Luft 3 by different routes when cars carrying them stopped in the dead of night to allow the prisoners to stretch their legs. As they stood with their backs to their Gestapo escorts, each member of the Fifty had been shot in the back of the head, at close range, by pistol. Several, including Bushell, had needed a second bullet to finish them off.

Brickhill's travel and living costs were eating into his reserves. Anxiety over money, combined with the crushing pressure he was putting himself under by working on two books at once, sent him to a London psychiatrist, a Dr Mason, who helped him prioritise. First priority, generate income. Second, focus on *The Great Escape* and tackle the 617 Squadron book later. As much as he hated returning to journalism, even briefly, in August Brickhill did a deal with London's *Daily Express* to write a series of features. These had similar themes: famous bankers who'd made enormous fortunes by financing war. 'The Masters of Money', featuring the likes of J. Pierpont Morgan, Lord Inchcape and Sir Basil Zaharoff, ran in the *Daily Express* over September-October. A follow-up series, 'The Money Men', appeared over October-November. Retaining the foreign rights, Brickhill sold 'The Masters of Money' to the loyal Port Pirie *Recorder*, to Sydney's *Sunday Herald* and to the Brisbane *Courier-Mail*. Even Victoria's *Shepparton Advertiser* bought it.

By Christmas 1949, Margot Slater and her sister Jeanette had taken a flat in northwest London's Swiss Cottage area. Teaming up with Pat Torr and Ruth Steele, two girlfriends from Richmond back home, the girls were playing tourist. And Margot was enjoying the attentions of shipboard suitor Paul Brickhill, who began seeing her regularly. Surrounded by four attractive girls, drinking champagne and eating heartily, this would be the best Christmas that Brickhill had experienced in a decade.

When 1950 arrived, Brickhill the author would arrive. And all his dreams, and his nightmares, would become reality.

17.

Enter the Author and Wife

In his New York City apartment, George Harsh sat gazing absently out the window. At his office several days earlier he'd received a package in the mail from Paul Brickhill in London – the manuscript to Brickhill's *The Great Escape*, neatly typed by the author on loose pages. Brickhill was asking for his colleague's comments, suggestions and corrections. Harsh took the manuscript home, and after dinner he and his new wife, Eleanor, had begun reading. Harsh would read a page, then pass it to her to read. She would pile completed pages on the floor between them. All through the night, as if possessed by some strange power, they read without pause. With the sun rising over Manhattan, Eleanor Harsh laid the last page atop the pile, and looked over to her husband. He continued to stare out at the city beyond their window. But she knew his mind wasn't in New York; it was in Sagan.

'Whew!' exclaimed Eleanor, lying back, physically and emotionally exhausted. 'Did all this really happen?'

'Yeah,' George murmured. 'It really happened.'[172]

Harsh soon sent the manuscript back to Brickhill, with his congratulations and his thanks. 'This book,' he would say, 'is the story of achievement against impossible odds.'[173] George seems not to have suggested any corrections, even when Brickhill wrote – after a quip by the American – that Harsh had been shot down over Berlin. He had actually been downed over Cologne. This was a minor detail in what Harsh considered a masterwork and a fine tribute to mutual friends. Brickhill subsequently sent the manuscript out to all the men he'd talked to in the course of researching the book. Armed with their comments, he did a final polish. On the agreed delivery date, he handed in the completed draft to David Higham, who passed it onto John Pudney at Evans Brothers. Basic corrections suggested by Pudney would follow, and then, months later, the galley proofs would come from the printer.

With all his books, Brickhill would correct and polish proofs up to the moment the book went to print. After his training at the *Sun*, he was obsessed with detail, and obsessed with getting the details right. Writing about how the tunnellers constructed Harry's air-conditioning system, he made a point of describing it step by step, almost as if writing a guide for would-be escapees. If more than one person was present for a particular conversation, he'd quizzed all parties about exactly what words had been used, chopping out troubling phrases or recollections that were not supported by the testimony of more than one man. With *The Great Escape* delivered, Brickhill had time to catch his breath before diving into detailed research for the 617 Squadron book.

Of late, his relationship with Margot Slater had blossomed into a full-scale romance. Margot was running out of money and talking about going back to Australia – Brickhill would say he ended up helping pay the rent on her NW3 flat, to keep her in London.[174] Finally, in the spring, he popped the question. On 22 April, thirty-three-year-old Brickhill and twenty-one-year-old Margot were married at St Michael's Church of England, Chester Square, Pimlico by Father Geoffrey Gray. It was a small affair. Margot's sister Jeanette was her bridesmaid, while Max Kempe, a journalist friend, was Brickhill's best man.

Brickhill had moved into a larger flat by this time, in a large pre-war brick block at 21 Cale Street in Chelsea. Whenever he walked into the city from Chelsea, he would pass a posh hotel in Sloane Street, the Cadogan, a handsome Queen Anne pile with a top-hat-wearing doorman out front. He booked his new bride and himself into the Cadogan for a three-day honeymoon; all he could afford. Brickhill's bank balance was sinking, and he was now living almost entirely on his great expectations. As for the honeymoon, it was not a great success. Margot would much later accuse Brickhill of declaring, at the end of their three-day tryst, that he'd made a huge mistake marrying her. Brickhill would deny this, and Margot would counter that, if he didn't voice the sentiment, she'd felt sure he was thinking it.[175]

Nonetheless, Mr and Mrs Brickhill set up home in the Chelsea flat, and Brickhill threw himself back into the research for the 617 Squadron book, again using the flat as his office. As Margot quickly discovered, Brickhill was still just as 'obsessional' as he'd been as a schoolboy. Working late into the night, he demanded absolute quiet. Plus, with many of the people he needed to interview only available at weekends, he was often away on Saturdays and Sundays. Margot was left to entertain herself with Jeanette and hometown friends Pat and Ruth – 'The Richmond biddies', Brickhill called them collectively.[176] Margot quickly became bored. As she would tell an Australian reporter three years later, she 'tired of sitting in their Chelsea flat and being told to keep quiet while her husband pounded on a typewriter'.[177]

Brickhill, for his part, quickly learned that his young wife had no proclivity for or interest in housework, and cooked infrequently. Exasperated by Margot's lack of domesticity, he gave her a list of household tasks to accomplish when he was away, only to come home to find few, if any, done. Brickhill blamed Margot's lack of domestic skills on a spoiling mother. Meanwhile, independent Margot wouldn't be told what to do by anyone. Their flat quickly became a battleground. She told him to get a housekeeper, he told her to get a job. Margot registered with a modelling agency and started winning freelance modelling assignments, and Brickhill hired a housekeeper. For the rest of their married life, Brickhill would employ domestic help for Margot.

When Margot implored Brickhill to take her out, or to bring people home, he took her to the cinema, to see the movie version of Eric Williams' *The Wooden Horse*. It wouldn't have been Margot's idea of a fun film, but to Brickhill this tale set in the camp where he'd been a prisoner was personal. He learned that the film version of *The Wooden Horse* was shot on Lüneburg

Heath in northwest Germany, not at the actual site of Stalag Luft 3. The producers had canvassed the idea of shooting at Sagan, but Soviet authorities had refused permission.

Brickhill saw familiar faces in minor roles in *The Wooden Horse*; most noticeably, his childhood friend Peter Finch, playing the part of an Australian patient in Stalag Luft 3's East Compound hospital. The pair had lost contact, and unbeknownst to Brickhill, Finch had arrived in England from Sydney in 1948. Bent on realising his dream of acting success, Finch was steadily building his career on stage and in film. The other familiar face on screen was that of Briton Dan Cunningham, playing a prisoner helping the three escapees. Cunningham, who, like Finch, was striving to build an acting career, had actually been a Stalag Luft 3 prisoner. Ironically, he'd been one of the players in the compound's theatre who'd shown no interest in escaping.

Knowing that the sooner he delivered the 617 Squadron manuscript the sooner he would secure an Evans Brothers contract and a new advance to prop up his flagging finances, Brickhill ignored his new wife's pleas to spend more time with her, and pushed on with the project. Gripped with anxiety, he worried about money, and worried about how he would tackle this new book. This would be a very different project from the last. At least this book's title had been written for him, by history. When the British press exuberantly reported the dams raid in 1943, it had dubbed the squadron 'the dambusters'. Shortly after, 617 Squadron, which had been formed especially to make the dams raid, officially adopted the title the Dam Busters, along with the motto of 'After me, the deluge'. So, *The Dam Busters* it would be.

That was the easy part. In writing *The Great Escape*, Brickhill had been describing people and events he knew. But he wasn't intimate with anything or anyone related to 617 Squadron. His research involved wading through reams of official documents and private papers, plus months of face-to-face interviews. John Nerney put him in touch with people who could help. One was Harry Humphries, adjutant of 617 Squadron through most of the war, who'd kept a set of squadron diaries.

Humphries would later reveal he was initially reluctant to let Brickhill see these diaries. He didn't say why. Perhaps it was because Brickhill was an Australian fighter type, or maybe Humphries harboured plans to write his own 617 Squadron book. Humphries revealed that he 'was later persuaded to make them available' to Brickhill by Nerney. He would also later grumble that Brickhill used the diaries 'without acknowledgment'.[178] Yet Brickhill interviewed Humphries, and the adjutant would feature considerably, and favourably, in Brickhill's subsequent narrative.

Once again, Brickhill went looking for the 'guts of the story'. Having undertaken to write a history of the squadron, he was obliged to describe all its operations throughout the war, not just the dams raid – 617 had subsequently carried out a number of special raids through 1943–45. What he needed was a common factor, a core to the story. Above all, he needed a Roger Bushell, an heroic figure battling against long odds.

Initially, that heroic figure appeared to be Guy Gibson, who'd been awarded a Victoria Cross for leading the dams raid. Gibson had arrived at the new 617 Squadron a handsome twenty-five-year-old wing commander who'd had the Distinguished Service Order and Distinguished Flying Cross pinned to his chest by King George VI. Gibson had subsequently been killed, in 1944, flying a Mosquito fighter-bomber – according to a 2011 revelation, shot down in error by Bernard McCormack, tail gunner of a British Lancaster.[179] Pushed by the RAF in 1943, Gibson had written a patriotic memoir, *Enemy Coast Ahead*. This was good reference for Brickhill, but only the last two chapters referred to 617 Squadron, and Gibson had left 617 following the dams raid. At best, Gibson's involvement in the squadron's story would end halfway through Brickhill's book.

Following Gibson, the squadron had a number of charismatic commanding officers including an easy-going Australian from Sydney, Harold 'Micky' Martin, who'd played a leading role in the dams raid. Martin's successor was Leonard Cheshire, a charitable Englishman who won a VC for his later work with the squadron. But all these changes in heroic lead were not helpful to an author seeking continuity of narrative. Changing lead actors multiple times wouldn't work in a movie, and it wouldn't make for a bestselling book.

As he dug deeper and further, Brickhill struck gold. The so-called 'bouncing bombs' used by 617 on the dams raid had been invented by an obscure and eccentric defence scientist, Barnes Wallis. For security reasons, the British Government hadn't permitted Wallis' name to be made public during the war. Consequently, Guy Gibson, in *Enemy Coast Ahead*, had referred to Wallis as 'Jeff'. This was a little joke on Gibson's part. During the bomb's test drops, Wallis had worked closely with Vickers-Armstrong test pilot Mutt Summers.

'Mutt and Jeff' was a widely syndicated American newspaper strip cartoon which even made it to stage and screen. In his book, Gibson had Mutt and 'Jeff' collaborating on development of the bouncing bomb. Gibson may have even been aware that Jeff the cartoon character had originally been an insane asylum inmate; Wallis was certainly considered crazy by some government officials.

Researching Wallis' involvement, Brickhill found that the massive 'Grand Slam' and 'Tallboy' bombs dropped by 617 Squadron later in the war had also been developed by Wallis. Here was the continuity, and the hero, that Brickhill was looking for. Now, five years after the war, the Government wouldn't prevent Brickhill from revealing Wallis' name and wartime role. So, after receiving an invitation from Wallis to visit him, in the summer of 1950 Brickhill headed down to Surrey, to Wallis' farmhouse home. This was White Hills House, at Effingham, just to the southwest of London.[180]

The author received a warm welcome from the man he described as 'the white-haired patriarch, pink-faced, gentle and abstracted'.[181] On his drawing board, the inventor enthusiastically showed Brickhill his design for a new aircraft, a swing-wing bomber. In the event, Wallis' design would be turned down by the British Government, only to be taken up by the Americans and the French. On this same drawing board, Wallis had designed his bouncing bomb.

During the war, the same security restrictions that had prevented the press and Guy Gibson from naming Barnes Wallis had also stopped them revealing the exact nature of this bomb. Those security restrictions remained in force in 1950, in case the Cold War developed into a hot war and the weapon had to be employed against Russian dams at some time in the future, preventing Brickhill from describing it accurately. In reality, the bouncing bomb was a very large depth charge, not unlike the kind used at sea against submarines. The revolutionary aspect of Wallis' dam-busting theory had been the low-level, skidding delivery to the dam face, after which the bombs sank, to explode many metres below the surface, right beside the dam.

As Wallis described his process of invention to the author, he explained how he had met and overcome numerous infuriating bureaucratic obstacles during the development of this unique weapon, only to have to overcome many frustrating technical problems, right up to the day of 617 Squadron's 1943 dams mission. Brickhill came away from their meeting knowing he had the makings of an interesting narrative, and a central figure; a driven man who'd overcome great odds to succeed.

In addition, like *The Great Escape*, the story would have the element of tragedy. Of the nineteen Avro Lancaster bombers that had taken off to bomb the Ruhr dams from very low level, eight had been brought down. Fifty-three airmen from a number of countries aboard those downed bombers were killed, with just three surviving to become POWs. And very few of the aircrew who started out with 617, which became known in RAF ranks as a 'suicide squadron', lived to see war's end. Most of the men who did survive were saved by appointments to administrative jobs.

Close to half the squadron destroyed on their very first operation represented a heavy loss, one that weighed heavily on Barnes Wallis' conscience after the dams raid. Because two of four target dams had been breached, and because the press had trumpeted it as a triumph which would alter the course of the war (it didn't), those losses had been glossed over by government and media. Brickhill would be honest in his account of the human cost, but, in focusing on Wallis' struggles with bureaucrats and bombs, his narrative would divert the attention of readers from that cost.

Brickhill went on to interview a number of key former 617 Squadron personnel, men such as Micky Martin and Leonard Cheshire, who were happy to talk to a fellow pilot about issues personal and professional. 'They were too modest to talk about themselves,' Brickhill would later say about these men, 'so I got them to tell me about the others. And vice versa.'[182]

During these interviews, Brickhill learned of a connection he'd almost had with 617 Squadron in 1944. That December, Cheshire had planned a special Christmas present for the inmates of Stalag Luft 3. He'd been determined to lead 617 on a mission to parachute food to the RAF prisoners. Cheshire was only talked out of the drops when it was pointed out that when the prisoners rushed to the drops, German machine-gunners in goon towers could think the packages contained weapons for an uprising, and would have opened up, mowing down hundreds of POWs. Brickhill, having always been at the forefront of everything, would probably have been one of them. Cheshire had almost been the cause of Brickhill's premature death.

While quite deliberately failing to point out that he was Australian, Brickhill would make sure that the Australians on the squadron got their fair dues in his narrative. In addition, among the photographs from the Air Ministry and Imperial

War Museum he collected to include in the book, he chose one that showed a group of 617's Aussies: Micky Martin, 'Spam' Spafford, Dave Shannon, Les Knight, Bob Hay, Lance Howard, Bob Kellow and Jack Leggo.

Probably to the surprise of John Nerney at the Air Ministry, the book that Brickhill wrote would begin with mission mastermind Barnes Wallis, just as *The Great Escape* began with escape mastermind Roger Bushell. It would not be until the fourth chapter that Guy Gibson and 617 Squadron took the stage. Wallis' story would continue to be threaded in and out of the narrative and hold it together through all the later episodes in the squadron's history following the dams raid. Nerney would approve.

From the US in the middle of the year came good news from Brickhill's literary agent Mike Watkins. A Los Angeles production company was interested in doing a sixty-minute television drama version of *The Great Escape*, to be aired on NBC. The production company was Showcase Productions, headed by Fred Coe. Only two years older than Brickhill, Coe was producing NBC's successful Philco-Goodyear TV Playhouse, with each drama in the 'anthology' series a one-off, standalone production.

The deal being offered by Coe gave Showcase Productions the option to also later make *The Great Escape* as a feature film. Agent Watkins would specify a standard ten-year reversion clause in the contract which meant that, should Coe fail to exercise his right to go ahead with a movie within ten years of signing, the feature film rights to *The Great Escape* would revert to Brickhill, unencumbered and free of cost. The money on offer for the TV drama rights was not huge, but as a marketing exercise it would put the book in front of millions of Americans. Coe was talking about airing the production the following January. Excited by the immediacy of production and the future possibilities it offered, and seduced by the fact that his work would be appearing on American TV, Brickhill agreed.

From August 1950, with *The Great Escape* hitting bookstores, press reviews came thick and fast. Brickhill, sensitive to both constructive and destructive criticism, read every review. They were glowing. 'Written as a really gripping, illuminating story should be,' said the *Times Literary Supplement*. 'The high-water mark of all active prisoner-of-war books,' declared the *Telegraph*. 'One of the most unputdownable stories of the war,' said the *Observer*. 'Mr Brickhill tells it very well indeed,' wrote the reviewer in the *New Statesman*. 'Has an exciting quality whose cream I mustn't take off,' said *Country Life*'s reviewer. 'It moves at a breathless pace,' said the *Scotsman* in Edinburgh.

It was the reviewer for the *Listener* who recognised another aspect to Brickhill's book. It wasn't the scale of the escape alone that set the work apart from other stories, he said, it was the quality of the writing. 'For there is present all through it, as well as in its outcome, the authentic strain of tragedy.'[183] In framing his book as a tale of glorious failure, Brickhill had unwittingly written a tragedy which touched sympathetic chords with his audience.

Reviews of *The Great Escape* in America over the following months were equally laudatory, and perceptive. 'It is much too mettlesome a story for fiction,' said New York's influential *Herald Tribune*. 'It happens to be the truth. Brickhill tells it with a patient anger that has its own eloquence.'[184] 'For sheer suspense, puts the fictioneers to shame,' wrote the *Boston Globe*. 'Puts the average war book so far in the shadow it's not even funny,' waxed the *Dallas Times-Herald*. 'Tense, thrilling, fabulous,' said the *Philadelphia Inquirer*. 'Will hold you spellbound,' declared the *Boston Herald*.[185]

In Sydney, Del Fox clipped an article about the reception for *The Great Escape* from a local newspaper and filed it in her Paul Brickhill collection. Before long aware that her former flame had married, it was the last item about Brickhill that Del would retain.

In the English autumn, *The Great Escape*'s good reviews and rocketing sales brought sudden notoriety to Brickhill, not the least among the Australian expat community in London. Urged by Margot, Brickhill begrudgingly set aside his *Dam Busters* manuscript every few weeks so they could host parties in their small Chelsea flat.

It was mostly fellow Australian writers that Brickhill attracted. One was Jon Cleary, a reporter with the Australia News and Information Bureau in Fleet Street for the previous two years. Apart from a shared Sydney journalistic background, Brickhill and Cleary had a lot in common. Of a similar age, they were the same height, blue-eyed and had a passion for fast cars and motor racing. Both had met their future wives onboard ship while sailing to England. And, like Brickhill's parents, Cleary's mother and father had been wiped out by the Great Depression. As a consequence, like Brickhill, Cleary loathed debt. In 1947, Cleary's first novel *You Can't See 'Round Corners* had been published. It hadn't been successful enough for him to give up his day job, but, like Brickhill, Cleary dreamed of worldwide success as an author. It was a dream both would achieve before long. Although Cleary would transfer to New York shortly after this, he would return the following year and become a regular at Brickhill 'do's', with the pair becoming long-term mates.

Another new Australian literary friend in London was Ian Bevan, a London book editor of note, who introduced Brickhill to Russell Braddon. Five years Brickhill's junior, Braddon had written *The Naked Island*, a novel based on his years as a prisoner of the Japanese on the Burma Railway, which became a multi-million seller as well as a stage play and film. Both Braddon and Bevan had flats at Dolphin Square in Chelsea. This massive Thames-side apartment complex with central heating and a swimming pool was then, as it is now, considered rather fashionable.

Bevan introduced Brickhill to other literary Australians in London, among them journalist and nonfiction writer Chester Wilmot and biographer and military historian Alan Moorehead. In October, another Dolphin Square resident sent the Brickhills an invitation to a party in his flat – Peter Finch – whose star was, like Brickhill's, on the rise. Apart from his growing film career, Finch was taking the West End stage by storm.

October 18 was the opening night for Orson Welles' production of *Othello* at the St James Theatre, with Finch playing Iago to Welles' Othello. That night, the party in Finch's ninth-floor Dolphin Square flat was in full swing by the time Finch and his wife, Tamara, themselves arrived, late, following curtain calls at the St James. Brickhill and Margot were there. Looking across the crowded room, Brickhill spotted his boyhood friend, champagne glass in hand.

Seeing Brickhill at the same instant, Finch, smirking, slowly raised his glass to him. 'Success! Success!' he called above the hubbub.

Breaking into a smile, Brickhill raised his glass in a return salute. 'Success! Success!' he called back.[186]

Brickhill reflected on their shared teenage dream. Finch was on the London stage, but not as a result of an urgent call from across the seas. And Brickhill hadn't flown him there in his own plane. Finch had brought himself to England and fought his way up through the acting ranks, while Brickhill was a pilot who was now afraid of flying. The pair would restart their friendship, although the bond would never again be as strong as it had been in their youth.

Margot wasn't happy. Between promotion for *The Great Escape* and continuing work on *The Dam Busters*, Brickhill was labouring around the clock and had little time for his wife. They agreed she should get away for a break on her own. Eve Norton, a mutual friend living in Dublin, invited Margot to come and stay, and, in November, Brickhill farewelled his wife as she set off for the Irish capital. Grateful for peace and quiet, he went back to work on *The Dam Busters*. Within a week of Margot going to Ireland, Brickhill received a telephone call from Eve. She told him that Margot had suffered a nervous breakdown under her roof. Dropping everything, Brickhill rushed to Dublin.

The doctor attending Margot told Brickhill that his wife was suffering from hysteria and hallucinations, and recommended she receive psychiatric help. When Brickhill brought Margot back to London in December, he put her under the care of Dr Mason, the same psychiatrist who'd helped him the previous year. Margot would see Mason for the next six months.[187] While now treating Margot with kid gloves, Brickhill still had to complete his book, and without delay. Like all publishers, Faber & Faber paid its authors royalties every six months. With a royalty cheque for *The Great Escape* still a long way off, Brickhill needed the advance that would come with delivery of *The Dam Busters*.

The immediate success of *The Great Escape* gave him the confidence to use his now-accustomed descriptive licence in the new book. Of Air Marshal Sir Arthur 'Bomber' Harris, chief of Bomber Command, for example, he wrote: 'Harris, it was freely acknowledged, could crush a seaside landlady with a look.' And, as he had with *The Great Escape*, he leavened the story of death and destruction with amusing anecdotes, such as the tale of how, after the dams raid, Micky Martin was approached by Australian authorities seeking items for the Australian War Memorial in Canberra. Martin had written back: 'I am very interested in your museum and am sending you, enclosed, the Moehne Dam.' He had an Australian colleague on the squadron, Toby Foxlee, write underneath:

'Opened by the censors and contents confiscated by the Metropolitan Water Board.'[188]

It was no wonder, as Brickhill was to tell Brisbane journalist Roy Connolly, that once he was able to deliver the draft *Dam Busters* manuscript to John Pudney at Evans Brothers at the end of 1950, it 'was eagerly seized by Evans'. The advance, he told Connolly, was handsomely into the five figures.[189] John Nerney would convince Lord Tedder, Marshal of the Royal Air Force, to write a foreword, and even though the book read like a gripping novel, as this was an official unit history endorsed by the Air Ministry, Pudney commissioned an index.

The first screen version of *The Great Escape* went to air in the US on 28 January 1951. Produced by Fred Coe, it was directed by Gordon Duff, who'd been directing anthology television drama since 1949. Brickhill was credited as author of the book, but no screenwriter was named. The screenplay had been the work of Coe and Duff, who failed to give themselves a writing credit because they weren't members of the writers' union.

The Coe-Duff script called for sixteen speaking parts. American actor John C. Beecher played Roger Bushell. Another American, the older Horace Braham, played SBO Massey. Polish-born, fifty-four-year-old Kurt Katch, who'd made a career in American movies playing character roles of mostly sinister types, was cast as the German commandant. Among the supporting players were a young Rod Steiger,

E. G. Marshall and Everett Sloane. To spice things up, Coe and Duff had also written in a part and a storyline deviation for a woman. The production, shot entirely in the studio, was broadcast live. It wasn't recorded for posterity. Once aired, it was lost to the ether. As Brickhill learned, the drama's tunnel set won praise from American critics for its realism. But he himself never saw it.

Six months later, a year after doing the deal with Coe, Brickhill's American agent would receive another approach for the screen rights to *The Great Escape.* This would come from a forty-one-year-old American who'd been directing B-grade movies, mostly westerns, for the past four years. John Sturges read *The Great Escape* when it appeared in abridged form in *Reader's Digest* in the US in 1951. A member of the United States Army Air Force during the war, he found the story resonated with him, even though he himself hadn't been a POW. Sturges became besotted with the book, and its cinematic possibilities. Told the rights weren't available, and unaware of Coe's option, he glumly went away. But that wouldn't prove the end of the matter. Over the next decade, Sturges would prove a persistent suitor.

David Higham had meantime negotiated a deal which allowed the BBC to put a *Great Escape* radio special to air in 1951. BBC Radio's producer for the special, David Porter, had been a Stalag Luft 3 kriegie, and he convinced several other former camp inmates to participate in the special, which would air in May. The book's author would at least hear this adaptation of his work, before, on 26 June, setting off for the south of France to find a rented villa. Brickhill's plan was for Margot to join him there once she completed her psychiatric treatment. He himself was exhausted after knocking out three books in two years, and was looking forward to a rest.

In a valley below St-Paul-de-Vence, a picture-postcard hill village in Provence between Cannes and Nice with Mediterranean views, Brickhill found his idyllic villa. The locale had been recommended by Eve Norton, who holidayed there, and had a literary connection – D. H. Lawrence had died at the former Roman town of Vence, six kilometres away. Today, St-Paul-de-Vence crawls with tourists, but then it was relatively quiet. The large villa sat on an acreage, had a pond and was blessedly private. With royalty cheques now flooding into Brickhill Publications Limited, Brickhill could comfortably afford to live here. Envisioning a life of writing in the sun free from cares while Margot brought out easel, canvas and paints, and brushing up the French he'd polished in Stalag Luft 3, Brickhill signed a long lease, hired a housekeeper and a maid, and sent for his wife. Moving in and setting his typewriter on a table outdoors, he began correcting *The Dam Busters* proofs.

Even though Margot didn't have a driver's licence and they didn't own a car, she insisted on driving to Provence. Taking a driving course and quickly gaining her licence, she purchased a gleaming new Alfa Romeo roadster, getting Brickhill to arrange payment from France. He paid for it through his company, but ground his teeth with annoyance when Margot registered the car, not in the company's name, but in her own. With a friend who was an experienced driver beside her, Margot drove down to St-Paul-de-Vence. The problem was, the friend stayed, and every casual acquaintance in London that Margot had invited to come to visit did just that over the next few months. Brickhill's dream of a peaceful idyll became a nightmare.

'I need you to protect and insulate me from the world!' he complained bitterly to Margot. 'So that I can work.'[190]

18.

Bader, the Man with Tin Legs

Contentedly, Brickhill sat back and puffed a cigar. He'd just enjoyed a fine dinner in a posh London restaurant, at someone else's expense. Across the table sat Douglas Bader (pronounced 'Bahder'), and his wife, Thelma. Bader, a handsome, round-faced forty-one-year-old with a cheeky grin and a mischievous twinkle in his eye, was also sucking on a cigar. His demure wife looked the image of Princess Elizabeth, the future Queen Elizabeth II. All evening, the couple had been quizzing the Australian.

'Look here, Brickhill,' said Bader now, 'we have a lot in common, you and I. We both flew Spitfires and Hurricanes in the war, and both bailed out, to spend years in German prison camps. We both use rude language, and dislike pompous officials. You might not make too abominable a mess of my story.'[191]

It was October 1951. *The Dam Busters* had been published in September, and it had immediately become clear that

Brickhill had another runaway bestseller on his hands. Among the first of millions who would read the book was Bader, a man who'd made a name for himself as a Battle of Britain fighter pilot with twenty kills, despite having lost his legs in a flying accident before the war. Bader and his wife had both been enthralled by *The Dam Busters*, with Bader later saying he'd been impressed by Brickhill's gift for bringing people and events to life, for creating a sense of immediacy and actuality, despite having never known any of the men of 617 Squadron before embarking on the book.[192]

Thelma would remember her husband slapping the cover of *The Dam Busters* after they'd finished reading it. 'If anyone writes our story,' he'd said to her, 'it must be Paul Brickhill.'[193]

So Bader had written a letter to Brickhill, proposing dinner in London to discuss a potential literary collaboration. After Brickhill received the letter at St-Paul-de-Vence, the invitation had intrigued him enough to agree to meet. Leaving Margot in Provence, he'd returned to England and come to dinner. On Belgrave Square in exclusive Belgravia, the airy Belfry restaurant was housed in a former Presbyterian church. Today, as Mosimann's, it's just as posh as it was back then. In May 1945, within days of being released from German imprisonment and returning to London, Bader had been taken to dinner here by Spitfire pilot chums including Johnnie Johnson and Adolph 'Sailor' Malan. It had been his regular haunt ever since, when he could afford it on his salary as a mid-level executive with Shell.

Brickhill already knew a lot about Bader, a former RAF group captain, although he had never met him before. He'd written several hundred words about the man in *Escape to*

Danger, referring to his escape attempts when a POW. Some of his information had come from Wings Day, who had flown with Bader in the 1930s and shared prison camp with him in the 1940s. Like Brickhill, Bader had been an inmate of Stalag Luft 3, although he'd been transferred elsewhere by the time Brickhill arrived there, ending up at the Colditz Castle maximum security camp, Oflag IV-C.

As Brickhill was aware, Bader's reputation was mixed. Gordon Sinclair, a pilot who'd flown with him, would remark, 'Bader was not everyone's cup of tea.'[194] In fact, Bader had an abrasive personality and a 'take the piss' sense of humour which rubbed many people the wrong way. Harry Broadhurst, who became an RAF Air Chief Marshal, would recall that, after he'd been wounded in the backside during the Battle of Britain, Bader had greeted him with a slap on the painful rear end, saying, 'Hello, hello. Run away from the Hun again?'[195]

When a prisoner of the Germans, Bader had made himself very unpopular with some fellow POWs. Said one of them, Victor Gammon: 'His imperious manner, unreasoned and frequently unreasonable efforts at escape, without thought for the consequences for others, did not endear him to those who had spent a couple of years in careful planning, or even to those who believed that attempting escape was a game for idiots.'[196] It hadn't helped that the Luftwaffe had treated Bader as a VIP prisoner, providing him with a chair at Appell and allowing him to ride in vehicles with his guards while other POWs were made to walk.

Leaving aside what he'd heard about Bader, Brickhill came to the Belfry dinner both flattered and fearful. Flattered by

Bader's approach, and fearful of tackling a full-on biography for the first time. He would also admit to being uncertain about how to act towards a man with no legs. Would Bader be sensitive about his prosthetics? 'Did one refer to them casually, or not at all?' Brickhill pondered.

That question was answered by Bader as they sat down to dinner. 'Just a minute while I fiddle these ruddy legs under the table.'

As they chatted over the meal, Brickhill realised that Bader was no shrinking violet. There would be no gradual reveal of the man's personality. 'It hits you like a bolting steamroller,' Brickhill would say three years later. 'A glowing, dominating charm that can change to disconcerting brusqueness.'[197]

If he were to take this book on, Brickhill told Bader as they puffed their Havanas, Bader must appreciate that he would be the Australian's guinea pig as he experimented with the biographic form. Bader seemed unfazed. And Brickhill's interest was piqued, especially when Bader offered to give him his flying logs, combat reports, press clippings, original photographs, more than 2000 letters, and other bits and pieces. Most interesting of all, Bader revealed that he had already attempted to write his story himself, bringing in another unnamed author to help. That author had taken their manuscript to the Rank Organisation, hoping to interest them in a feature film based on Bader's story. When Rank rejected the idea, the previous author had walked away. Bader also offered to give Brickhill the 100,000-word manuscript that he and that unnamed writer had produced.

Brickhill went away to think on it. No longer desperate for money, he had no pressing need to rush into a new book. The various incarnations of *The Great Escape* were by now lining his pockets, and Associated British Picture Corporation, which was forty per cent owned by Warner Brothers of Hollywood, was very interested in taking an option on the screen rights to *The Dam Busters*.

There was just one hurdle to that film deal. While Associated British's managing director Robert Clark was enamoured with the book, and with its huge sales and subsequent ready-made film audience, filming the book in its entirety, with its numerous raids and personnel, was just not feasible. To work, a *Dam Busters* film would need to be very focused. Before Clark committed to the picture he needed to be convinced that it could be successfully adapted to the screen.

In a meeting with Clark in early October, Brickhill agreed to drop everything and write a film 'treatment' of fifty or sixty pages which spelled out his vision for how *The Dam Busters* could be realised on film. He would do it without payment, knowing that, if Clark liked what he saw, the producer would commit to a film. To help Brickhill with his first-ever film treatment, Clark teamed him up with Walter Mycroft, sixty-one-year-old Director of Productions with Associated British. Mycroft had a hunched back and was just five feet four inches tall, but he had a wealth of experience in every aspect of filmmaking.

Basing himself in a Chelsea flat, and with Mycroft's help, Brickhill dashed off a *Dam Busters* film treatment, a cinematic overview in which he deliberately concentrated on the dams raid, to the exclusion of later 617 Squadron operations. And, as he had in the book, he focused on Barnes Wallis and Guy Gibson. By October's end, after delivering the treatment, he turned his full attention to the Bader proposal.

As he read Douglas Bader's manuscript, his logs, press clippings and letters, Brickhill became convinced there was drama aplenty here; another story of a man overcoming great odds. But Bader was also keen for Brickhill to make the book as much Thelma's story as his own. 'Make no mistake,' he had said, 'it was *our* story, not only mine. Without Thelma I could not have survived.'[198]

The more that Brickhill delved into the couple's life together, the more he agreed with Bader. Although Thelma had been working as a waitress at a country tearoom when Bader first met her, she came from a well-to-do family, was educated, refined, and very loving and loyal. She had married Bader despite the fact he was by then walking on tin legs following his 'accident'. He'd actually lost his legs after showing off, doing a prohibited low-level stunt. Thelma had been his strong supporter ever since.

Brickhill's mother was a strong woman. He was attracted to strong women; to women generally. He wouldn't have noticed that, when penning his feature articles from Germany and Hungary in 1945–46, he'd rarely named the men he mentioned. Always more interested in the women, he'd named them all. Even when talking about Frau Gades' starving children in Berlin, he'd given the names of her daughters, Brigide and Lise, but not her sons. Now, Mrs Bader interested him. To Brickhill's mind, the calm, cool and collected Thelma could make an interesting literary foil to the hell-raising Doug.

David Higham, immediately seeing the potential of a Bader book, encouraged his author to do it. With the ongoing success of *The Great Escape* and *The Dam Busters*, Higham was confident a fat publishing deal could be brokered. One autumn evening, Brickhill went around to Bader's Kensington flat, and they agreed to collaborate. Brickhill would write the book, and he offered to share the royalties fifty-fifty.

More than the potential ego-enhancing glory, Bader was interested in the money that would come out of this arrangement. He and Thelma had never owned their own home, and he wanted his biography to buy them a London house. For his part, Brickhill stipulated that Bader must make himself available for repeated interview, for as long as Brickhill needed. He would only commence writing when he felt he had everything at his fingertips. Bader agreed. There was no written contract. Theirs was a gentleman's agreement, sealed with a handshake.

Higham was soon able to attract the interest of William 'Billy' Collins, the future Sir William, colourful chairman of venerable multinational publishing house William Collins and Sons. Billy Collins assured Higham his company could make Brickhill's Bader book a worldwide publishing success, the equal of their last World War Two bestseller, Eric Williams' *The Wooden Horse*.

Another Collins author at this time, Winston Graham, best known for his Poldark novels, described Billy as 'cheerful, jolly, enthusiastic', as well as 'very likable but slightly unknowable'. Collins loved sport, and was an ardent cricketer and tennis player well into old age.[199] He had a very paternal and possessive attitude to his authors. Another writer, George Greenfield, would recall that, after one well-known Collins author died unexpectedly, the chairman exclaimed, 'Dead? After all I've done for him!'[200]

Brickhill agreed to sign with Collins. But, as he later told John Pudney, he felt extremely guilty about deserting both him and Evans Brothers, who had been so influential in his success to date. In part compensation, Brickhill had Higham negotiate an agreement with Pudney that would see Brickhill putting together a new book for Evans Brothers while he was researching the Bader biography. It would be an escape anthology.

Rejoining Margot at St-Paul-de-Vence after the productive six-week break in London, Brickhill began sending out Bader research letters and started work on the escape anthology. John Pudney would call this book *Escape Or Die*, and set down publication for the autumn of 1952.

To gain access to the sort of stories needed for *Escape Or Die*, Brickhill approached Air Chief Marshal Sir Basil Embry, chairman of the Royal Air Force Escaping Society (RAFES), formed to organise escaper reunions, to help escapers' widows, and to aid the families of Europeans who had given their lives to help RAF escapees and downed aircrew evade capture by the Germans. Brickhill offered the society fifty per cent of the book's royalties, and also convinced RAFES to follow his lead and incorporate to minimise tax. 'I am grateful to him,' Embry would say.[201]

Once Embry put Brickhill in contact with men who told him a raft of hair-raising stories of escape set in Europe and the Pacific, the author would churn out eight gripping true tales. Yet even though Brickhill was becoming a household name in Britain via *The Great Escape* and *The Dam Busters*, his self-confidence was only skin deep. Feeling the book needed the credibility a major literary name would lend, he suggested to Pudney that they seek a 'name' author with military writing credentials to write a preface, and Pudney put on his thinking cap.

There was soon further movement on the movie front. David Higham contacted Brickhill with the news that film producer Robert Clark liked his treatment. As it happened, the viability of the *Dam Busters* film had just been enhanced by the Air Ministry informing Clark he could borrow several Lancasters for filming for next to nothing. Through November, Clark and Higham haggled over a film-rights deal.

That deal was announced in early December. Clark was promising to commit more money to this project than Associated British had spent on any previous film. Although some newspapers would speculate that Brickhill would receive as much as £15,000 from the deal, Clark's total budget for both screen rights to the book and the writing of the screenplay was £7500.[202] Of this, £5000 was likely allocated to Brickhill, with the remaining £2500 going to the film's screenwriter.

Escape Or Die and Bader research kept Brickhill busy until January 1952, when he went back to London for ten hectic days of meetings, once again leaving Margot in Provence. In London, he put the final touches to *Escape Or Die* in close collaboration with Pudney, caught up with the Baders, met with producer Robert Clark and lunched with prominent novelist H. E. Bates.

The meeting with Bates had been set up by Pudney, who had interested the author in writing the *Escape Or Die* preface. Herbert Ernest Bates, who, like Brickhill, started out as a journalist, had gained a measure of success with rural novels and short stories before the war. His wartime novels had made him famous. Like Pudney, Bates had been employed by the Air Ministry's Creative Writers Unit expressly to write patriotic works for public consumption. Using the pseudonym Flying Officer X, he'd produced *The Greatest People in the World* in 1942, and *How Sleep the Brave* the following year. In 1944, using his own name, he'd written *Fair Stood the Wind for France*, the story of a British bomber crew forced down in occupied France. In later years, his successes would include the Darling Buds of May books, which would become a TV series that launched the screen career of Catherine Zeta-Jones.

Now, as Bates lunched with Brickhill to discuss how he might approach an *Escape Or Die* preface, he posed the Australian a question that had puzzled him for years. 'Why did not flying men, especially bomber pilots, go over Germany wearing fully prepared civilian disguise under their flying suits, so that they could begin organised escape immediately on hitting German soil, instead of afterwards toiling in tunnels?'

After giving the question thought, Brickhill responded, 'I suppose no RAF man ever had a final and absolute belief that he would be shot down, and that, if by some unfortunate accident, he were, he would never be captured anyway.'[203]

Bates would write a thoughtful preface, and, although one of the least known of Brickhill's books today, *Escape Or Die* would prove a great success, going into its seventh reprint within a year of publication. The downside for Brickhill would be that, after seeing what he'd done for RAFES, and reading of his high literary earnings, charities and individuals would plague him, begging his time and money. At first, he would give something to everyone. 'I tried to do all I could,' he would later say. But the more he gave, the more was asked of him. 'I found I was on the sucker list.' Over time, he would become increasingly selective about which charities he supported.[204]

Brickhill's latest meeting with Robert Clark proved productive. At his Elstree Studios at Borehamwood on London's northwest fringe, Clark informed Brickhill that he had made his choice of screenwriter for the *Dam Busters* movie. After initially considering novelist C. S. Forester, noted playwright Terence Rattigan and other leading screenwriters of the day Emlyn Williams and Leslie Arliss, Clark had settled on R. C. Sherriff. A successful playwright who'd first found success in the West End with *Journey's End* in 1928, Bob Sherriff had more recently built a career as a screenwriter on hit films such as *The Invisible Man, Goodbye, Mr Chips* and *Odd Man Out*. Clark passed Brickhill's book and treatment to Sherriff, who agreed with Brickhill – for maximum dramatic impact, a *Dam Busters* movie must focus on the dams raid, and on Barnes Wallis and Guy Gibson. An August delivery date was agreed for Sherriff's screenplay.

*

On Brickhill's February return to the French villa at St-Paul-de-Vence, his maid took him aside and confided that, while he'd been in London, his twenty-three-year-old wife had blatantly conducted an affair with a visitor, a Douglas Gordon, in Brickhill's marital bed.

Though shocked to the core by his wife's infidelity, Brickhill said nothing. But unable to live in the house where Margot had betrayed him, he announced that they were returning to London at once. Leaving her to pack everything, on 22 February he set off to drive the Alfa Romeo back to England. Unaware of the reason for the sudden relocation, Margot angrily followed by train, bringing all their trunks and suitcases. She joined him at the Cumberland Hotel in London, where they stayed until a Chelsea flat became available.

Leaving Margot in the flat, trying to put St-Paul-de-Vence behind him and to contain his anger, Brickhill told his unfaithful wife to go back to modelling and to hire a maid, then spent eleven days in a quiet hotel in Kent correcting *Escape Or Die* proofs. On his return, Margot had hired the maid, but was still at home, under his feet.

Across the Elstree Studios meeting table from Brickhill on 7 March sat screenwriter Sherriff, producer Clark and several of Clark's production executives. Sherriff had by this time read both Brickhill's book and treatment and had formed an idea of how he would approach the *Dam Busters* script.

'The story should be told simply and naturally,' Sherriff told the meeting, 'with no recourse to tricks of any sort.'

Brickhill was in full accord. As was Clark – his goal was always authenticity and realism.

'And there should be no effort to introduce a feminine influence,' Sherriff added.[205]

Again, agreement was voiced around the table, although Clark would reserve his judgement on that issue.

With Barnes Wallis at the core of the story, six days later Sherriff went down to White Hills House to meet with him alone. He came away convinced that the film should open with Wallis experimenting at his farmhouse with the home-made catapult and a bucket of water with which, a decade earlier, he had established that a bouncing bomb could, in theory, work. It was agreed that Brickhill, Sherriff and the production executives should visit Wallis to see the experiment in action.

With his customary soft smile, Barnes Wallis greeted his guests, then conducted them to his workshop. It was 22 March, and Brickhill had led a small expedition to Wallis' Surrey farmhouse. With him and Sherriff went two Associated British production chiefs, Walter Mycroft and production supervisor W. A. 'Bill' Whittaker. In preparation for the visit, Wallis had set up his original 'scientific' apparatus.

'It's just as it was at the time,' Wallis assured Brickhill and his companions. 'Now I'll show you how it works.'[206]

He didn't. And couldn't. To the scientist's acute embarrassment, no matter how many times he tried, Wallis was unable to successfully replicate the original experiment for his visitors. Still, Brickhill agreed with Sherriff that this charmingly innocuous home experiment, which had led to a breakthrough in arms development, and to so much death and destruction, should form the opening scene of the film. Of course, through the magic of cinema, the experiment would succeed on celluloid. And a 'female influence' would be snuck into the opening scene and several later scenes, in the person of an actress playing Wallis' supportive wife.

With his opening in place, Sherriff set off to talk with Micky Martin and others intimately involved with the dams raid.

Between February and August 1952, while the *Dam Busters* script was being developed, Brickhill focused on Douglas Bader book research. Regularly, he would take an after-dinner stroll around to the Baders' Kensington flat from his own in Chelsea, toting a recording device. This being before the era of the portable tape recorder, Brickhill's device was a dictating machine. Then state of the art, it looked like a portable record player, which it was, in reverse. A blank 78 rpm record was placed on the turntable, and a stylus recorded whatever the microphone picked up, onto the disc, creating a series of grooves. It took exactly an hour for the stylus to fill the disc. So, exactly an hour after Brickhill pressed the 'Start' button, his recorded chat sessions with Bader ended. The following day, Brickhill would mail the record to a secretarial service. Twenty-four hours later, he received a typed transcript. By the time Brickhill concluded his interviews with Bader, he'd filled 123 discs.

The routine for their after-dinner chats was the same. Brickhill sat in an armchair in the Bader flat, microphone in one hand, glass of beer in the other. Across from him sat Bader, puffing on a cigar. Bader had always been a pipe smoker, even in Spitfire cockpits. He added cigars to his smoking armoury after meeting Luftwaffe fighter ace Adolf Galland, who ended the war a general with 120 kills. Galland had been a lieutenant-colonel commanding JG26 at Wissant in France in 1941 when Bader was brought there to meet him after being shot down. Galland was famous in German ranks for his cigar smoking, even puffing away on the operating table after being shot down.

Once Brickhill made Bader famous via his biography, Bader would be approached by Galland to write a foreword to the 1955 English version of his autobiography, *The First and the Last*. Bader would provide the foreword, finishing with 'Galland is a brave man, and I personally shall look forward to meeting him again anytime, anywhere, and in any company.' They did meet again, with the former enemies becoming friends. While Bader was at Wissant airfield, Galland had permitted him to sit in the cockpit of an Me 109. After the war, Galland sent him a photograph which showed Bader in the Messerschmitt cockpit, with Galland and his subordinates crowded around. Only then did Bader notice that one Luftwaffe officer held a pistol – in case Bader attempted to take off in the German fighter.

As Brickhill and Bader talked during their interview sessions, Thelma Bader sat unobtrusively sewing, taking everything in. She rarely spoke. When she did, it was invariably to act as an impartial referee as the discussion between the men became heated. 'Now, now, you two!' she would say, immediately taking the sting out of the contretemps, with both men retreating under her maternal gaze.[207]

Early on during their chats, Brickhill felt that Bader was not being honest with him. Having learned that Bader had been up for selection in the England rugby team before he lost his legs, Brickhill was, in his own words, callously fascinated with how he would describe the feelings of an athlete who wakes up in hospital to find both legs missing. As delicately as he could, he asked Bader what he'd felt at that time.

'My dear chap,' Bader replied, 'I didn't mind a bit.'

Knowing how he would have felt in that position, Brickhill couldn't believe this, and said so. When Bader persisted with that line, Brickhill, shaking his head, urged his subject to come clean.

Bader scowled at him. 'My dear chap, would you kindly get into your unbelievably thick skull that I know what happened and you didn't. And I'm telling you what happened. I do not happen to be a liar.'[208]

While still disbelieving, Brickhill changed the subject, for the time being. He found that patience was required with Bader – something he was having to develop in all his relationships. The following evening, the author decided to again probe his subject on the same question. This time Bader was even more vehement in his denials. It was some time before Brickhill absorbed the fact – Bader had genuinely not been upset at losing his legs.

'I know that sounds unbelievable,' Brickhill would say, 'but it is true, and the reason is that he is a rare freak with enough guts to recognise tragedy that cannot be altered, to accept it without tears or wishful thinking, and carry on from there to endure it or overcome it.'[209]

In another session a little later, Bader said, 'You know, the months in hospital after I lost my legs were among the happiest in my life.'[210]

This wouldn't make sense to Brickhill until, in the course of interviewing Dorothy Brace, a nursing sister who'd looked after Bader at Royal Berkshire Hospital in 1931, it became clear to him that, perhaps for the first time in his life, in hospital Bader had been surrounded by people who really cared about him.

As the year unfolded, Bader relaxed totally in Brickhill's company. In his flat, he would remove his trousers and stomp around the room with his shirttails hanging down over his prosthetics. Made of yellow-painted metal, heavy and unbending, by today's standards those prosthetics were primitive. Brickhill was to marvel at how Bader got around on them, appreciating for the first time how he took his own flexible ankles for granted. To walk, Bader would heave a leg in front of him, then lean forward until he overbalanced, then move the other leg; and so it went. Bader had only taken up golf after losing his legs, and now he had a handicap of just four, which put him in the same class as professional champions.

For a while, Brickhill thought the man totally insensitive, until Bader one evening began to passionately recite the verse of A. C. Swinburne. The poet's work tended to be dark, and the lines quoted by Bader had a cynical edge to them. But at least, Brickhill concluded, the man had a poetic side.

Brickhill also found that Bader held views towards women that were typical of many men of the day. To Bader, a pinch on the backside should be considered a compliment by the female recipient. He also held the view that it was in order for a man to put his wife over his knee and give her a spanking if she became difficult to handle. Yet Bader would never pinch Thelma on the bottom, or even think of putting her over his knee. For Brickhill, 'The jigsaw of a very complex character was fitting together.'[211]

Interspersed with the interviews of Bader and many who knew him, Brickhill enjoyed getting away for golf breaks. His fairway partner in March was actor Anthony Bushell, a founding member of the Laurence Olivier Players, of which Peter Finch was a member. Over dinner with Brickhill that night, Bushell expressed the view that Finch didn't have what it took to be a West End star.[212] It would be another twenty-four years before Finch crowned his acting career with Golden Globe and Academy Award success.

In the spring of 1952, while research for the Bader book was ongoing, Brickhill teamed up with Ian Bevan to form the Australian Artists Association in London, an organisation for Aussie expats in the arts. This new group attracted a number of playwrights, authors and actors, among them Hugh Hastings, Alan Stranks, Charmian Clift and Robert Helpmann. With the support of Australia's High Commissioner to the UK, Sir

Thomas White, himself a published author, they launched the association with a function in the basement at Australia House. Peter Finch turned up for the launch, looking his usual dishevelled self – Russell Braddon described him as 'the worst-dressed man in Dolphin Square'.[213] Also among the artistic throng was a young bearded Australian entertainer with a stuffed kangaroo under his arm, Rolf Harris.

Feeling there was also a need for an organisation that supported Aussie authors in the UK, Brickhill was instrumental in the creation that October of the Society of Australian Writers (SAW), becoming one of the society's vice-presidents. Bevan and playwright Hastings again took leading roles, bringing in writers such as Chester Wilmot and Alan Moorehead to form an Australian literary mafia in London. Former Cambridge University professor Gilbert Murray was an early leader of the band, while Russell Braddon became SAW's chairman, a position he would hold for twenty-five years. Braddon was looking for a new book subject, and with an introduction and encouragement from Brickhill he would soon begin researching and writing the biography of 617 Squadron's Leonard Cheshire, a book which would be well received when published in 1954.

Although Elizabeth II had been queen since the death of her father, King George VI, in 1952, her official coronation would not take place until June 1953. She and Prince Philip would make a royal tour Down Under in early 1954. With the impending regal visit in mind, Ian Bevan convinced William Collins to publish a collection of patriotic essays about the many facets of Australia, under the title *The Sunburnt Country*, which would be presented to Her Majesty in her coronation year as a lead-up to the royal tour. Bevan, who would edit the book, invited fifteen noted Australian writers to contribute, SAW members Brickhill, Braddon and Wilmot among them. All the authors assigned their royalties to a charity to be nominated by Prince Philip.

With so much else on his plate, Brickhill rattled off an earnest though lacklustre piece for *The Sunburnt Country*, about the contributions of science to farming in Australia. He particularly applauded the work of the Commonwealth Scientific and Industrial Research Organisation (CSIRO), for whom his father-in-law, Edric Slater, was now working as a nature photographer. In part, Brickhill described the history of the war on the rabbit plague in Australia ever since British rabbits landed with the First Fleet in 1788, culminating in the CSIRO's use of the mixomatosis virus, or 'myxo' as it became known to Australians, to destroy rabbits wholesale.

In June, Douglas Bader informed Brickhill that he and Thelma were spending three weeks' annual holiday in Cornwall in August. Brickhill still had plenty of questions for his subject, so the Baders invited him to join them on holiday to continue the interviews. Bader said that the men could play golf together during the day and resume their after-dinner recording sessions each evening. Brickhill readily agreed, and, with a meeting at Elstree Studios set down for 12 August to review Bob Sherriff's draft *Dam Busters* screenplay, booked a room at the same hotel as the Baders to share the first ten days of their holiday with them.

When Brickhill told Margot that he was going to join the Baders on their holiday, she asked why she couldn't go too. Brickhill responded that this wouldn't be a holiday, it would be work. Flaming rows ensued, with Brickhill accusing his wife of being 'capricious, aggressive, irrational, uncooperative and extravagant'.[214] This culminated in an argument on 16 June which grew from a disagreement over the placement of a tea tray. According to Brickhill, Margot lost her temper and laid into him with her fists. Grabbing her wrists, he held them firmly until she desisted. An hour later, a heated dispute erupted over a nail file. This time, he forced her right arm behind her back until her anger subsided.[215]

A week later, they were again arguing about Brickhill's upcoming Cornwall trip. Tapping her cheek with his index finger, Brickhill declared, 'I'm not going to be henpecked by you, Maggie!'

He would claim that she reacted by attempting to slap and then scratch him. Grasping her wrists, he forced her back, sitting her down in a chair.[216]

The arguments lasted up until the moment Brickhill left for Cornwall, when, as he was going out the door, Margot suddenly changed her tune. She informed him she didn't want to accompany him anyway, as she was going to stay for three months at Taplow, a Buckinghamshire village on the Thames opposite Maidenhead, to the near west of London.

At Porthleven on the south coast of Cornwall, twenty kilometres from Penzance, the Baders and Brickhill checked into a small seaside hotel overlooking the bay. Typical of hotels of the day, the establishment had no en-suite bathrooms. Instead, the bedrooms on each floor shared a single bathroom. This didn't bother the Baders, although Douglas soon tired of having to strap on his legs each morning to cross the corridor to the bathroom, where he would only have to unstrap the prosthetics again to get into the bath.

'Stand "cave" for me, old boy, there's a good chap,' said Bader to Brickhill.

So, most mornings, Brickhill would stand at Bader's bedroom door and let him know when the coast was clear. Bader would then bounce out legless, on hands and rump, and cross the corridor to the vacant bathroom. To shave, he sat in the bath, having hoisted himself in, using what Brickhill described as 'arms developed enough to choke a gorilla'.[217] The first morning that Brickhill acted as crossing guard, he stayed outside the bathroom, chatting with Bader through the closed door.

Bader, as he heaved himself from the bath, bellowed, 'Some clot of a woman I'd never met before asked me what was the hardest thing to do without legs. I told her it was drying my stern while sitting on a stool after a bath. She was speechless – first time in years, they told me.'[218]

They played two rounds of golf a day throughout most of their stay. One day, after their morning round, Bader suggested they forget golf that afternoon and work on the book instead.

'You're getting soft, chum,' said Brickhill flippantly.[219]

Bader only responded with a scowl. The next day, Brickhill discovered that his companion had dented the socket of his right prosthetic, and when he'd removed the tin leg it had stripped the skin off his thigh, leaving it red raw. Bader picked up the phone and sent for a spare right leg, and the following morning it arrived by train, in Bader's cricket bag. They didn't golf that morning, but by the afternoon, Bader, with his thigh bandaged and the new prosthetic in place, was back out on the course. When he'd first been fitted with his tin legs, he'd routinely fallen over twenty or thirty times a day. The only time that Brickhill saw Bader fall over was one day on the Cornish golf course, when he tripped over Brickhill's golf bag. Cursing liberally, and waving Brickhill away, Bader pulled himself back to his feet.

Brickhill was determined to get the book's dialogue right, and at one point Bader spoke about an incident with a colleague when he was in command of 242 Squadron, whose other pilots were all Canadian. Years later, Bader would recall that, when he couldn't remember the exact words the other fellow had used, Brickhill responded, 'Tell me the *sort* of thing he would have said.'[220]

Once the book was produced, Jill Lucas, a friend of the Baders who'd known both them and the men of 242 Squadron during the war, remarked to Thelma, 'The extraordinary thing is that Brickhill never met any of those Canadians, yet he has got them so right.'[221]

In the second week of the Cornwall stay, a letter turned up at the hotel for Brickhill. It was from a firm of Chelsea solicitors. The lawyers informed him that they were acting on behalf of his wife, and she had instructed them that he had deserted her, had gone to live in Cornwall and had left her destitute. What was Mr Brickhill's response? Stunned, and angry, he wrapped up the sessions with Bader and hurried back to Chelsea. Only years later would Brickhill learn, from Margot herself, that, before she engaged the solicitors, she'd gone to Chelsea Police and told them that her now-famous husband had bashed and then deserted her. The police had recommended she get a lawyer.

Back in London, Brickhill found that Margot had kept her threat and rented a flat in Taplow. In the hope of impressing his style-conscious wife and winning her back, he now emulated Peter Finch, Ian Bevan and Russell Braddon by moving into a Dolphin Square flat, renting number 527 Rodney House. He even had a letterhead printed, featuring his name and the prestigious address. In the same complex, up on their block's flat roof, Finch's wife, Tamara, sword in hand, helped her husband practise his fencing for his stage roles. Brickhill's wife, meanwhile, was still living apart from her husband. Brickhill tried to talk Margot into coming back to London, but she refused, and demanded he send her money to pay her rent, which he did.

When he turned up at Elstree Studios on 12 August for what would prove to be intense *Dam Busters* script-assessment meetings, Brickhill pretended all was sweetness and light in his personal life. Joining Brickhill at the meeting table to read through Bob Sherriff's script were Clark, Mycroft, Whittaker, the film's art director, Robert Jones, and scenario editor Frederick Gotfurt – somewhat ironically a German by birth, whose imperfect English sometimes made his interpretation of dialogue problematic.

Sherriff's screenplay closely followed the build-up to and execution of the dams raid as Brickhill had written the story.

Brickhill liked Sherriff's script, as did everyone else at the table. But, despite this universal approval, many points of detail proved sticking points for one or more of those at the meeting. Over the next three days, they worked through each one of them in exacting detail.

Some deviations from fact in the final script would have irked Brickhill. Yet when proposed story changes were run by Barnes Wallis, the pragmatic scientist was unconcerned by the filmmakers' concessions to budget or the need for an exciting, fast-paced cinematic narrative. 'No one scene is the truth,' Wallis would say when the film was released, 'but the whole thing adds up to the truth.'[222]

Among the liberties taken in the final screenplay were the truncating of the time it took Wallis to develop his weapon, and incorrectly crediting Gibson with a spotlight system which the squadron used to gauge height at low level. The script also gave Wallis a memorable invented line. In the film, to acquire a Wellington bomber for trial flights Wallis asks if it would help if the authorities were informed he'd designed the Wellington? In reality, he didn't say that, and he'd only been responsible for the structure of the 'Welli's airframe and wings.

With the film now scheduled for production the following year and Bader research almost completed, over the next few weeks Brickhill devoted his time to convincing Margot to come back to him, sending her express-delivery letters almost daily and ringing her frequently. Suspecting that she was homesick for Australia, he proposed that, as soon as he completed the Bader book, they would go back to Australia for a year, see their families, live in a big house by the sea, and save on the tax that would accrue on the big earnings he was expecting from the Bader project – he'd learned that the top marginal tax rate in Australia was seventy per cent, as opposed to 97.5 per cent in the UK.

In a 29 August telephone conversation, Margot refused to say whether she would accompany him back to Australia, and, when he pressed her to see him, she declared, 'There's no point in our meeting, Paul.'[223]

The next time he telephoned, in early September, Brickhill decided to go on the offensive, revealing for the first time that he knew Margot had committed adultery with Douglas Gordon at St-Paul-de-Vence. Margot was stunned. Overnight, her attitude changed. She became, Brickhill was to say, 'solicitous and affectionate', and was amenable to getting back together. Brickhill had meanwhile not been sleeping, and his doctor recommended that he and Margot only cohabit again once he'd completed the Bader book.[224]

Like a dating couple, they began seeing each other again at weekends, and a month later they were once more making love, in the Dolphin Square flat, although they continued to live apart. This October get-together was prompted by a celebration. Margot had returned to the modelling agency that had previously employed her, and it secured her five days' mannequin work with fashion designer Norman Hartnell, famed as the Queen's couturier. Hartnell liked Margot's elegant walk. This, he said, could not be taught. At the end of the engagement, he offered Margot a full-time job as one of six mannequins who would model his Coronation range up to the Coronation the following June. Margot gleefully accepted.

In November, Brickhill announced to the press that he and his wife would be sailing from England to Australia aboard the liner *Orontes* the following July, for an extended stay. *Australian Women's Weekly* would herald their return in a 3 December issue featuring a fashion spread of Margot and other Hartnell mannequins modelling their employer's gowns.

19.

Reaching for the Sky

IN JANUARY 1953, David Higham finalised the contract with William Collins and Sons that would cover the publication of the Bader book in Britain and the Commonwealth, right down to a scale of royalty percentages – the more books that sold, the higher the percentage return to the author. Billy Collins also guaranteed to publish all of Brickhill's future books. This was like a security blanket to the Australian. He told the chairman that he now felt comfortable with, and confident in, his new publishers. 'I am extremely glad that I took the plunge and went with you.'[225]

He was keen to get into fiction, and his sessions with Battle of Britain ace Bader had prompted an idea, which he floated by Higham, who took it up with Collins. Brickhill was thinking about writing a novel about a Battle of Britain fighter pilot. Billy Collins immediately ran with the idea. This, he declared, would be Brickhill's next book after the

Bader biography. The author subsequently backed off, saying he had first to write the Bader book before he could think seriously about a novel.

Unbeknowns to Collins, Brickhill was considering another escape book, this time set in Burma and probably inspired by stories told to him by Russell Braddon. He also had vague ideas for another couple of novels.[226] Still, it was encouraging to know that his publisher was ready, willing and waiting. Meanwhile, in New York, the Ann Watkins Agency had secured a contract with Norton & Co for publication of the Bader book in the United States.

Brickhill's relationship with Margot was better than it had been in ages, and she was showing genuine interest in his work. Over the Christmas break, the Baders had read Brickhill's first 15,000 words of the Bader book, and were delighted. Brickhill wrote to Billy Collins in late January: 'My own wife, who is a fairly sound judge, agrees.' Margot had also seen the next 10,000 words, and Brickhill said she was 'more enthusiastic than I have ever seen her. Frankly, I myself cannot tell.' Nonetheless, he was beginning to feel more confident that the book would end up as he'd hoped.[227]

Margot was meanwhile hard at work in the world of high fashion. Though only being paid eight guineas a week, she was receiving double the wage of casual mannequins. The low pay didn't concern Margot; she was in her element. Her days in the Hartnell studio began at 10.00 am. Mornings were taken up with fittings in the workshop, afternoons with showings to wealthy clients who sat in gilt chairs in a grey-carpeted showroom as the mannequins glided by. At one point, Hartnell took his models to Scotland for fashion shows.

Another time, Hartnell's models featured in a Society of London Fashion Designers show at Claridge's hotel, with Her Majesty the Queen and her sister, Princess Margaret, guests of honour. Relaxing after the show, Margot and other models were sitting in their gowns in the dressing room, chatting and smoking, when the Queen and Princess walked in, trailed by a royal entourage. Swiftly stubbing out their cigarettes, Margot and her friends jumped to their feet and curtseyed, before being introduced to the royal pair.

In early March, Margot moved in with Brickhill at the Dolphin Square apartment. He'd sealed their reunion by offering her £5000, in two instalments, on condition she invest it. This was a substantial sum. At the time, the average annual salary in Britain was £500, and the average house price £2700. A brand new Rolls-Royce could be had for £4700.

Just after he parted with the first instalment, Brickhill heard from David Higham that film producer Robert Clark was having grave doubts about *The Dam Busters* going into production.

'In view of falling box office receipts,' said Clark, 'it's becoming a financially dangerous proposition.'[228]

This rocked Brickhill back on his heels, and caused him to immediately tighten his financial belt. Meanwhile, he still didn't have a title for the Bader book, and nothing suggested by Collins or Higham appealed. In desperation, Brickhill had Margot run a competition for a title among the models at Hartnell's studio. That didn't bring the necessary result either, and in the end he would give Margot credit for the title *Reach for the Sky*. She felt it a joint effort, saying she'd thought of it only a second or two before he did.[229] Still,

Brickhill wasn't entirely sold on the title; for now, it would remain provisional.

He was also struggling to make headway with the manuscript. Having set the July departure for Australia as the deadline for delivering the finished book to Collins, Brickhill decided that the only way he was going to complete it in time was by secluding himself away, in the sun, with a peaceful water view, writing nonstop. He booked a passage to Jersey in the Channel Islands, 'To live in a cave to finish my new book,' he told *Australian Women's Weekly* London correspondent Michael Plant. 'London is the worst place in the world to try to write a book.'[230]

His plan was to remain on Jersey until July, when he would travel overland to join Margot aboard the *Orontes* at Gibraltar, after she'd sailed with the ship from Southampton. When Plant asked Brickhill what he planned to do in Australia, the author replied, 'Buy a little house at Palm Beach and just lie in the sun.'[231]

Before Brickhill set off for his Channel Islands hideaway, he and Margot hosted an SAW hot-chocolate soiree at Australia House. By this time, SAW membership had grown to include women writers such as Florence James and Dymphna Cusack, co-authors of *Come in Spinner*, and young Irish-Australian author Catherine Gaskin, who would complete her novel *Sara Dane* on her twenty-fifth birthday the following year.

According to Brickhill, Margot was 'habitually and incorrigibly late for appointments'.[232] Nonetheless, for the press and public at the SAW event they put on 'the faces', as Brickhill called their smiling public personas.[233] Margot was impeccably dressed in suit and hat, but it was Brickhill's plum-coloured, pearl-buttoned vest that attracted most attention.

With William Collins keen to generate pre-release publicity for the Bader book, a reporter from Australia's *People* magazine sat husband and wife down together for an interview which ranged over both their backgrounds. As the pair spoke at length with the reporter, Brickhill was cheerful and friendly, and neither he nor Margot let on that, until just weeks before, they'd been living apart for eight months, or that twelve months prior to this Margot had been undergoing psychiatric treatment. To cover up that treatment, Brickhill told the reporter they'd moved to St-Paul-de-Vence four months earlier than had been the case.

The resultant *People* article, which would run over more than three pages in May, would drip with envy over the couple's apparent glamorous and lavish lifestyle, while disparaging Brickhill's books as merely 'a series of reports', granting that *The Great Escape* was 'a brilliant report'. The *People* reporter would go on, 'After the Bader story, the man who has made a fortune out of reporting in three busy years will write another escape book – about prisoners-of-war in Burma this time – then he will tackle one, two, or three novels, after that a film or two.'[234]

Brickhill was eager to get away from London, where unanswered fan mail piled up along with letters and cables about serialisations, foreign translations and article requests. There were lunch invitations from people who wanted something from him. Five men mentioned in *Escape Or Die* were asking for contact details about other former chums. An acquaintance had sent his own escape manuscript for comment. Someone wanted Brickhill's help hitching a lift on a NATO aircraft. Then there was a dentist's appointment and arrangements for garaging the Alfa while he was overseas.

'I sometimes wonder whether it's worth trying to write books at all,' Brickhill told the *People* reporter with exasperation born out of his anxiety over the unfinished Bader manuscript.[235] Yet while he was prepared to hire staff to keep Margot happy, he would always be too frugal to emulate other successful authors and employ a personal assistant to free him of day-to-day annoyances.

In the last days of March, loaded down with his typewriter and several suitcases, and clutching an attaché case containing his partly written Bader manuscript, Brickhill landed on Jersey. One suitcase was entirely filled with notes and transcriptions of interviews with Bader and others.

He took a single room in a house called 'Koi Hai' in the parish of Grouville. On the southeast tip of the island, it wasn't far from the capital, St Helier, and possessed sweeping views across a broad sandy beach and the waters of Royal Bay. By repute, the shallows here could be pleasantly warm in summer; Brickhill, a strong swimmer, would be able to take a daily dip once the weather improved. And his landlady was a Mrs Joy.[236] All boded well for a pleasant stay.

Writing enthusiastically to Billy Collins at the end of the month, Brickhill said:

> Above is my new address, which is exactly what I wanted, a large and pleasant room in a modern house with sun pouring in the wide windows and peace on all sides. There's nothing to do except get on with the job, which I am doing. In these circumstances I don't expect much trouble in having my m/s finished by mid-July.[237]

He'd commenced the letter with 'Dear Collins', a little jab at English pomposity and class consciousness. When he'd first written to the chairman, he'd begun with 'Dear Mr Collins'. In his responses, Collins persisted in addressing him with 'Dear Brickhill', so now Brickhill returned the compliment. In a postscript to this latest letter, he asked Collins not to give out his address to anyone travelling to Jersey. 'I'm a working hermit now.'[238] He would not tolerate drop-in visitors such as those who had helped ruin the stay at St-Paul-de-Vence.

As Brickhill settled down to work, Margot spent the Easter weekend in France. The Hartnell models were giving a show at the Le Touquet casino. The preceding week they'd chosen their favourite delicacies in advance, having worked out they would be served 'at least five first-class meals' in France.[239] On Jersey, Brickhill resumed his former frantic working pace. Several times, Margot flew out to weekend with him on the island, but otherwise he wrote without interruption.

June 2, Coronation Day in Britain, saw Margot on temporary seating in East Carriage Drive with thousands of others, cheering the Queen's golden carriage as it passed on its way to and from Westminster Abbey. Indifferent to the royal occasion across the Channel, on Jersey Brickhill worked like a man possessed. With his emotional life back on an even keel, he'd rediscovered the old magic. In under three months he expanded his initial 25,000 words to create a manuscript of 150,000, completing it three weeks ahead of schedule. He knew it was overlong and that he could probably chop 10,000 to 15,000 words, but he would leave a decision on length to his publishers.

On 22 June, he sent his typescript to David Higham in London, who would pass copies on to William Collins in London and Norton & Co in New York, along with Brickhill's observations on where cuts might be made. Asking that Collins provide him with a detailed forensic report by the time he set off for Australia in mid-July, he intended to work on cuts and revisions on the voyage to Australia, putting the reworked manuscript in the mail to Higham in London when the *Orontes* docked at Fremantle, Western Australia, in August.

Brickhill had previously arranged that Bader and his wife come to Jersey to holiday with him in June and discuss the final draft. Periodically, he'd fed stages of the manuscript to Bader, who'd responded with his comments. Not long before the couple was due to set off for Jersey, Bader sent Brickhill a letter which Brickhill felt was intolerably rude. In his lengthy response, Brickhill argued his case while holding nothing back. After the Baders flew in to Jersey on 23 June, Brickhill wasted no time referring to his last letter.

'What letter, old boy?' Bader came blandly back, looking innocent. 'I received no letter.'

Brickhill had kept a carbon copy, which he handed to Bader, who read it quickly, nodding. 'After some fairly impassioned dialogue he apologised with great charm,' Brickhill would later say, 'and we were out playing golf the next morning with the old amiability.'[240] He knew in advance that Bader was happy with his work. 'Bader thinks the book is splendid,' he'd written to Billy Collins, 'which is a bit remarkable as he is somewhat a "difficult" person.'[241]

There was only one early chapter that troubled Bader, and he wanted it out. 'I feel too ruddy naked!' he protested.[242] The chapter covered the amputation of Bader's legs and his postoperative physical and mental difficulties, accounts of several car crashes while learning to drive with tin legs, pay rises he'd received, and Bader's secret registry office marriage to Thelma in 1933 – family and friends had thought their 1937 church wedding their first. Brickhill felt strongly that the episodes covered by the chapter should stay. 'I would not want to eliminate them in any circumstances as they are important to the story, showing early struggles after losing his legs.'[243]

For three days he discussed the book with Douglas and Thelma, holding his ground. In the end, the trio agreed that the contentious chapter should remain, but with two paragraphs removed. 'Apart from that everything is fine and he approves the lot,' Brickhill reported to Billy Collins.[244] Years later, Bader would say that he had no quarrel with the way the book ended up, although he thought Brickhill 'had pressed the point too far' when writing of an inner demon which he believed had driven Bader to succeed through the 1930s and 1940s.[245] In fact, with the skill of a trained psychologist, Brickhill had laid bare Bader's soul.

On 6 July, Brickhill left Jersey feeling pleased with himself, but worn out. After stops at Saint-Malo and Bordeaux, he would spend a week or so in Gibraltar winding down until the *Orontes* arrived.

At the Dolphin Square apartment in London on the morning of 7 July, Margot was packing. She was due to board the *Orontes* at Southampton in ten days' time. Her luggage included numerous clothes trunks, and hatboxes filled with hats by St Cyr, Hartnell's French millinery associate. Margot had made herself several cotton outfits for the warmer Australian climes, but the rest of her new wardrobe had been purchased from Hartnell before she left the designer's employ in June. Brickhill, who'd been given a discount by Hartnell, had forked out between £500 and £600 on his wife's outfits.[246]

Before she departed London, Margot would go into detail with a Sydney newspaper correspondent about the Hartnell wardrobe she was taking to Australia. When asked why they were going, she replied, 'My husband needs a rest, and we hope to find a home near the sea.'[247]

But Margot was unhappy. Not only was her husband leaving her to organise the packing and transport of their things to the ship at Southampton, she was peeved that he hadn't given her the rest of the money he'd promised in March. As she packed, the phone at Dolphin Square rang. She found Billy Collins on the line. Collins told her he'd tried to call her husband on Jersey, but just missed him. He was delighted with Brickhill's Bader manuscript, he said, and, while his marketing chief Ronald Politzer was still reading it, he felt the book would even outsell *The Wooden Horse*.[248]

Brickhill's editor at Collins, Mark Bonham Carter, was just finalising a detailed report on the manuscript, and Collins knew Brickhill was anxious to get his hands on it, to guide his revisions. At this point, the chairman didn't know whether that report would be ready for Margot to take with her when she left for Southampton. In the event, Bonham Carter completed the report, which ran to thirteen pages, on 16 July.

The only forwarding address that Collins had for Brickhill at that point was the *Orontes*' shipping agents in Gibraltar. Rather than risk it going astray, and knowing that Margot was not leaving London until 17 July, Bonham Carter had the report hand-delivered to her at Dolphin Square. Margot's discontent with her husband was multiplied by being used as a courier. On receiving Bonham Carter's report, she slipped it in among a collection of her own papers she was leaving in England until their return. When she and her baggage went out the door to go to Waterloo Station on the morning of 17 July, she left the editor's report behind.

Brickhill drew his wife into his arms when he joined her on the *Orontes* in Gibraltar on 20 July. Only once they'd celebrated their reunion did he broach the subject of business. While spending eight days waiting in the Rock Hotel in Gibraltar he'd received letters from David Higham and William Collins making comment on *Reach for the Sky*. Higham's letter included suggestions for improvements from his associate Paul Scott, who felt that Brickhill had allowed Bader's bad qualities to overtake the good as the narrative progressed, losing the reader's sympathy for the man. The Collins letter was less helpful. It combined the comments of three people including marketing chief Politzer, and ran to just over two pages. Essentially, it was merely praise for a job well done.

Where, Brickhill asked, was the detailed Bonham Carter report that Collins had promised would be sent to Margot before she sailed? Margot could only shrug.

In completing the manuscript at breakneck speed, Brickhill had exhausted himself. And now he was bitterly disappointed, feeling that his publisher had let him down, had cast him to the literary wolves. 'I won't pretend I wasn't a bit upset by it,' he would later say. In fact, he was 'quite aggrieved'. He had always struggled to get Evans Brothers and Faber & Faber to give him full and frank reports. Such independent and detached views of his work were invaluable to him, he would later tell Mark Bonham Carter. For, like many an author, after living and sleeping with his work in progress for months and years, he tended to lose objectivity.[249]

As the *Orontes* sailed on, putting him increasingly out of easy contact with London, Brickhill could only stare at his manuscript and wonder what he should do to improve it. He gave it to Margot to read, hoping she would be able to satisfy unanswered questions troubling him. She had, after all, previously made valuable comments about the early chapters. But Margot had made new friends in the ship's first-class lounge and was engrossed in onboard activities. By the time the ship docked in Sydney, Margot would not have read past page 6. Spiralling into depression aboard ship, Brickhill began taking meals in his cabin. At each port on the voyage,

Margot arranged shore excursions with fellow passengers, expecting her husband to join in. But Brickhill didn't like his wife's new friends. At Port Said, he accused her of making him wait in the Simon Arzt department store for two hours while she shopped.

'The trip was pretty foul,' Brickhill would later tell Billy Collins.[250] He wasn't referring to the weather. When the *Orontes* docked at Fremantle, Brickhill kept out of sight, as the press, alerted by the presence of Margot Brickhill, Hartnell model and wife of famous author Paul Brickhill, poured aboard to interview her, photographing her posing in Hartnell clothes. A similar press reception awaited the couple at the *Orontes*' stops in Adelaide, Melbourne and Sydney. In Adelaide, Margot told reporters they would buy a house in Sydney.[251]

Brickhill finally spoke to reporters once they reached Melbourne. 'I will give away the writing of war thrillers,' he announced, adding that *Reach for the Sky* would be his last of that genre. He had by this time gone cold on the idea for the Battle of Britain novel, and would soon be discouraging Billy Collins from mentioning in the blurb for *Reach for the Sky* that this would be his next Collins release. 'I plan at present to write three books on Australia,' Brickhill told the press, 'one on city life, and possibly two on country life.' The return to his homeland had stimulated a desire to write the great Australian novel, although he had no detailed plots in mind. 'I have also discussed the possibilities of an Australian film before I left London.'

In answer to a question about previously announced plans to make a film version of *The Dam Busters*, he said, 'They had begun, but they were curtailed when the 3-D film industry started.' In fact, although Brickhill didn't then know it, producer Robert Clark had regained his confidence in the project and was moving towards commencing filming *The Dam Busters* at London's Elstree Studios within four months.

When asked whether a film version of *The Great Escape* was likely, Brickhill replied, 'The film option on *The Great Escape* has also been sold.' He didn't elaborate, or identify Fred Coe as the producer holding the option.[252]

Landing at Sydney in the third week of August, the couple were met by William Collins' industrious manager for Australia, Freddy Howe. Brickhill was worried that he would be stung for massive import duties for Margot's trunkloads of expensive clothes and hats, but Howe sweet-talked Customs and smoothed the path for a cost-free entry into Australia. Howe was 'magnificent', Brickhill would gleefully report to Collins. 'The Collins organisation seems to be able to turn on anything, anywhere, at any time.'[253]

After catching up with Brickhill's family in Sydney, the couple went to stay with Margot's mother at Richmond. By the end of the month, Brickhill had moved in with his proud parents at Greenwich Point. His father retired from the newspaper game this same year, but would stay active as president of the Lane Cove Progress Association. Margot, meanwhile, remained at Richmond. The couple's pressure-cooker relationship, progressively strained by the voyage out, was at exploding point.

Brickhill's income continued to multiply. Higham was negotiating with British filmmakers about *Reach for the Sky* screen rights. The *News of the World* had made a hefty serial rights bid. Considering the paper too downmarket, Brickhill plumped for *John Bull* magazine, and when it offered £12,000, twice as much as it had previously paid to serialise any book, both Brickhill and Bader were delighted, and Higham sealed the deal. *John Bull*'s serialised version would start appearing a week before Collins released the book the following April. Deals were also done for serialised versions in Australian newspapers in 1954. With a mixture of amusement and annoyance, Brickhill would read that the British press had anointed him the highest-earning author in the UK in 1953, estimating his income for the year at £115,000. He had certainly earned more than enough to pay off his parents' house, a priority from the beginning.

In the meantime, Margot's mother, a member of the Country Women's Association, had arranged for Margot to co-judge the Miss Manning Contest at the CWA Ball at Taree in Northern New South Wales, with Sydney opera singer Eric Starling. In mid-September, mother and daughter headed north to Taree. The town's newspaper declared that Margot 'possessed all the attributes of a good and conscientious judge', expressing confidence that 'her charming personality would immediately bring out the best in the girls'.[254]

While Margot told the press that she and her husband were both staying at Richmond, Brickhill remained at his parents' house, from where he wrote to Billy Collins, 'Australia seems very sunny and prosperous, but I'm missing London very, very much and couldn't bear to think of myself as a long-term exile.'[255] For now, he had a job to do. On the afternoon of 31 August, secure in his parents' bosom, he started polishing *Reach for the Sky*. During September, as he worked, he learned that his old 92 Squadron flying partner Neville Duke had just become famous in Britain. A test pilot now, Duke had broken the world air speed record.

Within several weeks, Brickhill had completed his Bader book. Without the guidance of Bonham Carter's report, he'd decided not to make major cuts. In the US, Norton & Co were planning to reduce the book from 150,000 words to 100,000, but that didn't bother Brickhill. He felt the British version much more important. And he was having second thoughts about the title. He wrote that month to Higham and Collins that he thought it should become *Foothold in the Sky*. 'I don't press the point, but I feel *Reach for the Sky* is just a shade too light, slightly hackneyed and faintly reminiscent of a cowboy story.'[256] Higham didn't agree, and Collins felt that such a title would be seen as a bad pun on Bader's legs, or lack of them. For a while, Collins considered *One of the Few* as an alternative title, but in the end preferred to stay with *Reach for the Sky*. From Sydney, Brickhill concurred.

By the time the author mailed the revised manuscript to London on 12 September, he'd dedicated the book to Thelma Bader. 'She was the luckiest break Douglas ever had,' he would say in a press article he wrote to promote the book on its release.[257] Thelma was, in fact, the sort of wife he would have liked for himself.

Once the book was in the mail, Brickhill could relax, play golf and do a little sailing on Sydney Harbour. He also tied down opportunities to exploit his books locally. A visiting Australian radio producer and budding author by the name of Morris West had come to one of Brickhill's Chelsea flat parties in 1951, and the pair had kept in touch. West had also met Jon

Cleary at that party; they subsequently became best friends. Brickhill now did a deal with West for his Australasian Radio Productions to record three Brickhill books as commercial radio dramas, with actors playing the roles. Brickhill himself recorded an introduction for each series. *Reach for the Sky*, longest and last of the three series, would run to fifty-two half-hour episodes. With television only reaching Australia in 1956, these radio serials had millions of listeners when they went to air in 1953–54.

Sydney actor Rodney Taylor would appear in all three Brickhill radio serialisations, playing increasingly important roles: one of the prisoners in *The Great Escape*, Dave Shannon in *The Dam Busters* and Douglas Bader in *Reach for the Sky*. In 1954, once recording of *Reach for the Sky* was completed, Taylor would set off for England. Travelling via Los Angeles, he would be waylaid there by offers of acting work, and stay. As Rod Taylor, he would become a Hollywood star. Taylor's last, brief role, before his death in 2015, would be as Winston Churchill in Quentin Tarantino's 2009 movie *Inglourious Basterds*.

Margot, meanwhile, was enjoying the limelight. Before leaving London, she had contracted Australian modelling jobs for renowned textile designer Miki Sekers of the West Cumberland Silk Mills in England's northwest. In October, she helped show a range of Sekers' new nylon garments at the Myer Emporium in Melbourne and Prince's Restaurant in Sydney. Her husband now put a proposition to her from Freddy Howe, who'd asked Brickhill to do a *Woman's Day* feature with his wife as advance publicity for *Reach for the Sky*. With the magazine proposing to make Margot the cover girl for the issue, she agreed. In early November, the couple did the interview and a studio photo shoot, with neither revealing they'd been apart for months. Margot fronted the magazine's 16 November issue, with a story about the couple and the upcoming book on page 2 along with a photo of them together.

Margot got on well with her in-laws, driving Dot around in a borrowed car. But her relationship with Brickhill was on the brink. In November, as the couple walked on the grassy reserve that sloped down to the Lane Cove River near 41 George Street, Brickhill was thinking that divorce was probably the best course for them. It was then that Margot dropped a bombshell. She announced that she was pregnant.

'Oh, God, no!' Brickhill exclaimed.[258] Conception had apparently occurred shortly after they'd reunited aboard the *Orontes*. A child was the last thing Brickhill wanted. Now, they would have an explosive marriage plus a baby.

For the sake of the child, both Brickhill and Margot that day vowed to make the marriage work. Going back to George Street, they informed Dot and George that they were going to be grandparents. Margot gave up smoking, and Brickhill booked a room for the third week of April at St Margaret's Maternity Hospital in Darlinghurst.

Now, too, Brickhill took a lease on 'Kambah', a pricey furnished house on the Northern Beaches. On Cabarita Road at Avalon's Stokes Point, it overlooked the calm waters of Pittwater, a short hop from Palm Beach. The couple moved in, and in mid-December, while Margot went Christmas shopping, Brickhill opened a package from London containing *Reach for the Sky* proofs. In accompanying letters, Bonham

Carter and Billy Collins urged Brickhill to remove all the 'by Christs', 'by Gods' and 'bloodies' colouring the text.

While these suggested deletions were partly at Bader's request, the chairman observed that the recurrent swearing, while true to life, would limit the Collins sales team's hopes of getting the book into every school library in the land. He recalled that one phrase in *The Wooden Horse* had significantly limited its sales to school libraries. At the same time, the publisher had good news for Brickhill: Collins' initial print run would be a massive 100,000 hardback copies. Buoyed by this, Brickhill began the task of expunging Bader's expletives.

Meanwhile, Bader was causing Brickhill headaches of a different kind. Bader had been surprised by the amount of money that *Reach for the Sky* now seemed likely to generate. And scared. At this rate, he said, after tax, he would end up netting only fifteen per cent of his fifty per cent share of the book's royalties. To relieve him of a heavy tax burden, he asked Brickhill to scrap their fifty-fifty arrangement and renegotiate their deal. Agreeing, Brickhill sent him Collins' and Norton's sales projections. Based on these, there was some difficult haggling, with Bader's officious accountants demanding to know why Brickhill's agent David Higham was involved in the negotiations.

Finally, both sides agreed that Brickhill Publications Limited would pay Bader £10,500 as 'expenses', with Brickhill relieving Bader of tax liability on that amount, plus £2625 for 'services', on which Bader would pay tax. There, the deal was capped. Bader would receive £13,125 in total. If royalties failed to meet projections, Brickhill would be out of pocket. If they exceeded them, he would make more than Bader.

This time, their deal went into a written agreement, which both Brickhill and Bader signed.

That same month of November, *The Sunburnt Country* was released in Britain, to a warm reception. UK sales would be healthy, generating new editions in 1954 and 1955. The book wouldn't reach Australian bookshelves until January, but an advance review in the Australian press in November about this mostly expat view of Oz from afar was not complimentary. The review particularly focused on a female contributor who'd declared that Australian women were 'lousy cooks'.

Angered on behalf of his co-authors, Brickhill complained to the local press about the lack of a comprehensive review of this well-intentioned book whose royalties were all going to a good cause. In response, Eric Baume, a Sydney writer and broadcaster, blasted him in the *Sydney Morning Herald*: 'You have a very high reputation, and are a world best seller, which few writers can say. Leave it at that. Give the critics the same right as your own to say what they want.'[259] Brickhill did not respond.

For the first time in five years, now as a married man with a baby on the way, Brickhill spent Christmas with his parents and brothers. This same month, Russell Brickhill ran for Lane Cove Council; he would serve as an alderman for many years and as mayor of Lane Cove in 1963 and 1964. Brickhill was also able to catch up with literary friends from London who were spending Christmas in Australia, Russell Braddon, Alan Moorehead and Chester Wilmot among them. Surrounded by friends and family, he enjoyed his best Christmas in years.

It was the calm before the storm; 1954 would prove one of the most difficult years of Brickhill's life.

20.

The Dam Busters Crisis

THE YEAR BEGAN well enough. In the first week of January, David Higham announced from London that a deal had been signed with independent British film producer Major Danny Angel for the film rights to *Reach for the Sky*, for 'a record amount', rumoured to be £25,000. To make the film, Angel would partner with the Rank Organisation, then Associated British's only competitor in Britain's restricted film-distribution market. Higham also announced that shooting of Associated British's production of *The Dam Busters* was expected to finally begin that month.[260]

The cameras would not in fact start rolling on *The Dam Busters* until April. After considering Laurence Olivier and Jack Hawkins to play Barnes Wallis, producer Robert Clark signed Michael Redgrave for the role. Australian actor Bill Kerr would play Micky Martin, and two future stars would have minor roles: Patrick McGoohan and Robert Shaw – whose career would surge decades later after he co-starred in *Jaws*. To play Guy Gibson, Clark cast Richard Todd. Like Gibson, Todd was short but handsome. 'No other role has appealed to me so much in all my acting career,' Todd told the press.[261]

But, very quickly, Brickhill's year took a downhill trajectory. On 10 January, Chester Wilmot was flying back to England when his BOAC De Havilland Comet jet crashed into the Mediterranean near Elba, killing all thirty-five aboard and snuffing out a lauded writing career. The disaster only heightened Brickhill's dread of flying. This same month, Brickhill's Sydney accountant delivered even more disastrous news. Between British and Australian taxation and what he'd promised to pay Douglas Bader, Brickhill would soon be up for a staggering £65,000.

As Brickhill panicked, his accountant offered a solution; if he moved to New Zealand, where the top marginal tax rate was then sixty per cent, he would be able to limit his liabilities. But he must do it at once, and not set foot back in Australia, or Britain, for several years. Brickhill gave two options to Margot, by this time six months pregnant. She could accompany him to New Zealand, or remain behind in Sydney. He conceded that, apart from a few Air Force chums of his, they knew no one in New Zealand. But if he didn't go there, he said, they could end up penniless. Shattered by the thought of having the baby alone, Margot found herself between the devil and the deep blue sea.

'I have no alternative,' she glumly responded.[262]

On 11 February, Brickhill and his wife sailed for New Zealand. After staying at Auckland's Trans-Tasman Hotel for a fortnight, they rented a flat for another six weeks at pretty

Mission Bay, on Auckland Harbour. Setting up his typewriter, Brickhill again attempted to begin a novel. But work quickly stalled as sickness levelled him – the severe bronchitis he'd suffered in Stalag Luft 3 returned. Margot was sympathetic, bringing meals to his bed. Then, as he was recovering in March, a letter arrived from Billy Collins. A letter which rocked Brickhill, and his world.

For the first time, Billy dispensed with 'Dear Brickhill', beginning this letter with the more solicitous 'Dear Paul'. Sales of *Reach for the Sky* looked like exceeding all expectations, and Billy was seeking Brickhill's agreement to reduce the author's royalty set out in his publishing contract to make it a flat ten per cent for all sales, instead of lifting to fifteen per cent for sales above 20,000 copies. Collins' argument, which made no sense to Brickhill, was that the more copies they sold, the less the publishers made, until they ended up losing money. To Brickhill's mind, it would surely be the other way around. Collins even split hairs on whether 'Australasian' sales included New Zealand. He claimed that no one in New Zealand felt the term 'Australasian' encompassed their country as well as Australia. Author George Greenfield, who fell afoul of Collins around this time, would declare that Billy frequently resorted to money-grubbing 'venal tricks'.[263]

It was not the first time that Brickhill had been the victim of such behaviour from publishers. Faber & Faber and Evans Brothers had both attempted to renegotiate his royalties down, similarly because his books had been much more successful than expected. Brickhill was already disappointed with William Collins for what he saw as their failure to provide him with a detailed editor's report. This grab for his money sapped all confidence he had in his publishers. For a week he fretted over what to do, before it all became too much. Totally disillusioned with the whole business of writing books, he spiralled into depression, and was soon overcome with exhaustion so total he could barely find the strength to get out of bed. When he did arise, he wrote to David Higham, asking him to sort out everything with Collins.

In April, at Kohimarama, just around the point from Mission Bay, Brickhill found a house to rent. On the crest of a ridge in Allum Street, the house was spacious, although far from luxurious. Its best features were dramatic views east over playing fields below and south across the harbour. Local shops were a five-minute walk down the hill, with a sandy, tree-lined beach reminiscent of Manly Beach another few minutes away. Hiring a housekeeper, Brickhill and his wife moved in.

Work still proved impossible. A hundred *Reach for the Sky* press reviews flooded in from London and New York. His breath bated, Brickhill read every one. With rare exceptions, such as fellow Stalag Luft 3 kriegie Robert Kee, who, in the *Observer*, damned Brickhill's writing as nothing more than competent journalism, press critics had woven their reviews with the gold cloth of praise. Brickhill had to drag himself away from the adulation to rush Margot to Auckland's Wakefield Private Hospital. On 14 April, a week earlier than expected, she gave birth to a son, 7lb 3oz Timothy Paul.

Knowing that AAP in London would disseminate the news to newspapers of the world, Brickhill sent a revealing cable to the news agency, announcing the new arrival:

> He seems pretty good for a first edition. Very bold type-face, requiring extra end papers. Well received by the critics. No cereal rights yet. I won't be reprinting for some time – the first impression is regarded as adequate.[264]

An unfinished letter sat in his typewriter. Immediately following his son's birth, Brickhill returned to his desk to complete this missive, to John Pudney in London. He would add a handwritten postscript about the birth of Timothy, but was writing in reply to a December letter from Pudney that had found its way to him via Greenwich Point. Pudney, who had just changed publishers, joining Putnam's, had written a *Reach for the Sky* review for a London magazine. Brickhill thanked him for penning what he considered one of the best, most constructive critiques he'd received, complaining that so few reviews helped him improve his writing.

The catalyst for Pudney's letter had been a comment from a SAW member in London that Brickhill thought Pudney was 'hipped', or unhappy, with him for some reason. Brickhill wrote back that it was he who was hipped, with himself, for failing to include Pudney among the people he'd acknowledged in *The Dam Busters*. It pricked his conscience that he'd forgotten Pudney, the father of his fortune in many ways. Brickhill told Pudney that he planned to present him with a handsome present the next time he saw him in London, and nothing the editor did or said would prevent him from delivering on that intent.

'You are a pawn between me and my conscience,' he told Pudney. Appropriately, he would pay for this gift, he said, from the proceeds from the Pan paperback edition of *The Dam Busters*, published that year.[265] Brickhill always kept his word. And this edition of *The Dam Busters* would soon fill his gift-buying coffers to overflowing – within two years, it became the first Pan paperback to sell a million copies. It has been suggested, but not substantiated, that Brickhill subsequently gave Pudney an expensive gold watch.

As Margot remained in Wakefield Hospital for ten days, Brickhill initially visited mother and child twice daily. Feeling trapped in a volatile relationship, he was once more overwhelmed with depression. As his spirits dropped, so too did the frequency of his hospital visits. On one occasion, he gloomily lapsed into silence as he sat at his wife's bedside.

'Come on now,' said Margot impatiently, 'entertain me.'

He made no reply.[266]

The next day, in a doctor's surgery, Brickhill collapsed from nervous exhaustion. Days later, hiring a full-time nurse for the baby, he took mother and son home to Allum Street. Brickhill already slept poorly. A new baby crying at all hours meant he got no sleep at all. Moving out, he slept at an Auckland gentleman's club for two weeks, visiting his wife and child during the afternoons. Margot demanded to know why.

'I'm ill!' he replied in exasperation. 'Can't you see?'

'You are suffering from no illness whatsoever!' he would remember her retorting.[267]

Throughout May, William Collins' New Zealand manager drove Brickhill to signings at bookstores throughout the North Island. As a result, New Zealand sales of *Reach for the Sky* would approach those in Australia. With travel and public appearances exhausting him, and desperate for a rest, when Brickhill heard about a cancellation on a cruise ship departing Auckland in June, he booked a cabin; for himself, alone. For twenty days, he sailed around the Pacific.

When the cruise ship docked in Fiji, he caught up with aviation pioneer Harold Gatty, who by this time had founded Fiji Airways. Gatty told him about a philosophical book he was writing about nature and survival, and Brickhill would strongly recommend it to Billy Collins. The book, *Nature Is Our Guide*, would be published in 1958, a year after Gatty's death.

Prior to sailing away, Brickhill had given his wife a generous housekeeping allowance and money to pay the nurse's wages. Margot, who was exercising and dieting to regain her slim pre-pregnancy figure, which she would succeed in doing by the time her husband returned, was before long short of cash and asking her father in Australia to send money to pay the nurse's wages. Margot wouldn't tell Brickhill about this until a decade later. Brickhill, arriving back in Auckland to find his wife desperately lonely, flew Margot's mother over from Sydney to stay for many weeks. While Olive took care of the baby, Margot went looking for modelling work in Auckland, securing one week-long assignment.

In Brickhill's absence, letters from Billy Collins had piled up. Collins had clearly not approved of the author's lone Pacific jaunt, saying that he expected Brickhill's wife and son would be very pleased to see him again. He also said that recently, at a lunch, he'd seen Douglas Bader, who was far from happy with the success of *Reach for the Sky*. With the hardback print run now up to 300,000 and the film contract finalised, Bader had told Collins he very much regretted the deal he'd renegotiated with Brickhill, and questioned the sales projections provided at the time.

No one could have predicted the book's phenomenal success in advance – within several years, *Reach for the Sky* would become the biggest-selling hardback book in Britain since Homer's *Iliad* in the 1930s. Yet Billy Collins was siding with Bader, telling Brickhill he hoped he would sort the matter out with him. As far as Brickhill was concerned, the matter was already sorted. He hadn't heard a peep out of Bader about their revised agreement since they'd signed it. And he never would. As Collins continued to prod him about Bader's share, Brickhill, now commencing his letters with 'Dear Billy', spelled out in detail the lengths he'd gone to in accommodating Bader's requested revision of their deal. But the chairman never seemed to grasp the intricacies of it all, and Brickhill would always feel that everyone at William Collins felt he'd defrauded Bader of his fair dues.

Not that Bader came out of it a poor man. He would use money from his share of the book royalties to purchase and totally renovate a house in Kensington's Petersham Mews. It became his and Thelma's much-cherished home. Thelma would die from throat cancer in 1971, five years before Bader was knighted for services to the public and the disabled. Sir Douglas would retain the mews house as something of a shrine to Thelma. Although by then living in the country, Bader and second wife Joan would use Petersham Mews as their London pad after they married in 1973. In 2009, Sir Richard Branson would unveil a British Heritage plaque dedicated to Bader on the mews house's exterior. Branson's Aunt Clare had been a friend of the Baders, and at the age of seven, at his aunt's Norfolk house, Branson had stolen the famous tin legs and run off with them while Bader was swimming, only to discover that he was just as nimble on his hands as he was on prosthetics.

Bader would not complain publicly about his share of *Reach for the Sky* spoils, but his dissatisfaction with the way he and Brickhill split the money, at Bader's own instigation, led to the pair falling out. Bader no longer answered letters from the author, and their firm friendship dissolved the way family relationships dissolve over contested inheritances. 'I am sickened by the whole business,' Brickhill would lament.[268]

As Brickhill read the backlog of letters from Collins, he found the chairman returning to the subject of reduced royalties. Brickhill had thought that matter dealt with. He sent a negative response, and through July and August long, politely couched but combative letters flowed back and forth between the two. Still, Collins harped on royalty revisions. Seething, Brickhill asked for detailed sales figures for all territories, and withheld permission for a book club edition. Their disagreement on financial matters was, he told Collins, 'an awful business', and he deeply regretted it.

As he fought this continuing war of words, his drinking increased, and all inspiration for a novel deserted him. The only thing he took pleasure in now was his new son. 'He is pink and a ball of muscle,' he proudly told Collins, adding that tiny Tim had just let out his first full-bodied laugh.[269]

By August, Brickhill had tired of chilly New Zealand, and was missing big city life. An early return to London was ruled out by the taxation issue. Across the Pacific, US sales of *Reach for the Sky* were below expectations, so Brickhill decided that later in the year he would sail to America and spend six months in New York City promoting the book.

Margot insisted that, before she and Timothy joined him in New York, he send her back to Sydney to show off the newborn to family, then fly the pair to Hong Kong to spend a month over Christmas with Margot's sister Jeanette there. Brickhill agreed, adding that in March or April they would go somewhere warm for the rest of the year — he gave Margot the option of either Italy or the Bahamas. She chose Italy.

Jeanette had initially gone to Hong Kong to visit big sister Beth, whose husband had been transferred to the colony by the British Army. Finding employment in Hong Kong as secretary to a British barrister, Jeanette had married a local diamond trader, and Brickhill would send Margot to Honkers with money to buy jewellery wholesale from Jeanette's husband. As Margot told Billy Collins in an August letter, she was excited about seeing her sister, and about visiting Hong Kong and New York. She also revealed that she was looking forward to returning to England and settling permanently there, and declared that both Brickhill and she were besotted with baby Timothy.[270]

Come September, Brickhill was so displeased with Collins for his persistent requests for royalty reductions, and his support of Bader in the royalty split matter, he told the chairman he was seriously considering terminating his relationship with the publisher. Quickly backing off, Collins offered to fly to New York in January to meet Brickhill and iron out their differences. In the end, Brickhill would stand firm and refuse to alter his contract. He did concede that, with Collins still pushing him to write the Battle of Britain novel, he was prepared to accept lower royalty rates on future books.

Another storm now broke over the author. By the second week of September, the *Sydney Morning Herald* was reporting from its London office that *The Dam Busters* movie had been wrapped up and was in the can, ready for release.[271] That release was scheduled for November. In October, out of the blue, came a phone call to Brickhill from London. The film's release was on hold, perhaps permanently, and producer Robert Clark was blaming Brickhill. Guy Gibson's young widow, Eve, was threatening to sue Associated British Picture Corporation for using material taken from her late husband's book, *Enemy Coast Ahead*, without permission.

As Brickhill explained to Clark, he had obtained written permission from the publisher of *Enemy Coast Ahead*, Michael Joseph, to use selected extracts from the book in *The Dam Busters*. Clark wasn't satisfied with this. He wanted Brickhill to settle the matter with the widow, fast. When Brickhill said he couldn't possibly return to London, and was shortly setting off for New York, Clark told him to sort it out from America; but sort it out he must. If Associated British was prevented from releasing the film, they would sue Brickhill for every penny he possessed.

Brickhill crashed back into depression. He was so low when Margot and Timothy flew back to Sydney as planned, he couldn't get out of bed to see them off. Finally pulling himself together, Brickhill told Clark that if Gibson's widow appointed agents in New York, he would enter into discussions there. Make it quick, Clark responded. This was Associated British's biggest movie ever, and the only one wholly funded by the company. This crisis threatened to bankrupt them. To save time, and overcoming his prejudice against air travel,

Brickhill booked airline tickets to New York, via Suva, Honolulu and San Francisco.

Gibson's widow, meanwhile, arrived in London from South Africa. Besieged by the press wanting to know about the dispute over the film, she declared, 'I am not concerned with the financial aspect – I am just deeply hurt that they did not consult me.'[272] As Brickhill was to discover, it would prove to be all about the financial aspect.

As he nervously flew across the Pacific from Auckland, Brickhill wondered how Gibson's widow knew exactly what was in the film. No one outside Associated British had yet seen it. Then he remembered that, before filming began, Clark had sent the screenplay out to him, and everyone who'd been connected with 617 Squadron in 1943, for comment.

Australian former 617 Squadron member Jack Leggo had told the press he'd received his copy via his father, after the RAF informed Associated British he was dead. Harry Humphries, difficult former 617 Squadron adjutant, had added a few comments to his copy and returned it, considering it 'a fair reflection of the events'.[273] Gibson's father had seen and approved the script. So, Gibson's widow must have been sent the script by Clark – she'd been introduced to star Richard Todd prior to filming. Why wait until the film was ready for release before speaking out? Clearly, she must have had legal advice to hold off, to maximise her leverage.

At first, Clark publicly declared that Associated British was prepared to pay her compensation if she had been wronged, and remake the movie from scratch if necessary. But knowing his company didn't have the money for a reshoot, he quickly changed his tune. 'This film will never be shown until this matter has been cleared up,' he angrily told the press as Brickhill flew east. 'As far as we are concerned, it is a matter between Mr Brickhill and Mrs Hyman's agents.'[274]

Gibson's wife quickly attracted public sympathy. For she was twice a widow. After the war, she'd married a second time, to Jack Hyman, a former captain with the South African Army, and moved with him to Johannesburg. Hyman had within a few years also been killed, in a car accident. Now using the name Mrs Eve Hyman, the double widow would before long revert to the name of Mrs Gibson.

Brickhill knew that Eve had been chorus girl Evelyn Moore when Gibson began courting her. While the 1940 evacuation of Dunkirk's beaches was underway, and Brickhill was still a subeditor at Sydney's *Sunday Sun*, Gibson had been on leave in Brighton, haunting a theatre's stage door to see the petite dancer. They had married shortly after. The fact that Eve's marriage to Gibson had been on the rocks at the time of his death didn't come out until much later. Only in 2010 would Margaret Masters, a nurse with the Women's Royal Auxiliary during the war, come forward to say that she and Gibson had an affair in 1943–44, and claiming he'd intended leaving his wife.

Once Brickhill landed in New York, he took an apartment in the Beaux Arts building on East 44th Street, and, with the help of Mike Watkins, began a long, drawn-out conversation with the widow's US agents. Planning to commence researching a novel while in New York, Brickhill told Billy

Collins it would be on a subject he knew well and would be a perfect transition from war nonfiction. As December arrived, Brickhill reckoned it would take him a year to produce the novel, although he soon found this city which never slept a far from ideal place to be creative – as Collins had earlier warned him. But first, Brickhill had to sort out the Eve Hyman affair: 'The most bare-faced attempt at unjustified extortion I have ever encountered,' he told Collins. 'Their claims are quite untenable and we are, of course, calling their bluff.'[275]

Brickhill reckoned he'd taken quite a beating in 1954. The battering wasn't yet over. *The Dam Busters* battle would continue into the new year.

21.

A Slap in the Face

Across the table from him in Manhattan's swanky Hawaiian Room night club sat Margot, looking trim and healthy. On 11 January, she and baby Tim had arrived from Hong Kong. To please his wife, Brickhill had moved out of the Beaux Arts building and taken a suite at the Waldorf-Astoria Hotel, hiring a fulltime nurse to look after their eight-month-old. This night out was Brickhill's way of welcoming Margot back. With Timothy under the watchful eye of his nurse at the Waldorf, they'd taken in the Hawaiian Room's hula show, with Margot telling Brickhill how much she'd enjoyed seeing family and how fascinating she'd found Hong Kong.

As a waiter refilled their champagne glasses and withdrew, Margot reached into her handbag, took out a cigarette, and put it in her mouth.

'I thought you'd given up smoking,' said Brickhill with a scowl.

As far as he knew, she hadn't smoked since falling pregnant. Although a heavy smoker himself, he'd never liked to see Margot smoke. As she fished in her handbag for a lighter, Brickhill reached across the table, took the cigarette from her mouth, broke it in half, and laid it on the table in front of her. After looking at him in surprise for a moment, Margot calmly took up the halved cigarette, and stuffed the pieces into his champagne. The confrontation ignited into a row, which continued as Brickhill paid the bill, and flowed out onto the Lexington Avenue pavement. It was not the reunion that Brickhill had been hoping for.[276]

Their stay at the Waldorf-Astoria lasted fifty-five days, as Brickhill and Watkins continued the battle with Eve Hyman's agents. Finally, by March, an agreement was reached that would allow *The Dam Busters* to be released. With the marathon negotiations terminated, Brickhill tore an advertisement from a New York newspaper which promoted an imminent sailing to Naples of the liner *Roma*. Giving it to Margot, he asked her to book their passage. His return to Naples would be in considerably more style than he'd left it in 1943.

As the Brickhills sailed for Italy on 19 March, it was left to Robert Clark to implement the changes agreed with Hyman's agents. Details of the settlement were never made public. The production company's records are lost, and neither surviving film crew nor film historians have been able to shed light on precisely what was done to placate Gibson's widow. Brickhill clearly stuck to his guns and didn't part with any money.

He and Clark did agree to give Guy Gibson a screen credit. As the opening credits unfold, we see, following the film's title, 'Based on the book by Paul Brickhill', and, beneath that, 'and Wing Commander Gibson's own account "Enemy Coast Ahead"'. The term 'own account', rather than 'book', seems to draw a fine line to obviate the need to pay a rights fee.

Almost certainly, Brickhill also convinced Clark to shoot two short, additional cockpit scenes in the spring of 1955. Freddie Goode, assistant director on the film's second unit, would recall that filming of aerial scenes for *The Dam Busters*, supposed to last only ten weeks, ultimately extended over five months.[277] And Walter Mycroft is known to have written several additional scenes for the film. All this extra shooting contributed to a blowout in the film's budget from £200,000 to at least £250,000. By one account, it grew to £260,000.[278]

These two new cockpit scenes involved supporting actors, not Richard Todd, who had moved on to other projects. The two, virtually identical scenes, were superfluous. In the final film, as the first wave of three Lancaster bombers flying Operation Chastise flit low over the North Sea, heading for occupied Europe, the scene changes to the cockpit of Gibson's aircraft. Guy Gibson's navigator informs the rest of the crew that the Dutch coast is just ahead.

'Stand by, front gunner,' Richard Todd, as Gibson, then says, 'we're going over.'

The scene changes to the operations room, where Barnes Wallis, Bomber Harris and senior RAF Bomber Command officers tensely wait. An officer says that the second wave of Lancasters should now be coming up to the Dutch coast. The scene switches to the cockpit of the lead aircraft of the second wave, where the navigator says, 'Enemy coast ahead.' After seeing the second trio of bombers cross the Dutch coast and head inland, we cut to the cockpit of the lead aircraft of the third wave. Before he fastens his oxygen mask and these three planes also cross the coast, the pilot says, 'Enemy coast ahead.'

Neither Gibson nor Brickhill used the phrase 'Enemy coast ahead' in their books. Gibson only used it as his title. He wrote that his own bomb aimer, Australian Spam Spafford, actually said, 'There's the coast.' But Gibson made no mention of what was said in other aircraft. In negotiations, Brickhill would have pointed out that additional scenes using the dialogue 'Enemy coast ahead' would promote Gibson's book and generate more sales of it, and more royalties, which continued to flow to Gibson's widow, Eve. And this compromise seems to have been the centrepiece of the undisclosed settlement.

Finally, with Hyman seen off via the secret deal, and with two additional short scenes edited in and credits amended, Robert Clark had his film in the can. He announced that the movie would launch with a charity premiere in London attended by Princess Margaret, on 16 May, which would coincide with the twelfth anniversary of the night that 617 Squadron took off on the dams raid. Demand for tickets proved so high, Clark scheduled a second charity premiere for the following evening, with the Duke and Duchess of Gloucester officiating.

Rain teemed down in London on the evening of Monday, 16 May 1955, but that didn't deter hundreds of people from lining the streets outside Leicester Square's Empire Theatre. They'd come to catch a glimpse of film stars and royalty arriving for *The Dam Busters* charity premiere. Richard Todd and Princess Margaret garnered the greatest cheers. Among the special guests were mothers of men of 617 Squadron who'd died in Operation Chastise, and fourteen 617 survivors including five who'd been flown in from Canada.

Producer Robert Clark had pulled out all stops to make this a success. He had to. In 1954, Associated British had released ten pictures. This year, as a result of the Hyman dispute, it released just four. The futures of the company and Clark were riding on *The Dam Busters*. Two nights earlier, Clark had staged a special 617 Squadron reception at Regent Street's Criterion Restaurant. The centrepiece had been a giant model of the Moehne Dam, and Guy Gibson's seventy-eight-year-old father, Alexander, had told guests his son had deeply regretted the large number of farm animals drowned after he'd ruptured the dam.

Gibson made no mention of the 1294 civilians, many of them foreign forced labourers, who'd also drowned. That death toll was similar to the highest number of civilian deaths in London on the worst night of the Blitz of 1940–41. In 1943, Germany's propaganda ministry had labelled the dams raid a war crime. Now, in 1955, the German press was expressing deep regret at the release of this film, which they saw as a 'glorification of a gruesome act'.[279]

Moustachioed, paunchy producer Clark could be seen in the Empire Theatre's foyer at the world premiere, anxiously rubbing his chin. Hovering behind Princess Margaret, he whispered to her occasionally as she stood at the head of the official receiving line. One after the other, VIPs filed past the princess, bowing and curtseying. A slight, bird-faced blonde seemed in an inordinate hurry as she curtseyed nervously and went to move on. But Margaret held fast to her hand and spoke with her. Clark, it seems, asked Her Royal Highness to make a fuss of this young woman – Eve Hyman. He wanted no more problems from Guy Gibson's widow.

Brickhill had meanwhile arrived in Italy with his wife and son. After two weeks at Florence's Anglo-American Hotel, they settled into the Villa Tortoli at Tavarnuzze, outside Florence. During the fashion season, Margot secured work modelling for Victor Stiebel in Florence, leaving Timothy in the care of a nurse at the villa while she drove into the city in their Alfa Romeo, which had been shipped to Italy from storage in London.

Although the Hyman affair had been settled, Brickhill was just as worried as Robert Clark about the success of the *Dam Busters* movie. His concerns were exacerbated when Air Marshal Sir Robert Saundby, a former senior Bomber Command officer who'd attended one of the gala premieres, wrote to the *New Statesman* spluttering that the film and Brickhill's book were fundamentally wrong in making Barnes Wallis the hero of Operation Chastise. The RAF had been planning a dams raid for years before Wallis came along, he said. Saundby also claimed that much of Brickhill's dialogue was incorrect.

The letter was passed on to Brickhill in Italy, from where he sent a prickly response to the *New Statesman*. In his and Wallis' defence, he wrote that he had only used dialogue conveyed to him by multiple sources. And, as for destroying the dams, 'Who cares who first thought there *might* be a way?' he countered. 'Dr Wallis was the man who "hatched" the only idea that did, in fact, work.'[280]

Brickhill's blood pressure was going through the roof by this time, and he went to see a Florence medico, Dr Guiliani. The doctor prescribed Reserpine, a new 'wonder drug' first used the previous year. Today, the drug is banned in the UK and other parts of the world after its use was connected with suicide by users. For several months in Italy, Brickhill, gravely assured that his life depended on it, attended the doctor's surgery twice weekly for injections of Reserpine.

Now began what Brickhill called 'the horrors', for which he would later blame the drug. He'd been made aware of side effects such as congested nose, weight gain, vomiting and diarrhoea, but wasn't ready for others which included sexual dysfunction, depression, nightmares, inability to concentrate, inexplicable fears, and the return of his claustrophobia. With Brickhill totally unable to get himself organised, his typewriter gathered dust.

By October, the frustrated Brickhill and his bored wife were again arguing. Violently, this time. As Margot yelled at him, Brickhill pushed her back against a wall of their Italian villa. Three days later, when Margot became hysterical during an argument, Brickhill slapped her on the cheek with an open hand. Suddenly silenced by the blow, she took a step back.

'I suppose you enjoyed that,' she said after composing herself.

'Well, as a matter of fact, I did,' he responded, a little dazed.

'The only way you can handle a woman is by hitting her,' she spat, pushing by him.

'It might have come to that,' he retorted, 'if you made it impossible to deal otherwise with you.' Following her into the kitchen, he defended himself by saying that if she became hysterical again he would be forced to end her fit by again slapping her.

That night, neither of them could sleep. Overcome with remorse at striking his wife, Brickhill sat on the edge of their bed, head in hands, muttering to himself. On the recommendation of his doctor, both he and Margot sought psychiatric treatment from Italian specialists. Within weeks, Brickhill had another nervous collapse and was admitted to hospital.[281]

By December, Brickhill was off the Reserpine and feeling able to get back to work on his novel. Needing privacy, he rented a room in a house at Montecatini Terme, a Tuscan spa town between Florence and Pisa favoured by composer Giuseppe Verdi. Brickhill had been there a week when loneliness overwhelmed him. When he returned to the Villa Tortoli on Christmas Eve, Margot refused him entry. He was back next afternoon, Christmas Day, bearing a £200 gold necklace as a Christmas gift. This time, Margot let him in.

22.

End of Exile

THE DELAY IN the release of the *Dam Busters* movie had increased public interest, and receipts. It topped the British box office for 1955, and restored Associated British's fortunes. The news was of little comfort to Brickhill. In early 1956, he had a mental relapse and was again admitted to an Italian hospital.

By the spring, he'd recovered sufficiently to drive Margot to Fiesole from Florence along a narrow mountain road. Inevitably, they fell into an argument en route. When she praised her mother, Brickhill's temper flared.

'Your mother, and all women, are useless,' Brickhill declared. 'With the exception of my mother, of course.'

'How did you come to except your mother?' she snorted.

Brickhill's mother was, to him, beyond reproach, and his anger rose like an erupting volcano. Without warning, the back of his hand collected Margot on the side of the face.[282]

*

Flying in from Italy for five days, Brickhill and his wife were among the guests of honour at the world premiere of *Reach for the Sky* at Leicester Square's Odeon Theatre on 5 July. Among the VIP guests were Australian Prime Minister Robert Menzies and two senior British cabinet ministers. Brickhill would later say that Margot 'vindictively humiliated' him at the event. He wouldn't describe the nature of that humiliation, but, because of it, he vowed to never take Margot to another premiere. He kept his word, going alone to the film's Edinburgh and Paris premieres.[283]

Douglas Bader declined the Rank Organisation's invitation to attend the London premiere. He had visited at least one location during filming, and prior to the shoot he'd seen the first draft of the screenplay and had played a round of golf with Kenneth More, the actor cast to play him. More, who'd recently starred in *Genevieve*, a popular comedy about a man and his antique car on a rally to Brighton, didn't mind that Bader beat him on the golf course. He was taking in his legless companion's gait, which he would get down pat in the film. More had wanted the part the moment he'd read Brickhill's book, but Richard Burton had initially been cast as Bader. Only after Burton dropped out did More's agent receive a call from producer Danny Angel.

Bader would not only stay away from the film's premiere; bitter because he didn't make a penny from the film – as a consequence of the renegotiated deal he'd pushed through with Brickhill – he would never see the movie in a cinema. Not even the fact that Thelma's composer stepbrother John Addison wrote the film's score would induce him to see it. Eleven years after its release, with Thelma, Bader would watch the film for the first time, on television. From that time forward, Bader referred to the film, and the book, disparagingly as *Reach for the Sticking Plaster.*

Reach for the Sky became Britain's top-grossing film of 1956, breaking box-office records. It also won 'film of the year' at the British Academy of Film and Television Arts (BAFTA) awards. It cemented Bader as a national celebrity, and made More a major star. More would tour America to promote the film on its US release in 1957, but, seen as another film about Brits winning the war, like *The Dam Busters,* it didn't do well in the States. Released in Australia a year after its British release, it emulated *The Dam Busters* in becoming a major hit in Brickhill's homeland.

Brickhill's accountant had advised him he could now resettle in England, and as soon as the couple returned to Italy they commenced packing their twenty trunks. Still seething over Margot's perceived humiliation of him at the movie premiere, Brickhill then drove back to England in the Alfa, leaving his wife to make her own way back. Hers was a leisurely return, interspersed with stays at several French resorts.

They rented in South Ascot, and in August Brickhill went to Deauville to sail the Mediterranean with Stalag Luft 3 chum Johnny Dodge. On his return in September, Brickhill took his wife to a ball at the Savoy Hotel in aid of Leonard Cheshire's charitable home, with pianist Winifred Atwell among the entertainers. An Ashes cricket Test series was underway, and Australian and English players attended the ball, among them Keith Miller, Ray Lindwall, Tony Lock and Fred Trueman. A new dance craze, the Kangaroo Hop, had arrived in town with the Aussies, and a magazine photographer snapped Margot in the act of energetically kangaroo hopping with her husband's colourful publisher Billy Collins, who loved to dance.

Now, after years of renting in five countries, Brickhill committed to buying a house of his own. Overjoyed, Margot went scouting in the Alfa Romeo. With mind-blowing financial and critical success for Brickhill, and on the quest for their first real home, the Brickhills had every reason to be happy. And, for a time, their stormy arguments subsided. Their love life was reborn; Margot would later say that she had only started enjoying sex after she gave birth to Timothy.[284] In December, Margot again fell pregnant.

In early 1957, the Brickhills found their dream home, in Surrey's exclusive Wentworth Estate, outside Virginia Water. Set on 700 country acres, the estate was dominated by a golf course set around a nineteenth-century house, the Wentworths. Once owned by a brother-in-law of the Duke of Wellington, the Wentworths was now the golfing clubhouse, its championship course noted for hosting the first Ryder Cup. As a house owner here, Brickhill could play a round whenever he fancied.

The estate had been developed in the 1920s by W. G. Tarrant, who'd had the first houses built on large lots and in grand style. Most were half-timbered, with tall chimneys, gables, dormer rooms, leaded lights and handmade bricks and tiles. The largest houses featured stonework around their front doors and fireplaces, plus marble-floored entrance halls. The Great Depression had hit Wentworth Estate hard, sending Tarrant into bankruptcy in 1931, the same year that George Brickhill's disastrous financial decline had begun.

Paul Brickhill's company purchased 'Little Barr', a Wentworth Estate house with a large, mature garden for young Tim to play in. That garden backed onto the golf course, with a hedge separating the two. The Alfa Romeo would be joined in the garage by a new company car, a two-year-old Mark II Jaguar bought second hand by Brickhill in an attempt to excuse a long-held ambition with the gloss of economy.

Struggling to write his own work of fiction in 1957, Brickhill helped Morris West with his novel *The Backlash*, later filmed by Hollywood as *The Second Victory*. West, now Europe-based, set his book in Austria in 1945, just after the war, a time and place Brickhill knew well. When the book was published in 1958, West's dedication page would read: 'For Paul Brickhill.'

By this stage Brickhill was lusting after an exotic Northern Hemisphere residence with a warm climate, and considered Malta, Ghana, even Beirut. While on a scouting visit to Malta, he left Margot to entertain his visiting brother Lloyd and his South American wife, who spoke no English. After Margot showed no interest in any of Brickhill's foreign destinations, the idea was dropped. In April, with a brainwave for a new novel, set in France, Brickhill drove to Cannes. Staying a month on the Riviera researching the book, he spent time in Marseilles, home of Algerian immigrants, who would play a key role in his plot.

On his return to England in May, the family moved into 'Little Barr'. Brickhill employed a full-time children's nurse, a daily charlady and a part-time gardener, but Margot astonished him by working in the garden herself. She seemed happier than Brickhill could remember. Alas, by July, they were again fighting. When Margot, eight months pregnant, became overwrought, Brickhill twice slapped her face. The arrival of daughter Tempe Melinda in August should have been the highlight of 1957 for Brickhill. But following Tempe's birth, he became ultra-jealous, privately accusing Margot of improper behaviour with one man in London and publicly accusing a Wentworth neighbour of seducing his wife.

'If you continue your behaviour towards me, Paul,' a fraught Margot declared, 'I'll break down under the strain!'[285]

As Brickhill continued to wrestle with his latest attempt at a novel into 1958, his marriage disintegrated around him. Margot could not understand why he was not able to simply sit down at his typewriter and bash it out, the way he'd always done. And the more he said he was unwell, the less she believed him.

This year, John Sturges again came courting the film rights to *The Great Escape*. Still unaware that Fred Coe held the option, he was again sent away, unsuccessful. Brickhill was by this time living almost entirely on his investments. Book income had dropped significantly after his meteoric sales earlier in the decade. He would have been interested in talking to Sturges, but Coe's option still had more than two years to run.

In September, Brickhill came to his wife, eyes sparkling. 'I've had a breakthrough with the novel!' he declared.

'Too late!' she retorted. 'I'm leaving you.'[286]

She moved out on 21 September, rented a farmhouse at Croyde in Devon, and had a lawyer initiate a six-month legal separation. Margot much later revealed that she would have filed for divorce, but she hadn't lived back in England long enough to do so under English divorce law. A legal separation was her only option at that time. Brickhill, as he had in the past, tried to woo back his wife. In October, he undertook to take them back to Australia the following year. And he made a vow: 'Never again, under whatever provocation or circumstance, will I strike you. I'll prove to you I'm not totally evil.'[287]

Still they remained legally estranged. By December, Margot had moved to a house at Ascot. Brickhill paid her rent, and paid for a live-in maid. When Margot invited him to visit the children, he arrived with a £200 diamond brooch as a Christmas gift.

'What will the judge think?' Margot joked, as she accepted the offering.

Over Christmas they twice made love, but Margot asked him not to tell anyone. 'I wouldn't want this to happen too often,' she said.[288]

In the new year, they agreed to give the marriage another try. With the marital waters calmed, and as they began planning the trip to Australia later in the year, Brickhill had an idea for yet another book, a novel about British immigrants going to Australia. Approaching the Australian Government, he convinced them to agree to pay for Margot, the two children, a nanny and himself to travel on an immigrant ship to Sydney free of charge, in return for writing the immigration novel, which would have to be completed by a set date in 1960.

Through the first half of 1959 he made progress on his French novel, finding Margot mature and agreeable despite occasional tantrums if she didn't get her own way. Selling Margot on a ten-day trip to Paris as a second honeymoon, Brickhill took the family there in June. As Brickhill trawled Parisian backstreets to trace their layout, haunted sleazy bars to study their clientele, and applied a forensic eye to the work of the French police, he was in his element. Margot, meanwhile, complained there was almost nothing to do but eat. After Paris, in preparation for the trip home, Margot gave up potatoes, went to the hair salon every five days for blonde tips, and toasted herself under a sun lamp.

On 26 October, accompanied by twenty-two-year-old German nanny Margarete Haselwander, forty-two-year-old Brickhill, his thirty-one-year-old wife, and their five- and two-year-old children boarded the *Fairsky* at Southampton, and sailed for Australia along with 1400 British migrants.

23.

Return to Oz

AFTER THEY DISEMBARKED from the *Fairsky* in Sydney on 19 November, a chauffeur-driven limousine whisked Brickhill, his wife and their children to the Hydro Majestic Hotel at Medlow Bath in the Blue Mountains, where they were joined by the couple's parents. All spent twelve days there at Brickhill's expense, as the children enjoyed their first taste of Australia and enjoyed the attentions of their grandparents.

Before leaving England, Brickhill had arranged a lease on the same waterfront Stokes Point house they'd lived in back in 1954. The lease included the owner's car, and, to lower the rent, Brickhill allowed their landlord, who was in England, to use his Jaguar there. The Brickhills moved into the Stokes Point house in time for Christmas. During December, Brickhill recorded an ABC Radio interview, talking about his immigration book.

After this was aired on 29 December, the press quickly latched onto a comment of Brickhill's that British people were becoming less inclined to migrate to Australia. This would generate a rapid response from immigration minister Alick Downer, who blustered that, not only was there still a very strong flow of British immigrants, the government would soon launch a campaign to attract UK university graduates to Australia. Brickhill had trodden on the toes of the very man who'd approved the subsidisation of his immigration novel.

But Brickhill wasn't in Australia for the fallout from his radio interview. On Boxing Day, with Margot's keen encouragement, he flew out of Sydney to Los Angeles. The persistent John Sturges wanted to talk about filming *The Great Escape*. The urgency of his request, the lure of Hollywood and the fact that Sturges was paying the author's way, first class, in one of the new Boeing 707 jets that had started on the trans-Pacific route that year, combined to suppress Brickhill's dread of flying.

Sturges' star was now high in Hollywood. After a string of hit westerns including *Gunfight at the OK Corral* in 1957, his 1958 film was very different: *The Old Man and the Sea*. Adapted from the Ernest Hemingway novella, it earned Spencer Tracy an Oscar nomination for best actor. Sturges would soon be basking in the success of his 1960 blockbuster western *The Magnificent Seven*. Here was a Hollywood heavy hitter who might do *The Great Escape* justice on the big screen. By comparison, Fred Coe wasn't in Sturges' league. Coe's ten-year option still had eight months to run, but if Brickhill liked Sturges and what he had to offer, he might be able to stall him until the rights reverted in the second half of 1960.

In Los Angeles, Sturges laid out the welcome mat for Brickhill. He habitually put up guests at his palatial Hollywood home, and had a reputation for entertaining them royally. For the past two years, Sturges had been working successfully with the Mirisch Corporation on a non-exclusive production arrangement. The very day they brokered that agreement, Sturges had spoken excitedly to Walter Mirisch about wanting to film *The Great Escape*. It was following this that they'd made the unsuccessful 1958 approach for the rights. Now, Sturges and Mirisch teamed up to woo the Australian author on their home turf.

Mirisch would recall that, from his first LA meeting with Brickhill, the author played hard to get. Brickhill, while failing to reveal that the screen rights were not his to sell at that moment, or that he was keen to secure the money a Hollywood film deal would bring, was nonetheless truthful when he told Mirisch he was sceptical that American producers could authentically play out the details of the escape from Stalag Luft 3.

'I don't want an Errol Flynn picture,' Brickhill told Mirisch.[289]

As it dawned on the producers that this courtship could still be a long one, Sturges took Brickhill to his favourite hangout, the Polo Lounge at the Beverly Hills Hotel, where Hollywood A-listers went to see their peers, and to be seen by their peers. According to novelist Bill Gulick, who was similarly wooed, Sturges was 'a plain speaking man', but 'very hospitable'.[290] Sturges told Brickhill about his own Air Force service during the war, and quizzed him about every aspect of the book and the men who peopled his *Great Escape*. During these convivial sessions, Brickhill, glass in hand, told Sturges about his colleagues, his claustrophobia in the tunnel and his own escape plans. Sturges took it all in, filing details away in his mind as building blocks for the story he would tell on screen. Sturges told Bill Gulick, 'To me, the story comes first.'[291]

The sweet talking of Brickhill went on for two weeks. As they conversed, Sturges told Brickhill that, even though he hadn't been a POW, as a former airman he knew the kind of men who'd been in Stalag Luft 3, and knew their lingo. Sturges would remember a long lunch with the Australian during which he guaranteed his movie would stick to the facts of the story.

'We'll do the thing justice,' Sturges assured Brickhill, adding that this wouldn't be an American 'How we won the war' movie.

Brickhill seemed impressed, especially when Sturges gave him a written outline setting out how he would film *The Great Escape*.

'Have I convinced you I'm on the level?' Sturges asked.

'Yes, you have,' Brickhill acknowledged.[292] But who, he wondered, did Sturges have in mind to write the screenplay?

Sturges immediately nominated Walter Newman. He owed Newman a favour. They'd fallen out when the writer demanded his name be removed from the writing credits for *The Magnificent Seven* after Sturges brought in 'script doctor' William Roberts to polish Newman's original screenplay. Newman was known as a writer of snappy dialogue, and in years to come would receive three Oscar nominations for his screenplays, including 1965's *Cat Ballou*. Sturges thought Newman and Brickhill would get along, being the same age and both coming from journalistic backgrounds, and promised to put them together.

Days passed, without Newman appearing. The screenwriter was apparently caught up out of town. Brickhill's patience gave out. Flying to Hawaii, he told Sturges he could bring him back to LA if and when the screenwriter showed up. For five days, Brickhill swam in Waikiki's balmy waters and downed a Mai Tai or two. Finally, with still no sign of Newman, Brickhill telephoned Sturges to tell him he was going home. He also told him he felt duty-bound to run Sturges' outline by Wings Day and the relatives of Roger Bushell and other members of the Fifty before he signed over the film rights, just as the screenplay for *The Dam Busters* had been circulated to key insiders.

Brickhill was undoubtedly genuine in this desire, but it also provided a way to string Sturges along, potentially until the northern summer when the rights reverted from Fred Coe. Back to Sydney went Brickhill, praying that Sturges would wait.

Margot was to complain that Brickhill was fixated on film rights through 1960, and on his health, and was impossible to live with.[293] Brickhill was sweating on getting back the screen rights to *The Great Escape* from Fred Coe, without Coe learning that he was talking to Mirisch and Sturges. Had Coe found out, he may have done a deal with Mirisch Corp to assign the rights to them, for a share of the film and a credit as co-producer. This was how Hollywood worked, and still works; producers holding rights to a property like to make money from them.

In February 1960, back at Stokes Point, Brickhill began work on the immigration novel, driven by the delivery deadline and inspired by people he'd met and stories he'd heard aboard the *Fairsky*. By April, he'd produced four chapters, which he gave Margot to read. She was singularly unimpressed. Her lack of enthusiasm was enough to sap Brickhill's confidence. Casting the manuscript aside, he lapsed into despair. Daily, he would sit on a balcony gazing out over peaceful Pittwater. At midday, he started drinking wine or sherry. By late afternoon, he was almost incoherent.

One day, Margot overheard him mumbling that he should have married childhood sweetheart Mary Callanan. Picking himself up, Brickhill drove to the home of Callanan's parents. With a bunch of flowers, he arrived unannounced. When he returned, he overflowed with apologies to Margot. Confessing he'd possessed a 'nostalgic affection' for Mary, he now realised what an idiot he'd been. From Mary's parents he'd learned that she had indeed 'consorted' with an American years before. She had married Dr Hugo Baum and settled with him in Chicago, where they were raising a family.

In search of balm for his soul, Brickhill attended an evangelical Church Army Mission service. This inspired him to join the congregation of the Avalon Anglican Church, whose services, he assured Margot, were doing him good. After entering Stalag Luft 3 an atheist, he'd come out an agnostic, prepared to believe that some greater power governed human life, and death. Now, he found comfort in the Bible. Despite this, personal, creative and commercial pressures caved in on him, and, on 29 May, Dr Frank Ritchie admitted him to St Luke's Private Hospital at Kings Cross for a complete rest.

Brickhill's day nurse at St Luke's, on duty between 8.00 am and 8.00 pm, was Maria Lupp. Born in New Zealand, Maria had completed her nursing training in Sydney. She found Brickhill deeply depressed, and on any given day his condition ranged between lethargy, tears and anger. However, he never became violent, which many of Nurse Lupp's patients did. When his anger rose, she would calm him by being firm but kind.

'Now, settle down,' she would say. And, overcome with remorse, he would.

Brickhill's doctors had him on a cocktail of drugs for chronic depression and to help him sleep. Each morning after breakfast, he and Nurse Lupp went walking in the hospital grounds. For maximum rest, she encouraged him to sleep in the afternoons. He fought this, worrying that if he slept during the day he wouldn't sleep at night. Eventually, Brickhill managed to convince his nurse to go to a pub every second day to buy him a bottle of Scotch whisky. The Scotch was his only solace.

'Give us the whisky,' he would say to Maria. 'Just a little drop.'

She rationed the whisky as best she could. 'Settle down,' she would say when he became too demanding.[294]

Brickhill had few visitors at St Luke's. Margot came occasionally, discussing personal business in hushed tones. Their time together was usually tense. Nurse Lupp was unaware of it, but Brickhill felt that Margot was spending with abandon, which only increased his angst. Before he went into hospital, Brickhill had set up a joint bank account. Now, he would later complain, cheques written by Margot were bouncing.

Margot would say she couldn't imagine any bank bouncing the cheques of the famous Paul Brickhill.

'I'm living to the standard you require,' Brickhill would recall Margot saying.[295]

While Brickhill was furious about the cheques, fearing they would damage his cherished reputation as a man who never got into debt, he spoke not a word about his wife or his children to Maria Lupp, although they talked at length. Once, in tears, he said to her, 'You're so nice to me.'[296]

After five weeks at St Luke's, Brickhill discharged himself, feeling the rest cure wasn't working. In every waking moment his mind was still active, and short of extremely heavy sedation, he still wasn't sleeping. As he departed hospital, he promised to send Nurse Lupp one of his books.

On his return to Stokes Point, Brickhill, doped to the eyeballs on antidepressant 'happy pills', exclaimed to Margot, 'It's extraordinary! In five weeks, you have absolutely changed.'[297] In fact, it was he who had changed.

Maria Lupp had forgotten Brickhill's promise when, in July, a small parcel arrived at St Luke's – a copy of *Reach for the Sky*, with a note inside. 'I hate wrapping books and it takes me a long time,' said Brickhill. Describing himself as a 'troublesome patient', he went on, 'Thank you for your special attention – and your discipline. I'll have to go sick again and send for you.'[298]

Not long after Brickhill returned to Stokes Point, the house's lease ran out. While in hospital, Brickhill had lost all track of practicalities. Margot was far from happy when told they had just days to pack and leave. Brickhill's novelist friend Jon Cleary had become a major success, and had built a house on Stokes Point, in Riverview Road, just around the corner from the Brickhills in Cabarita Road. Cleary was then living in Europe. In desperation, Brickhill rang him, and Cleary told his mate to move into his house at once, and to use his garaged car as well. Days later, the family hurriedly moved into the Cleary residence.

It was now summer in the Northern Hemisphere, and finally the rights to *The Great Escape* reverted to Brickhill from Fred Coe. Fortunately for Brickhill, Coe was obsessed during this period with turning William Gibson's Pulitzer Prize-winning play *The Miracle Worker* into a feature film. This wrenching story of Anne Sullivan's struggle to teach blind and deaf Helen Keller how to communicate, starring Anne Bancroft and Patty Duke, would be released in 1962. With his focus on *The Miracle Worker*, Coe took his eye off *The Great Escape*. Immediately, Mike Watkins swooped, wrapping up a new rights deal with the Mirisch Corporation.

Walter Mirisch sighed with relief after what he characterised as rights negotiations with Brickhill that had been 'exceedingly difficult'.[299] He would never know the real reason for Brickhill's stalling tactics. Mirisch paid an option fee of £1000, against a final execution fee of £15,000 once production commenced.[300] The equivalent of US$60,000, this rights fee was below par by Hollywood standards. Bill Gulick was paid US$85,000 by Mirisch Corporation the following year for the rights to *Hallelujah Train*, which Sturges would film as *Hallelujah Trail*. Unlike Gulick, however, Brickhill was a comparative unknown in the US.

As soon as the rights were secured, Mirisch Corporation announced *The Great Escape* as one of fourteen movies it would produce over the next three years, and Sturges put Walter Newman to work on a first draft screenplay. This sent Brickhill's spirits soaring, along with his hopes, only for things to soon go quiet on the Mirisch Corporation front. Mirisch was having a hard time selling the project to film investors. The lack of progress again saw Brickhill lapsing into depression.

By the time the deadline for producing the immigration novel arrived that spring, Brickhill had made no further progress on it, and he repaid the Australian Government the entire cost of his family's *Fairsky* passages. To escape his moods, Margot took the children to Hong Kong for four weeks in November. In December, after her return, she took the children Christmas shopping, and stayed away five days. When she came back, she told Brickhill she'd only returned because she'd run out of money and clothes.

'Maggie,' Brickhill wailed, 'the furores you create will only have a bad effect on the children.'[301]

Several weeks later, when both their families came to Stokes Point for Christmas dinner, Brickhill only dragged himself out of bed thirty minutes before their guests arrived.

The new year saw movement on *The Great Escape* in Hollywood. In February, Mirisch announced that Steve McQueen, riding high on the success of *The Magnificent Seven*, had been signed to star, and that discussions were ongoing with Frank Sinatra and Dean Martin. Production was slated to commence in June. Sturges, unhappy with Newman's screenplay, which remained faithful to Brickhill's book, gave it to William Roberts to rework. Apart from his work on Newman's script for *The Magnificent Seven*, Roberts was best known for creating TV's *Donna Reed Show* in 1958.

With commencement of filming seemingly imminent, along with a £14,000 rights cheque, Brickhill bought a zippy Triumph Herald for Margot, and contemplated buying himself a Bentley. Despite Margot's encouragement, in the end he couldn't see past the massive import duties; he could have bought a Bentley for half the price in England. With Margot complaining she lacked financial independence, he gave her £2000. Brickhill also set up a £20,000 trust for his children, in his parents' name, assigning the deeds to 41 George Street to it. The trust soon purchased an investment property at Hunters Hill.

Brickhill's enthusiasm for the French novel returned, and when he assured Margot that, between a book and a movie, it could generate £50,000, she became his greatest supporter. Finding the study at the Cleary house too small, he took a flat down the street as his daytime writing roost. Margot even brought meals to him there, becoming a critical reader of his output as he typed away. 'The style of the writing is good,' she declared, 'and so is the general action of the plot. But the central character is too dull and colourless to grip the attention of the average reader.' She urged him to put it aside and resurrect the immigration novel.[302]

At first crushed, he subsequently rebelled against her opinion, deciding to return to England to finish the French novel in peace at 'Little Barr'. Margot and the children would join him there later, flying via a stop in Hong Kong. Brickhill also decided to finally buy a Sydney house and leave behind the rental cycle his parents' experience had ingrained into him. After his £33,333 offer on an Avalon mansion failed, he found 'Craig Rossie'. High on a bend at Palm Beach, the 1936 two-storey, five-bedroom, brick-and-stone house overlooking Pittwater had direct frontage to Sandy Beach and even possessed a boathouse. Its one-acre grounds encompassed a bowling green and gardener's cottage. Inside, 'Craig Rossie's wood-panelled walls and ceilings and stone fireplace were reminiscent of 'Little Barr'. Brickhill had found his Palm Beach dream house.

When he departed Sydney for England that Easter, he left Margot and the children excitedly preparing to move into 'Craig Rossie' once settlement was completed, giving her £5000 to furnish it as she wished and to pay for flights to Britain via Hong Kong in August. After taking up residence at 'Craig Rossie', Margot would feature in a *Woman's Day* photo-spread shot at the house. Brickhill would say he knew nothing about this at the time.[303]

Now that Brickhill had fine homes in Australia and England, he planned to move back and forth between the two, following the sun as he wrote his novels. That northern autumn, at 'Little Barr', he completed the French novel, *The Deadline*. Writing in the first person, he made his Australian hero Robert Mackay an auto engineer and racing car driver with, like himself, a love of Jaguars and Coopers. Putting Mackay in his twenties, at one point he had him rail against 'the tyranny of women'. In Brickhill's plot, Mackay is visiting Paris when he becomes implicated in a political assassination by Algerian terrorists. Mackay falls for Simone Dumail, a beautiful French girl. But is she one of the terrorists? The book's last act becomes a race against time as Mackay strives to prevent a terrorist from infecting the Paris water supply with deadly cholera bacteria, and, in the end, to save Simone and himself.

For the book's back cover, Brickhill had an artistically lit portrait taken in a London photographic studio. William Morrow in New York, who would publish the novel in the USA in 1963 under the title *War of Nerves*, didn't like the picture. To satisfy Morrow's request for a shot that made him look like a successful author rather than a shady hypnotist, he had himself photographed at 'Little Barr' leaning on the bonnet of his Jaguar, gold watch to the fore.

Through these months, Brickhill was writing regularly to Margot and the children. Initially, Margot wrote loving responses, but as time passed her tone cooled, and she put off the departure to England by the children and herself. In October, she wrote to say they wouldn't be coming to England after all. Sensing something was amiss, Brickhill jumped on a plane and rushed back to Sydney, to find that Margot had moved the children and herself out of 'Craig Rossie' and into a four-bedroom house at Turramurra, a bushland northern Sydney suburb well inland from Palm Beach. She now informed her husband that she wanted a divorce.

Brickhill spent Christmas with his parents. In February, he was served with a writ: Margot was suing for divorce on the grounds of cruelty and desertion. In 1962, divorce was a messy business. Margot, the applicant, would have to prove her husband guilty of cruelty and desertion in court. Today's no-fault Australian divorce law, introduced by the Whitlam Government, was still more than a decade away. In the 1960s, divorce cases could run for years, and make lawyers rich.

Brickhill thought that Margot was bluffing, was grandstanding for attention. And it infuriated him that the documents from Margot's lawyers were riddled with errors. His date of birth and birthplace were wrong; so, too, the date of their marriage. Tempe's middle name had been misspelled. Numerous other dates and details were incorrect. And Margot was making claims about his actions that simply didn't accord with the facts, as far as he was concerned. Most of all, it irked him that Margot was claiming he'd deserted her by going to England the previous Easter; shades of her earlier desertion claim when he'd gone to Cornwall with the Baders.

Brickhill, shocked, gutted, and alone at his dream mansion 'Craig Rossie', couldn't bring himself to address the legal documents, or the fact that Margot had gone this far. Casting the documents aside, he again lapsed into deep depression. His doctor readmitted him to St Luke's.

In the autumn of 1962, *Sydney Morning Herald* journalist Robert Willson was visiting a friend at St Luke's Hospital when he stumbled on another patient he recognised – Paul Brickhill. The author said he wasn't expecting any visitors that morning and encouraged Willson to stay and chat. With Brickhill lucid and in good spirits, they talked at length, with

Willson relishing the opportunity to discuss the famous author's books.

Before the reporter departed, Brickhill showed him the proofs for *The Deadline*, recently arrived from William Collins in London. He was slowly correcting them. Billy Collins was hopeful the novel would cash in on Brickhill's name, which would appear much larger on the cover than the title. And Brickhill would be cited as author of *Reach for the Sky*, his most recent hit in Britain. For the cover design, Collins hired John Heseltine, a leading British artist noted for illustrating the covers of the bestselling thrillers of Scottish author Alistair MacLean.

When Brickhill left hospital, he didn't return to Palm Beach. Encouraged by his parents, he joined them at 41 George Street. Dot and George, both unwell, had been using separate bedrooms for years. Although Dot had not long before recovered from the second of two strokes, she gave up her bedroom to her son and moved back into the master bedroom with George. There, at Greenwich Point, Brickhill completed correcting *The Deadline* proofs. Before he mailed them back to Bonham Carter in London, he added a dedication: 'For Dot and George, bless them.'

By the second half of April, he was feeling well. Clear-headed, he completed his detailed responses to the claims from Margot's lawyers. Now, several trunks arrived by sea from England. Brickhill was expecting them, having asked that all personal items left at 'Little Barr' be collected up and sent out to Sydney. Going through the trunk contents, he came across some of Margot's papers interspersed with his own. To his astonishment, among her papers he found Mark

Bonham Carter's thirteen-page 1953 *Reach for the Sky* report. Thoughtful and perceptive, this was by far the best editor's report Brickhill had ever seen.

But, what was it doing in his wife's papers? Had it reached Margot prior to her departure to board the *Orontes*, or after it? Only now did it occur to Brickhill that Margot may have kept the report from him. He could only imagine it'd been through neglect. On 24 April, he typed a letter to Bonham Carter, telling him he'd just unearthed the report, thanking him for it and apologising profusely for the misunderstanding and his complaints a decade before.

'Margot is a very nice girl in many ways, but a bit shaky on some respects of responsibility,' he told Bonham Carter. 'You may have heard that there is more domestic trouble between us. This time it is a somewhat nasty story but at least I'm fit now for the first time in a long, long time, and it won't throw me as before.' He went on, 'I've got two more novels all set to go, and as soon as I get rid of a few legal details, I'll be all set to go.'[304]

Bonham Carter passed Brickhill's letter on to chairman Billy Collins, noting on it that Brickhill seemed in an unbalanced condition.[305] In responding to Brickhill, Bonham Carter apologised for any confusion back in 1953. If he'd been a little more perceptive he would have realised that Brickhill had never received his report.

The 'few legal details' that Brickhill referred to involved his divorce case. More accusations continued to arrive from Margot's lawyers. She claimed that early in their marriage he'd twice taken Pat Dunne out for meals when she'd visited from New York, had contributed money to her divorce, and had corresponded with an Enid Trill and a Dorothy Fielder, all of which had made her feel very insecure. In his response, he said he'd taken Pat out with Margot's knowledge and agreement, had been unaware Pat divorced – let alone financed that divorce – and Enid and Dorothy were old platonic friends.

In addition, probably through the agency of a private detective, Margot's lawyers had learned that Brickhill had surreptitiously drunk whisky during recent hospital stays. He would counter that he'd done so with the knowledge and permission of his doctor and hospital staff, which is likely to have been only partly true. These latest rounds of legal back and forth succeeded in souring what should have been one of the most exciting times in Brickhill's life. Ahead lay the publication of his first novel. And filming of John Sturges' movie version of *The Great Escape* would soon get underway.

24.

John Sturges' Great Escape

As WALTER MIRISCH struggled to raise the finance, the northern summer of 1961 had slipped by without production beginning on *The Great Escape*. An escape movie where only three out of 220 escapers actually escaped didn't excite investor interest. Then there was the lack of a female romantic interest that Fred Coe had tried to overcome by writing a female character into his 1951 television production. In all, there would be eleven screenplay drafts, produced by six screenwriters – four more were used by Sturges after Newman and Roberts. Only two would be credited. One was prolific novelist and screenwriter W. R. (William Riley) Burnett, who made his name in the 1930s with screenplays for hit gangster movies *Little Caesar* and the original *Scarface*. James Clavell was the other. A British novelist, famous for *King Rat* and novels set in the Orient, Sydney-born Clavell had himself been a POW of the Japanese during World War Two.

By casting bankable stars, Mirisch and Sturges eventually secured their $4 million budget. In addition to McQueen, they brought in two more names from *The Magnificent Seven*, Charles Bronson and James Coburn, added *Maverick* TV star James Garner, and teamed them with classically trained British star Richard Attenborough and genuine former POW Donald Pleasence, plus solid British supporting actors including David McCallum and Gordon Jackson. The final screenplay would change the names of all the real characters, creating mirrors of some who'd been involved in the escape, inventing composite characters based on others.

Roger Bushell became Roger Bartlett, complete with sagging right eye. The character of SBO Ramsey was created to amalgamate SBO Massey and Wings Day, with Massey's limp and walking stick. American Harsh morphed into Hendley, the American scrounger. Von Lindeiner became Von Luger, and Glemnitz was turned into Strachwitz. Tailor Tommy Guest became Griffith. Escape controller Torrens was turned into security chief Sorren. Dispersal's Fanshawe was renamed Ashley-Pitt. Canadian tunnel king Wally Floody became Englishman Willie Dickes.

'Conk' Canton and 'Crump' Ker-Ramsey became Cavendish and 'Mac' MacDonald. Johnny Dodge was a loose inspiration for third American character Goff, played by Jud Taylor. The fact that all six Polish Great Escapers were executed guided the creation of Danny, Charles Bronson's Polish character. Based on real Polish escaper Stanislaw 'Danny' Krol, who'd also tunnelled from Oflag VI-B at Warburg and Schubin's Oflag XXI-B, Bronson's character was given Paul Brickhill's debilitating claustrophobia. Diminutive tunneller Ives was modelled on Henry 'Piglet' Lamond, with his nationality changed from New Zealander to Scot.

Steve McQueen's American character, 'Cooler King' Virgil Hilts, was a composite of Americans in Stalag Luft 3, most particularly Jerry Sage. Known as the Cooler King when in South Compound, Sage was, like Hilts, a baseball player. William 'Bill' Ash, a Texan in the East Compound Cooler during the Great Escape and a leading Schubin tunneller, may have influenced the character of Hilts, although Brickhill, key source for the filmmakers, had not known Ash.

Nigel Stock, the British actor who played Cavendish, had been in *The Dam Busters*, playing Guy Gibson's Australian bomb-aimer Spam Spafford with a bad Australian accent. Now it was James Coburn's turn to make a sad attempt at Strine, as he played the part of *The Great Escape*'s Australian tinkerer Sedgwick, modelled on Al Hake. This Aussie character seems also to have been a salute by Sturges to Paul Brickhill. For, in the film, Sedgwick would succeed in escaping solo, via France and Spain, as Bob van der Stock had done. Perhaps Sturges thought that portraying a successful escape by an Australian, and via Brickhill's intended escape route, would please the author and compensate for his wholesale character changes.

Colin Blythe, the movie's gentle forger losing his eyesight, played by Donald Pleasence and helped by James Garner's character Hendley, was modelled on Henry Stockings, the 'code user'. Stockings' eyesight progressively failed him as he toiled long hours in candlelight on secret codes. Hoping the Germans would repatriate him, he begged for eye tests. As it's easy to fake eye-test results, his requests were denied. Despite his appalling vision, Stockings stumbled through the march to Westertimke with Brickhill and his group, survived, and became a pig farmer in Norfolk after the war. He lived to the age of ninety-eight, only passing away in 2015.

In the film, Hendley and Blythe steal a Luftwaffe training aircraft but are forced to land after running out of fuel. This incident was based on a break prior to the Great Escape by Walt Morison and Lorne Welch, members of a kriegie party that had marched out the compound gate disguised as workmen and their guards. Morison and Welch almost succeeded in stealing a Junkers trainer from a Luftwaffe airfield before being caught. Both were subsequently sent to Colditz Castle.

Just as the escapees in 1944 had frequently gone out in pairs, the film's final script would cleverly partner actors in pairings of opposites: Garner with Pleasence, Attenborough with Jackson, Bronson with English actor and singing star John Leyton, and McQueen with Scotsman Angus Lennie. Lennie was always convinced he was cast to make McQueen look taller. In the film, Lennie's character says he's five feet four tall. In reality, Lennie was only five feet one, and five-feet-nine McQueen towers over him on screen. Meanwhile, SBO Ramsey had to be a loner by the nature of his position, as did successful solo escapee Sedgwick.

The film was originally to be shot in California, but outdoor locations there didn't look right. In March 1962, a year behind schedule, it was announced that the shoot was being transferred to Bavaria Film Studios at Geiselgasteig, outside Munich, after German authorities offered incentives to attract filming there. All interior sets of huts, offices, the

Cooler, police cells and the tunnels were built there, mostly by Germans.

When the studio's back lot proved too small for the POW camp set, permission was gained from German authorities to shoot in a nearby national forest. One thousand trees were cut down to create a clearing where the Stalag Luft 3 exterior was built. After filming ended, 2000 pine seedlings were planted by the production company to regenerate the cleared area. The exterior set only represented one compound, and gave no hint of the fact that the real camp involved five compounds containing 11,000 prisoners.

World War Two vintage vehicles were found in Munich junk yards and restored. A 1937 German aircraft was reconditioned. A steam locomotive was rented, and condemned 1940s rail carriages renovated. The railway scenes would be shot on the Munich–Hamburg line between regular train services. At Brickhill's stipulation, Wally Floody was flown in by Sturges to be the film's technical adviser. Floody ensured that the camp buildings and layout looked authentic, and spent long hours with the set builders to ensure the tunnel set and its fittings were exact. Even though one side of the tunnel was cut away to allow filming, and it was built above ground on the studio floor, it was too realistic for Floody, who began having nightmares.

To play both German soldiers and Allied airmen, Sturges cast hundreds of Munich university students as extras. When their number was insufficient for some scenes, Sturges put grips, wardrobe assistants and even his script assistant in uniform. But it was the stars who caused him most trouble. James Garner rented a Bavarian chalet near Sturges', and bought himself a Porsche sports car, but was soon bored, complaining to the American press that there was no nightlife in Munich, and telling reporters he wanted to go home.

Garner was a pussycat compared to Steve McQueen, who constantly made petty demands, or went AWOL, driving Sturges mad. At one point, McQueen demanded the rollneck sweater being worn on screen by Garner. He didn't get it. Another time, Sturges had to send Garner to placate McQueen. Then, once shooting began, McQueen decided his role wasn't big enough and demanded that a motorcycle chase be written in for him. There was no motorcycle chase in the true story, but to keep McQueen happy Sturges had the episode created. It would, of course, provide some of the most iconic and memorable images from the film. In several of the chase scenes, McQueen even played one of the helmeted German riders pursuing his character.

As for the movie's storyline, it kept close to the facts when depicting preparations for the breakout. Only when it came to the escape itself did it lurch into runaway fiction. The bitter, snowy weather, which had defeated so many real escapees, was overlooked. The motorbike and aircraft-stealing scenes were pure Hollywood. The nationalities of the three successful escapees were changed to Australian, English and Polish. But it would all make for good box office. And Sturges would dedicate it to the Fifty.

Brickhill didn't go to Germany to visit the set or the shoot. In the depths of a bitter divorce wrangle with Margot, he was fearful that if he were to leave the country, if only briefly, her lawyers might use his absence against him and he would lose access to his children. As it was, his lawyers had to battle for months before Margot agreed to allow him access for more than a day at a time – Tim and Tempe would spend the May school holidays with their father.

For the two weeks of the holidays, Brickhill had intended that the children share his mother's bedroom with him at 41 George Street, having rented out 'Craig Rossie'. But Margot's lawyers specified that he could not sleep in the same bedroom as the children. The implication was that the heavy drinking and bashing that Margot accused him of might cause him to harm the children if he slept in the same room. To meet this requirement, Brickhill put the pair in his double bed, and he slept on a couch outside the door. After four-year-old Tempe pleaded with her father to sleep in the same room as them, Brickhill explained that he wasn't allowed. Tim, meanwhile, had taken to calling him 'Bardo', a nickname which apparently originated with Tim's schoolmates, who knew his father was famous for making Douglas Bader famous.

Brickhill felt especially guilty that his mother Dot had given up her bedroom for him. So that month of May, via a company he'd recently set up in Canberra, he purchased a £20,000 block of six flats at 54–56 Blues Point Road on McMahons Point. A stroll from the North Sydney business precinct, it was less than ten minutes from his parents' house by car. It had been recommended to him by his father-in-law, Edric Slater, who knew it well.

Renting out five of the flats, Brickhill retained one on the first floor for himself. His new home had a single bedroom, a bathroom, a living-dining area and small kitchen, and a harbour view to the west. It was a comedown from 'Craig Rossie', but as far as Brickhill was concerned it would only be temporary. His own needs were always only minimal. His past grand accommodation choices had been made to please Margot. Besides, he firmly believed that his family would be reunited and they all would return to his Palm Beach dream house.

Margot had by this time enrolled nine-year-old Tim in a private boarding school, Tudor House, at Moss Vale in the Southern Highlands. Over the winter Brickhill stayed ten days at Moss Vale to spend time with Tim over two successive weekends; the school wouldn't let Tim out during the week. Throughout this period, papers from Margot's lawyers continued to land in Brickhill's letterbox. They contained counterclaims to his counterclaims, and, now too, financial claims. According to Margot, Brickhill had a large property portfolio in New South Wales and England, and her claim listed 41 George Street among his Australian investment properties. This incensed Brickhill, who, in his response, pointed out that the George Street house was his parents' home, and it was owned by a trust of which Tim and Tempe were the beneficiaries.

When Brickhill's lawyers urged him to arm them with accusations to lob back at Margot, he steadfastly refused to allow them to bring up her 1952 affair at St-Paul-de-Vence. But he was coming around to the view that, out of spite, Margot had held back Mark Bonham Carter's *Reach for the Sky* report in 1953. Needing proof, in June and July he wrote increasingly fraught letters to Bonham Carter, asking him to search the Collins records to establish who received the report, where, and when.

Bonham Carter wrote back that, according to the firm's records, his report had been delivered by hand to Margot at Rodney House, Dolphin Square, on 16 July, the day before she left for Southampton. Brickhill begged proof for use in court; a receipt signed by Margot, perhaps. He remarked, in a 10 July letter, 'Things are a bit bloody at the moment. I wouldn't mind if the childer [sic] weren't also involved.'[306] Bonham Carter was unable to provide proof of delivery.

Brickhill became gripped with the fear that, in a quest for a fat divorce settlement, Margot's lawyers would tip his ailing parents out of their home. By August, while John Sturges' filming of his version of World War Two in Germany was going over time and over budget, in Australia the strains of the divorce war proved too much for Brickhill. He collapsed, suffering another breakdown. On 4 August, psychiatrist Dr John Kerridge admitted Brickhill to Cabarisha Private Hospital at Castlecrag on the North Shore. There, Kerridge proposed that Brickhill undergo electroconvulsive treatment.

'It can do no harm,' Kerridge assured Brickhill.[307]

After considering the idea for a while, Brickhill agreed, and over two-and-a-half weeks he underwent a course of electric shocks to the brain. Following this, he was moved to Kirribilli Hospital on the lower North Shore to convalesce. On a cocktail of prescribed drugs, Brickhill left hospital and re-emerged into the real world in early November after being hospitalised for three months. Fearful of losing his children, Brickhill would deny he'd had treatment for a mental condition, claiming that he'd been suffering from a virus all this time.

Through his lawyers, the now-recovered Brickhill sought to have Tim and Tempe stay with him over the Christmas-New

Year holidays. Margot agreed, but her lawyers stipulated that he sleep apart from the children and on the day of their return he must drop them off at 5.30 in the morning. To see his children, Brickhill agreed to all conditions.

On the day of their return, after their stay at McMahons Point, Brickhill had to rouse the children well before dawn.

'I hate being bundled off,' complained bleary-eyed Tim.

As they drove up the highway to Turramurra in the early morning darkness, both children told their father how much they loved and missed 'Craig Rossie', their house beside the water at Palm Beach.

'Don't worry, kiddies,' Brickhill responded, trying to remain upbeat, for his sake as much as for theirs, 'we will be alright, and back in the house with Mama.'

Tim seemed unconvinced. 'Bardo, why did you marry her?'

Brickhill attempted to steer the subject away from their mother.

But Tim would not be distracted. 'Mama says that a divorce is going.'

'Don't worry, Tim,' Brickhill replied, 'I don't think there is going to be a divorce.' At that time, he seems to have genuinely believed this would be the case, and that, as they had in the past, he and Margot would get back together. When Tim said that he would ask his mother whether or not she would divorce his father, Brickhill responded, 'Oh, you had better not talk about these things with Mama.'

He duly dropped the pair off at Turramurra at 5.30 am. As they parted, Tim informed his father that, when he was thirteen or fourteen, he would come to live with him.[308]

*

While Brickhill continued to be embroiled in family dramas, *The Deadline* was published in the UK. Some reviews were excellent. 'Breathtaking,' said London's *Evening News*. 'A winner,' said *Books and Bookmen*. 'Highly topical,' a more muted *Guardian* would say – for, that same year, there had been another attempt to assassinate President Charles De Gaulle in Paris.[309]

When Morrow published the book in the US in 1963, they would unaccountably fail to mention that Brickhill was the author of *The Great Escape*, which would burst onto movie-theatre screens just months after the novel's release. Nonetheless, *War of Nerves* would quickly sell out its first edition and be reprinted. In the UK, *The Deadline* would do well enough to go into Fontana paperback. Unfortunately, neither his first novel's writing nor its reception compared with that of his war books. Margot's assessment of Brickhill's hero Robert Mackay proved accurate. We never know Mackay well enough to either love or loathe him. The villain, meanwhile, is a shadowy, one-dimensional figure. And the book lacks Brickhill's earlier wit.

The plot, hinged on bio-terrorism, was clever, but decades ahead of its time. Brickhill's denouement was gripping, but a tale of political assassination in Paris didn't then attract mass British or American readership. In 1962, British readers were devouring spy novels. Ian Fleming's *The Spy Who Loved Me*, the latest and most sexually explicit James Bond novel, came out this year. So too did Len Deighton's first spy caper, *The IPCRESS File*, and John Le Carré's second, *A Murder of Quality*. Brickhill's hero, a sexually timid Australian mechanic who was the victim of events, not the master of them, stood no chance in such company.

Times, and tastes, would change. Nine years later, Frederick Forsyth, another ex-journalist, would publish a novel whose plot revolved around an attempt to assassinate the French president. As it happened, Forsyth's plot was inspired by the 1962 attempt on Charles De Gaulle's life that had coincided with the release of Brickhill's novel. Forsyth's *Day of the Jackal* would sell millions and be made into an equally successful movie in 1973.

Post-production on *The Great Escape* was completed in Hollywood in the first half of 1963, with, among other things, composer Elmer Bernstein recording the film's memorable musical theme, a tongue-in-cheek play on military marches. On 20 June, Sturges' movie opened in London. Two weeks later, on 4 July – not coincidentally, US Independence Day – and backed by a massive marketing campaign from United Artists, the movie launched across the United States. Quickly achieving box-office success, it was praised and panned by critics in equal measure. The Australian premiere was scheduled for the end of the year.

Brickhill had little time to enjoy the moment. Margot had discovered from Tim and Tempe that when they holidayed with their father they now stayed in his McMahons Point flat, not at their grandparents' home. Investigating the premises and determining that the flat had just a single bedroom and Brickhill lived alone, Margot's lawyers demanded that another person be present whenever he had custody of the children. Brickhill fought this, with the result that he was summoned to be questioned before a judge in the Supreme Court on 9 August.

Alec Shand acted for Margot. A tall young barrister and future Queen's Counsel, he possessed a bulldog reputation. By coincidence, Shand was an officer in the RAAF Reserve, and had seen his own parents divorce when he was twelve. Once Brickhill took the stand, Shand quizzed him on his income, especially in the light of the success of *The Great Escape* at the American box office. In court filings, Brickhill said he had largely been living on his investments since 1957. He had also said, truthfully, that his income from *The Great Escape* movie could currently be expected to range between the option fee of £1000 and an execution fee of £15,000. The final amount he received, he said, would depend on how well the movie did at the box office. Taking into account the small percentage of net profit the contract gave him, this was true.

But Shand, unfamiliar with the movie business, was unaware that film-rights contracts invariably specified that execution fees be paid at the commencement of principal photography. Principal photography for *The Great Escape* had begun the previous June. In the past, Brickhill had arranged for publishers to delay major royalty payments to defer and reduce his tax liabilities. Almost certainly, he'd asked Mirisch to delay paying the execution fee until after divorce proceedings had been terminated one way or another, to prevent Margot's lawyers from including that in any potential financial settlement.

'My assets have diminished considerably,' Brickhill stated in court. 'I do not have the funds anymore.' When Shand asked him why he was not producing income, Brickhill responded, pointedly, 'I am mostly engaged in litigation.' Divorce litigation, that was.

In his resonant voice, Shand asked Brickhill to describe the layout of his flat, and the sleeping arrangements when the children stayed over. Brickhill replied that the children slept in his bed and he slept separately from them. In describing the layout of the flat, he said it had a lounge room and a dining room, but when required by Shand to draw a diagram he revealed that there was a single living room made up of lounge and dining areas. Having caught Brickhill out on this, Shand asked him to detail a conversation in which Brickhill had instructed Tim not to tell his mother that they had been talking about her and divorce.

Realising that Tim must have told his mother about this conversation on the day of the 5.30 am return to Turramurra, Brickhill answered, 'I'm reticent to talk about it.'

Shand demanded to know why.

'Tim and his mother don't always get along very well,' Brickhill returned. He explained that Margot had complained to him that Tim was very difficult to handle after returning from visits with him. 'I worry that there will be reprisals on Tim.'

'Reprisals?'

'I am afraid she is prone to shouting,' said the author. 'She shouts a lot at Tim. I don't think he receives very much in the way of affection.' For the benefit of the judge, he added, 'My wife is not very emotionally stable.'

The judge required him to write down the conversation in question for the court, which he did, with reluctance.

Shand then moved to Brickhill's illness of the previous spring. 'A virus? What kind of virus was it?'

'Just a virus,' Brickhill replied.

When Brickhill wouldn't elaborate, Shand demanded, 'Was it not a nervous breakdown you suffered?'

Brickhill, terrified that he would lose access to Tim and Tempe if he told the truth, denied he'd suffered from mental illness. Shand then wondered why Dr Kerridge, a psychiatrist, had been his admitting physician, to which Brickhill replied that Kerridge was a friend as well as a doctor. At this point the judge intervened on Brickhill's behalf, telling Shand not to pursue this line of questioning.

Shand asked Brickhill to specify the drugs he was currently prescribed. Brickhill gave his current drug regime as Percodan for pain in arms and legs, antihistamines and sleeping tablets, plus Phenobarbital and a chloral-hydrate sleeping mixture. Shand pounced on this, saying that, surely, all this sleeping medication must knock Brickhill out at night. What would happen in the event of a medical emergency or a fire when the children were staying, and they were unable to wake him?

Brickhill countered that he was a light sleeper, even with medication, and could be expected to wake, or be easily awakened, in an emergency. 'My wife used to punch into me as I slept,' he went on. 'On several occasions I was awakened with a punch.'

Shand proceeded to call several of Brickhill's tenants to testify about the state of his flat, his drinking and the lifestyle he led. If Shand was hoping for damning revelations, he was disappointed. Brickhill's only female visitors were secretary-stenographers he employed, and tenants stated that, as far as they could see, Brickhill was a caring father when his children visited. Brickhill's lawyers would subsequently nip this attack in the bud by producing affidavits from several neighbours who were trained nurses, who stated they were available to help Mr Brickhill and his children at any time if the need arose.[310]

The court subsequently allowed Brickhill continued access to his children, and without the need for another person to be present. One battle had been won. But this war still had a long way to run.

25.

War of Nerves

THE IMMEDIATE RESPONSE to the publication of *War of Nerves* in the United States in 1963 was an approach to Brickhill by a Hollywood producer interested in acquiring the screen rights. Dick Berg was a young television screenwriter and producer who came to Hollywood in 1957 and made a name for himself writing the 1959–60 Universal Studios TV detective series *Johnny Staccato*, starring John Cassavetes. With a long-term contract with Universal, Berg had interested CBS in a weekly drama anthology TV series which became the *Bob Hope Chrysler Theater*, with Berg as an executive producer. Each episode, which would be introduced by Hollywood entertainment superstar Bob Hope, would be a single story, unrelated to those which preceded or followed it.

With the release of John Sturges' production of *The Great Escape* imminent, Brickhill's new book caught Berg's attention. In acquiring the screen rights to *War of Nerves*, Berg would have the option of later making a feature film, but at this point his interest was in a one-off, one-hour TV drama for the new CBS series. This would be like Fred Coe's 1951 TV production of *The Great Escape*, but shot on film.

Brickhill's timely story, gripping ending, limited number of characters and mostly interior settings made *War of Nerves* ideal for TV. The few Parisian exterior scenes could be shot on Universal's back lot, in its permanent European street set. Berg wasn't offering Brickhill the sort of money that Sturges was paying for *The Great Escape*, but money wasn't everything. Besides, there was the possibility of a second payday if Berg did later make a movie version.

For Brickhill, the appeal of having the legendary Bob Hope introduce his thriller to America's television audience was enormous. His agent and US publisher would have also pointed out that this could boost the book's sales. Besides, Berg was able to reel off the names of some of the biggest film and TV stars of the era who would be appearing in the first series of *Bob Hope's Chrysler Theater*: Rod Steiger, Angie Dickinson, Claude Rains, Piper Laurie, Jason Robards, Susan Strasberg, Bing Crosby, Shelley Winters, Mel Ferrer, Diane Ladd, Roddy McDowall, Vera Miles, Cliff Robertson, Eva Marie Saint and Robert Stack among them.

The seduction was complete when Berg named the two male leads he had in mind for *War of Nerves*. Playing Brickhill's hero, Robert Mackay, would be handsome, muscular matinee idol Stephen Boyd. Northern Ireland-born Boyd was famed for his Golden Globe-winning performance in 1959's blockbuster *Ben-Hur*, playing the role of Ben-Hur's friend-turned-enemy Messala, who perished in the famous chariot race. Boyd had co-starred in three movies in 1961–62, and in 1963 was conveniently between roles. *War of Nerves*' villain would be played by Hollywood-based French box-office star Louis Jourdan, who had made his name in the 1954 hit *Three Coins in the Fountain*, followed by another box-office smash, *Gigi*, in 1958. Most recently he'd co-starred in 1960's *Can-Can* with Frank Sinatra and Shirley MacLaine.

The behind-the-scenes talent that Berg would bring to *War of Nerves* was less well known to Brickhill. Berg would personally produce the drama, and he would use a young director he was championing. Sydney Pollack had a short directorial CV, but Berg was convinced he was destined for big things. Pollack would in fact become one of Hollywood's most celebrated movie directors, with hits including *They Shoot Horses, Don't They?*, *The Way We Were*, *Three Days of the Condor*, *Out of Africa*, *Tootsie* and *The Firm*.

Berg's director of photography would be established cinematographer William Margulies. The musical score would be written by another young man being fostered by Berg. John Williams had written memorable scores for TV series *Peter Gunn* and *Bachelor Father*, and in the coming decades would create some of the most recognisable film scores of all time: *Jaws*, *Star Wars*, *Superman*, *Jurassic Park*, *Schindler's List*, *Indiana Jones*, *Home Alone*, *Saving Private Ryan* and *Lincoln* among them.

The screenwriting department was not as strong. Berg, a writer at heart, himself penned scripts on yellow legal pads, and had input into the scripts for every episode in the series. Of necessity, he also used a number of screenwriters.

To write the teleplay for *War of Nerves*, Berg employed his writing protégé Mark Rodgers, an ex-cop whom Berg was convinced would, like Sydney Pollack and John Williams, go on to bigger things. He didn't, instead bashing out scripts for episodes of TV cop shows over the years, among them *Kojak*, *Ironside* and *Hawaii Five-O*.

To fit the story into the series' short-form format, Rodgers abridged Brickhill's novel. And to ensure it appealed to American audiences, he overlooked the fact that hero Mackay was Australian. Unhappy that Brickhill's villain was an Arab, Rodgers made him a Frenchman. Berg succeeded in convincing Brickhill that this would not impact on his overall storyline, which remained unchanged.

With the court having confirmed access to his children, Brickhill felt able to now briefly leave the country. To Los Angeles he went in the American autumn of 1963 to see his first fictional baby realised before the cameras. *War of Nerves* was shot relatively quickly at Universal Studios. In the process, Brickhill met members of the coterie with whom Dick Berg surrounded himself. Berg didn't have much time for actors, but he loved writers. One of his best friends was screenwriter Rod Serling, who gained fame and a cult following with *The Twilight Zone*. Berg and Serling played paddle tennis and gin rummy together every Saturday morning.

Brickhill returned to Sydney in time for the December premiere of *The Great Escape* at Hoyts' Paris Cinema on the corner of Wentworth Avenue and Liverpool Street. The *Australian Women's Weekly*'s young social columnist Ita Buttrose was there, talking to excited local celebrities. She noted the presence of author Paul Brickhill, unaccompanied.

But Brickhill didn't hang around to talk to Buttrose or other reporters. He had pressing personal matters to attend to.

By early 1964, the latest bombardment of paperwork from Margot's lawyers contained explosive accusations which so alarmed Brickhill's Pitt Street solicitor Dick McIntyre that he wrote 'See us' in the margin of Brickhill's copy of Margot's new filing. Margot claimed she'd returned to 'Little Barr' one evening with another couple to find Brickhill lying on a bed with their Norwegian maid. Margot's lawyers also stated they would be calling the couple to testify to this, in Britain, and to testify, along with a female English friend of Margot's, that they had seen Brickhill strike Margot on several occasions at 'Little Barr'.

Brickhill vehemently denied any impropriety with the maid. And he challenged the other side to produce any witnesses to testify he'd struck Margot in their presence. He was adamant that he'd never touched Margot in front of others, and that he'd never raised his hand to her again following his sworn commitment seven years earlier not to do so whatever the provocation. Brickhill had to wonder what had sponsored these latest allegations.

Only now did it dawn on him that Margot fully intended divorcing him. For she had recently been seen in the company of mutual friend Devon Minchin. Three years younger than Brickhill, a former 145 Squadron pilot in North Africa, Minchin had even penned a novel in 1944. Now the colourful and wealthy owner of MSS, Australia's first and largest security firm, which had the contract to provide security for the Beatles' upcoming 1964 Australian tour, Minchin would later write *The Money Movers*, a novel filmed by Bruce Beresford.

Friends had recently told Brickhill that, back in the second half of 1961, when Margot's letters had cooled and she subsequently flatly refused to join Brickhill in England, Minchin had left his second wife, Betty, whom he had since divorced. Margot was proposing to send Tim to Knox Grammar; Minchin was a former Knox boy. Putting two and two together, Brickhill demanded that Margot keep Minchin away from his children. She denied any impropriety with Minchin, but Brickhill, realising she'd found a replacement for him, now went on the attack. Counter-suing Margot on the grounds of desertion, he detailed a litany of alleged sins, starting with Margot's adultery with Douglas Gordon at St-Paul-de-Vence in 1952 and including bouts of uncontrolled hysteria, chronic lack of punctuality and wild champagne parties with her sister and friends at 'Little Barr' when he'd been absent.

Weeks passed, and then came a response from the other side – a white flag. Clearly advised that the value of a final divorce settlement would be diminished by any lack of honesty, Margot now acknowledged that she'd had sexual intercourse with Douglas Gordon, but declared she hadn't conducted adulterous relationships with anyone else. She also acknowledged she'd become hysterical at times during the marriage, that she had not always been punctual and that Brickhill had been generous with money. She also confirmed that she had indeed deliberately held back Mark Bonham

Carter's *Reach for the Sky* editor's report in 1953; because, she said, her husband had failed to give her promised funds. Now, too, Margot's lawyers advised that they would not be tendering the previously flagged evidence of English witnesses.[311]

A settlement was reached. As Margot dropped 'cruelty' from her suit, Brickhill withdrew his suit altogether and agreed to pay her £20,750 plus weekly maintenance for each child. He also agreed to cover Tim and Tempe's education expenses until they were nineteen, and to pay Margot's £2500 divorce lawyers' bill. Margot also received the contents of 'Craig Rossie' – both 'Craig Rossie' and 'Little Barr' were sold. The Sydney doctor who bought 'Craig Rossie' in 1964 still uses it today, as his weekender. Brickhill sold the Alfa Romeo for £600, and shipped the Jaguar to Australia.

On 20 July 1964, the Brickhills' divorce became official. Within months, Margot married Devon Minchin. As Margot Minchin, she receded from the spotlight. She and the children moved in with Devon and a son from his first marriage, Nick Minchin, a future senior Liberal Party senator and member of the Howard Government. Margot and her new husband would have two children together.

Two months after his divorce, Brickhill lost his father. George passed away at the age of eighty-five. Almost exactly a year later, eighty-year-old Dot would follow George. The house at 41 George Street, so important to them for so long, and to Paul, was sold.

26.

The Artful Dodger

IT WAS 1965 before Brickhill returned to his typewriter. After the huge worldwide success of *The Great Escape*, the movie that would, along with *The Magnificent Seven*, symbolise John Sturges' career, Brickhill decided he would write movies from now on. A forty-page treatment was nowhere near as exacting as a 350-page book. For his first subject, he chose the wartime adventures of his American Stalag Luft 3 friend Johnny Dodge, who'd passed away in 1960. Brickhill sent his completed treatment, *The Artful Dodger*, to John Sturges in 1966. Seeing it as a sequel to *The Great Escape*, Sturges promptly optioned it.

Via his new production company, Kappa Corporation, Sturges teamed with Mirisch to announce they would co-produce *The Artful Dodger*, with Steve McQueen and Warren Beatty being considered for the lead. Sturges wanted Stirling Silliphant to write the screenplay, based on Brickhill's treatment. Brickhill approved of Silliphant, who'd written several episodes of *Bob Hope Presents the Chrysler Theater* for Dick Berg before co-writing the script for Sydney Pollack's 1965 film directorial debut, *The Slender Thread*, starring Sidney Poitier and Anne Bancroft. Silliphant would later soar to prominence as writer-producer of the *Shaft* movies, and of *The Poseidon Adventure* and *The Towering Inferno*.

But the choice of Silliphant meant a long delay. Right through 1966, Silliphant was hard at work for Mirisch writing and rewriting the script for the Sidney Poitier/Rod Steiger feature *In the Heat of the Night.* That screenplay would win Silliphant a 1968 Academy Award. It would only be in March 1968 that Silliphant would be officially announced as screenwriter for Brickhill's project.[312] Even without a script, Warren Beatty soon came on board to play Johnny Dodge, giving Brickhill confidence the film would be made.

With the Dodge project stalled, Brickhill decided to write a screenplay, based on the adventures of another wartime colleague. Friends Jon Cleary and Morris West routinely wrote the screenplay adaptations of their novels. How difficult could it be? His subject would be Harry 'Wings' Day. Brickhill's typewriter was soon clacking away in a flat he purchased that year in the Lower North Shore beachside suburb of Balmoral. This modest apartment would be Brickhill's Sydney home for the rest of his life.

On 20 December, Brickhill celebrated his fiftieth birthday. By the end of 1966, he had completed two thirds of the

Wings Day screenplay. Only then did he make contact with Day, suggesting they meet to discuss the project. Day was spending the northern winter at a villa in Monaco, and he promptly invited Brickhill to come over and stay, telling him he was also working on a project with their former fellow kriegie Sydney Dowse. This latter news would have alarmed Brickhill. Concerned that Dowse might prove competition, Brickhill resolved to suppress his dislike of flying to get to Day as soon as possible. In the middle of February, he flew to London with script and typewriter in his baggage.

In London, on Wednesday, 25 January 1967, Brickhill caught up with an AAP colleague at his old Fleet Street workplace, and over a drink told him about his Wings Day project. Two days later, under the headline 'Brickhill's New Film', a news item about Brickhill's Wings Day project appeared in the Australian press.

'He said the script would be ready in two or three months,' reported the news service journalist, 'and the film would be produced by an American. He would later write a book, based on the script, and this would take him about a year.'[313] The likely producer concerned was John Sturges.

To Monaco went the expectant author, to a warm welcome from the courtly Wings Day. And a shock. The project with Sydney Dowse was Wings' biography, being written by Dowse under the pseudonym of Sydney Smith. Still, Wings was not overly happy with the way the book was panning out. Dowse's style didn't suit him, and he didn't like the way Dowse was portraying him. In contrast, Wings liked Brickhill's script and his approach. With his financial picture at the time not as bright as he would have preferred, Wings wanted both Dowse's book and Brickhill's movie to go ahead. He had a share of Dowse's proceeds from the book deal, and Brickhill was offering him fifty per cent of any film deal he secured based on his screenplay.

When Brickhill pointed out that each project was directly competitive, and Wings couldn't have both, Wings chose to go with Brickhill, the man with the Hollywood connections. By comparison, Dowse was an amateur. Wings made up his mind to get out of the deal with Dowse. But this wasn't going to be easy. Dowse and his publisher had a written agreement with Wings, and that included the film rights. When Wings showed the agreement to Brickhill, the Australian's heart sank. Dowse had contracted the book to Brickhill's own publisher, William Collins, and Brickhill knew what a tough cookie Billy Collins could be when it came to contracts.

Sure enough, Collins would not let Day out of the agreement. And Brickhill knew the publishers would take legal action against anyone infringing their rights to Day's story. Dowse's book, *Wings Day*, would be published by Collins the following year. It would do quite well, despite being error-strewn – when talking about the Great Escape, for example, Dowse got both the date and number of escapees wrong. He also got the date of Day's earlier Schubin break wrong. Not surprisingly, having become aware that Brickhill had almost snatched his Wings Day project from under his nose, Dowse failed to mention Brickhill in his tome. Read Dowse's book, and you would never know that Brickhill had been at Stalag Luft 3, let alone a leading light in X Organisation, or had authored *The Great Escape*, the book that gave Wings a public profile in the first place.

Brickhill was devastated. He had wasted the best part of a year on his Wings Day project, which had now to be jettisoned. His screenplay was worthless. However, he would have saved himself a lot of trouble had he contacted Wings earlier. Meanwhile, there was still no movement on the Johnny Dodge project.

Precisely what happened to Brickhill following this great disappointment is a mystery. He would not return to Australia until almost three years later. Brickhill himself said he went to live in Canada. Where and why is unknown. His relocation may have been inspired by Wally Floody, who encouraged George Harsh to move from the US to the Canadian town where he lived, which he did.

For the next two years, Paul Brickhill disappeared off the map.

27.

Back, for Good

WITH MOST CELEBRITIES now arriving in Australia from overseas by jet, the press' habit of grabbing interviews with 'name' arrivals by ocean liner had almost died out by 1969. Just the same, the first day of December was a Monday, a slow news day, and a reporter for Perth's *West Australian* thought he might get a few paragraphs out of one particular passenger aboard the Lloyd Triestino liner *Galileo* after it docked at Fremantle following a voyage from Europe. The reporter had spotted a name he knew on the ship's passenger list – Paul Brickhill. Fifty-two-year-old Brickhill, with receding hairline and gaunt face, looked tired as the reporter waylaid him with his opening question.

'Why are you back in Australia, Mr Brickhill?'

'I'm returning to Sydney to do more writing,' Brickhill replied, without elaborating.

Brickhill's hackles were raised when asked why he hadn't released more books in the past decade and a half.

'I've virtually finished writing books,' he airily replied. 'I found I was working for the tax man, the publisher and the accountant. I was getting little for myself.' He went on to lament the high cost of hardback books, and the high number of paperbacks vying for bookseller attention. 'I had intended concentrating on writing for films,' he explained, 'but the film industry is now sick.'

There was a little bitterness in his tone, as he declared that Hollywood was no longer the centre of the film world, with just a few features being made. Television movies were now all the rage, he growled, and low-budget sex films. He'd been told, no doubt by John Sturges, that big budget action movies like *The Great Escape* rarely as much as broke even these days.[314]

Brickhill wasn't bothered by the press when the ship docked in Adelaide, as it traced the same route around Australia's southern shores followed by the *Orontes* and *Fairsky* in years gone by. When the *Galileo* docked in Melbourne the following Friday, the local press likewise showed no interest in Brickhill, considering him a Sydney boy. By the same token, several Sydney papers thought his arrival would interest their readers, and sent reporters to meet him. And Brickhill, initially at least, was more amenable than he'd been in Fremantle. He gave Graham Cavanagh of the *Australian* a lengthy interview.

Cavanagh began by asking where Brickhill was heading, and why, after so many years in 'non writing exile'.

'I'm heading for a little pad in Sydney, where I'll settle down to write three books,' Brickhill replied. 'I pulled out of the rat race and I've been sitting around doing nothing since. But it's no kind of life, and so I go back to work.'

'A comeback?' The surprised Cavanagh pressed him to describe the trio of books he would work on, sixteen years after his last major work.

Brickhill declared he would pen two books with a war base, one of which would be made into a film by an independent Hollywood film company, and a third nonfiction work, which he wouldn't go into detail about. The latter was actually an update of *The Dam Busters* for Pan in London, stimulated by the release earlier that year by the British Government of thousands of pages of previously classified documents relating to 617 Squadron and its top-secret weapons. Although he revealed nothing to Cavanagh about any of his planned projects, the other two war books were Johnny Dodge's story, on which John Sturges still held a screen rights option, and Wings Day's story. Both offered rich source material for fiction, and Brickhill was thinking of turning them into novels.

When Cavanagh continued to press him about the reasons for his long absence from writing, Brickhill trotted out the same excuse he'd used at Fremantle. 'There was no point in working for the tax collector all the time,' he flippantly replied, keeping well away from the real reasons, the breakdown of both his mental health and his marriage.

He went on to list all the others who'd made big dents in his literary income – his lawyer, accountant, literary agents, friends and relatives – before complaining about all the approaches for money he'd received over the years. 'I just got sick of all the bums and the bludgers that gathered around.' He recalled a year when his accountant had told him he'd earned a quarter of a million dollars. 'Christ!' he'd thought at the time. 'The trouble that's coming out of this.'

Now that he'd uncorked his frustrations by letting fly at all who thought he was rich, he vented against those who thought that writing a bestselling book was easy. He couldn't imagine anyone holding down a full-time job and writing a book. There would not be any mental energy left for creativity, he said. And if there was, it would be destroyed by the demands of a man's wife and children. He returned to his hobby horse that too many books were being published, before the reporter's apparent condescension had him reminding Cavanagh that he had sold more than five million books in seventeen languages, and sold more hardbacks than Homer.

Brickhill added that his novel, *The Deadline*, had been published seven years back, so the last decade had not been entirely wasted. When Cavanagh responded that he'd never heard of that book, Brickhill dismissed it as 'a lesser work', and changed the subject. Cavanagh would mention Brickhill's lone novel in his subsequent article, but would get its title wrong, calling it *The Dead Lion*. To Brickhill, it had been more of a dead squib.[315]

The interview with Cavanagh had ruffled Brickhill's feathers. When he was shortly after tackled by a reporter from Sydney's *Daily Telegraph*, he was like a bear with a sore head. The exchange would stimulate an article describing him as 'kicking out at everything'. According to the *Tele*'s reporter, who exhibited a turn of phrase which emulated Brickhill at his best, the author 'approached his topics like an advancing circular saw'.

Brickhill allegedly said that: sex films were out – which contrasted with his statement at Fremantle that they were in; that Australia was dull and insignificant; that Hollywood was finished, but Australia could not hope to attract filmmakers. And he was quoted as saying, 'I loathe writing war novels, but for one I am committed to Hollywood.' In fact, he was hoping for the Dodge movie to go ahead so his novel could ride on the back of it. 'And the other is something I have wanted to get off my chest for some time.' This would be his answer to the Sydney Smith book that had wrecked his earlier plans for a Wings Day movie.[316]

The ship sailed on. By the time the *Galileo* terminated its voyage in Sydney, the far from complimentary *Daily Telegraph* article had appeared. A reporter from the *Sydney Morning Herald*, now a stable mate of Brickhill's old paper the *Sun*, ambushed Brickhill as he landed, with orders from his news editor to get a quote from the author from some fresh angle.

In answering the stock question about his reason for returning to Australia, Brickhill made his first mention of Tim, now fifteen, and twelve-year-old Tempe, with the paper reporting the following Monday: 'He will visit his two children and start work on two novels.' The brief article would be headlined 'Author Hits Textbooks'. After the reporter sought comment from him on the state of school textbooks, Brickhill observed that the Department of Education should employ 'rewrite men' to edit back the turgid prose in textbooks and inject a touch of humour.[317]

Brickhill then retreated to his Balmoral Beach apartment, opening it up for the first time in more than two years and letting the sea air and sunlight flood in. Setting his typewriter on the table and unpacking the notes he'd compiled after going through the declassified 617 Squadron material in London, he set to work on the rewrite of *The Dam Busters*.

Privately, Brickhill conceded that his return had brought him back to Australia for good. In the new year he applied to the Australian Government's Repatriation Department for treatment for ailments including what today would almost certainly be diagnosed as Post Traumatic Stress Disorder, or PTSD, stemming from his war service. In 1970, too, Brickhill finally registered to vote in Australian elections; another acknowledgement, to himself and the world, that he was home to stay.

He would still make the occasional overseas jaunt. His return by air from a trip to Hong Kong attracted snapping newspaper photographers at Sydney Airport when they spotted him sporting a huge black eye. He told the press he'd scored the 'shiner' after a fall while rushing to catch Hong Kong's Star Ferry. Those who knew him intimately would suspect the fall had more to do with his heavy drinking.

No longer could he dash off a manuscript in a few months. For a year and a half following his 1969 return to Sydney, Brickhill laboured over his rewrite of *The Dam Busters*. Still hooked on booze and sleeping-draughts, he found it a monumental struggle, but he rated himself the kind of person who never gave up. By the time he completed the task, he'd deftly inserted another 12,000 words into *The Dam Busters*. In early 1971, he completed correcting proofs of the new edition.

Pan's British editors subsequently disappointed him by deleting the photograph of 617 Squadron's Australians included in the original edition, and by dedicating a page to photographs of British COs of the wartime squadron, but leaving out Micky Martin, the unit's Australian commander.

This new edition of *The Dam Busters* would sell well, but would never achieve the sales figures of the original.

As for the two novels Brickhill had referred to in December 1969, he continued for several years to hold hopes of turning *The Artful Dodger* into a novel, and of novelising the Wings Day screenplay. John Sturges commissioned Stirling Silliphant to write eight screenplay drafts, briefing the screenwriter to have Johnny Dodge escape from Stalag Luft 3 and combine with the French Resistance to fight the Nazis. He also asked for loads of railroad action, having purchased a vintage steam locomotive. Retitling it *The Yards at Essendorf*, Silliphant set the story in European railway marshalling yards, and with each draft it had less and less to do with the true story Brickhill had committed to paper.

Unhappy with Silliphant's efforts, Sturges passed the project to TV dramatist Mayo Simon, asking for a climactic scene where two locomotives crashed headlong into each other. Mayo worked on it for another year before the project was shelved in 1970, with Silliphant blaming its failure on Sturges, who he thought was diverted by his passion for building a luxury yacht at the time. Sturges would blame both scriptwriters for failing to deliver a winning screenplay, plus lack of studio interest in another grand-scale war movie.

Without the incentive of the movie going ahead, Brickhill couldn't bring himself to tackle the Johnny Dodge novel, let alone start the Wings Day book. Increasingly, he cut himself off from most old friends, and had nothing to do with the Australian Society of Authors, which Morris West had helped found in 1964, serving as its inaugural vice-president, or with any other organisation. Brickhill's early meteoric success and subsequent lack of productivity were making him feel a has-been, and a bit of a literary fraud. He'd come to find the whole business of being a successful author and public figure a charade.[318]

West was again living overseas by the time Brickhill resumed residency at Balmoral, but another mate, Jon Cleary, returned to live in Australia in the 1970s, building a house on a block at Kirribilli opposite the new Sydney Opera House, only ten minutes by car from Brickhill. Cleary and others urged Brickhill to get on with his planned novels.

'Just sit down to the typewriter and write,' they said. 'It'll come.'[319]

It didn't come. And, irritated by his friends' seeming lack of understanding, Brickhill became a veritable hermit. No longer did he communicate with writing or air-force chums abroad. In the Balmoral apartment, years of unanswered letters gathered dust in ever-growing piles. Brickhill ignored invitations to Stalag Luft 3 reunions. Others, including Wings Day, Jerry Sage and Wally Floody, thrived on these get-togethers. At the twenty-fifth anniversary of the Great Escape held in London in 1969, which Brickhill didn't attend even though he was in England that year, Day and Sage had recited the *Jabberwocky* together, as they had in North Compound's theatre in 1943. They'd then proceeded to get very drunk, doing Cossack dances with arms around each other's shoulders.

Brickhill now passed his days swimming at the beach on his doorstep and putting in two-mile walks around the hilly Balmoral area. His flat was equipped with radio and TV, but he rarely turned them on, preferring to read newspapers and magazines for news on current affairs – on which he held strong opinions, even though he had hardly anyone to share them with.

He closely followed the career of his childhood friend Peter Finch, whom he still credited with starting him down the road to success as a writer. In many an interview over the years, Finch spoke with affection of growing up in Sydney, mentioning Norman Johnson, Donald Friend and others who had figured in his life back then. But never once did he mention Brickhill. That didn't seem to bother Brickhill, or diminish his regard for his childhood mate.

By 1976, Finch had garnered five BAFTA awards in Britain as best actor in various films, winning the latest for *Network*, in which he played the role of demented news anchor Howard Beale, delivering the epic line, 'I'm mad as hell, and I'm not going to take this anymore!' He won the best actor Golden Globe award that year for the same role, and was nominated for an Academy Award. Finch had been nominated for an Oscar before, but he was a hot favourite this time, despite his competition including Robert De Niro for the lead role in *Taxi*.

On 13 January, in Los Angeles where he lived, Finch taped a studio interview with Johnny Carson for that night's *Tonight Show* on NBC. The following morning, due to appear live on ABC's *Good Morning America*, he rose early, and walked to the Beverly Hills Hotel to meet director Sidney Lumet, a fellow *GMA* guest. There, sitting in a chair in the hotel's lobby, Finch suffered a heart attack. Rushed by ambulance to the University of California hospital, he was declared dead at 10.19 am. In the Academy Awards ceremony on 28 March,

Finch was awarded the best actor Oscar for his *Network* performance, becoming the first actor to receive the award posthumously.

Brickhill, like many others, was shocked and saddened by the sixty-year-old's unexpected death. There was so much that Brickhill had wanted to say to his old friend, and thank him for. Less than two years later, when he read in the Sydney press that American actor and author Elaine Dundy was in Sydney seeking out people who had known Finch, for a biography she was writing about him, Brickhill threw off the recluse's cloak and made contact with her, inviting Dundy to visit his Balmoral 'cave'.

The pair spent a memorable morning reminiscing together, for Dundy had known and worked with Finch. Not long after, when a British TV crew came to Sydney filming a segment on the Australian actor for a documentary series, Brickhill similarly invited them in, so that he could record his memories of, and gratitude to, his friend.

By 1978, Brickhill had given up hope of becoming a screenwriter. 'Don't kid yourself,' he said to himself, 'you're not going to make it.'[320] After John Sturges had successfully returned to World War Two with 1976's *The Eagle Has Landed*, based on Jack Higgins' bestselling novel, Brickhill had realised that Hollywood was a closed club, and he was nothing more than a beggar at the servants' entrance. This realisation sent him descending back into the depths of depression.

A year later, he picked himself up and went back to the biographical format that had served him so well thirty years earlier, pulling out his Johnny Dodge notes and starting work on a Dodge biography. He'd known much of Dodge's story for years – the Dodger had opened up to him during their Mediterranean sailing holiday together. To fill in the gaps, Brickhill now wrote to Dodge's family in Britain, who gladly helped. He then began bashing out a manuscript.

It was slow work. Much slower, and harder, than during his heyday. But it gave him enormous pleasure to be creating again. By March 1981, he had completed eighty per cent of the book – enough to agree to an interview about it with Liz Porter of Sydney's *Sunday Telegraph*. She visited him at the Balmoral flat for the interview, and was blown away by the fabulous views from his picture window.

Brickhill had bags under his eyes and looked a weary old man, but he was cheery, talking quickly and with enthusiasm. Still remembering the savaging he'd taken at the hands of the *Daily Telegraph* back in 1969 when he'd run off at the mouth on various subjects, he tried to keep the interview focused on Johnny Dodge's story. He only talked about himself to explain his role in the Great Escape and his long-term lack of productivity.

'Largely because of ill health, I haven't written anything of substance for years.' His creativity had been crippled by that ill health for twenty-six years, he said. 'By the time *Reach for the Sky* came out in 1954, I was coming apart at the seams.'

A *Telegraph* photographer snapped a shot to accompany Porter's article, showing Brickhill looking rather childlike as he played, at the photographer's behest, with a model Lancaster bomber. But Porter's article would paint a glowing picture. She went away from the Balmoral flat convinced that Brickhill had the makings of a new bestseller, and would open her subsequent article by declaring that Brickhill was about to make a literary comeback with a book 'even more thrilling than *The Great Escape*'.[321]

Her acclaim would prove to be a little premature.

28.

The Final Chapter

SYDNEY MORNING HERALD journalist David Langsam stood looking at the bland red-brick block at 6 Wyargine Street. Was this really where the famous Paul Brickhill lived? From the street, it looked just two floors high. But on the harbourside, five storeys tucked into the steep hill, with the ground floor sitting beside the golden sands of little Edwards Beach. Langsam had contacted Brickhill, requesting an interview. He would learn from the man himself that it was the fact he'd learned to fly in a Tiger Moth, as Brickhill had, that won him an invitation to the Balmoral flat. *Reach for the Sky* had inspired Langsam to fly, just as it'd inspired him to skip school in England to see Douglas Bader at one of his public appearances.

Climbing the concrete steps to the top-floor balcony, Langsam walked to the door to flat 53, and rang the bell. A figure appeared on the other side of the door's rippled glass. A portly man in thongs, shorts and open shirt opened the door. His moustache was grey, his face flushed. It was April 1982, and this was Paul Brickhill, looking all of his sixty-five years. Inviting Langsam in, Brickhill ushered him past the small kitchen to a living room just large enough for a dining setting and two winged-back, fabric-covered chairs facing each other beside a large picture window.

Langsam didn't know it, but the view from Brickhill's flat was reminiscent of that from 'Craig Rossie'. The beach sat immediately in front, complete with palm trees under the window. Rippling blue water extended as far as the eye could see – in this case, Middle Harbour and North Harbour stretching to Sydney's heads, and the Tasman Sea beyond. Topless bathers lay blithely on the sand below. Yachts lazed in sheltered coves. In the distance, green-hulled Manly ferries charged through the rolling ocean swell with the urgency of corvettes on convoy duty.

Brickhill credited this view with keeping him sane. 'If I had a unit,' he said to Langsam, 'say, in some side street in Gladesville or wherever, I would have gone around the twist years ago.'

Sitting in his armchair by the window, throughout their long chat Brickhill chain-smoked Summit Lights and drank Tab cola from a glass. By this time having recognised that he had a drinking problem, Brickhill no longer kept alcohol in the flat, and only drank when occasionally catching up with an old flying chum.

As Brickhill spoke quickly but quietly, skipping from one subject to another, Langsam found him conversant with current affairs. Politics, though, held little interest for Brickhill.

Neither did the books of other authors. A bookshelf in the flat was lined with foreign editions of his own books in twenty languages, and a statuette of Greco-Roman god Pan presented by Pan Books for his 1956 *Dam Busters* million-seller.

On a coffee table lay a copy of *Vogue* magazine, with Brickhill's daughter, Tempe, on the cover. After graduating from the NSW Conservatorium of Music, majoring in piano, Tempe had studied stage management at London's Royal Academy of Dramatic Arts before following her mother into modelling. There was no decoration in the flat's main room; the walls were starkly bare, like a hospital ward, or a prison cell.

Brickhill had only given three interviews in thirteen years – to Dundy, the British TV crew and Porter. He'd treated those as duties. Relaxing with Langsam, he opened up about his life and his 'horrors'. He confessed that even the slightest stress now floored him, and he expressed sympathy for former South Australian Premier Don Dunstan, who'd recently been diagnosed with stress disorder. Brickhill reckoned that, personally, he'd suffered a nervous breakdown in England and had never fully recovered since.

He also spoke of losing his religious faith following his divorce. 'The requirement to believe a literal interpretation of Christian folklore turned me away from the church and filled my newfound belief with guilt,' he confessed to Langsam.

Six years back, a book had come to him in the mail. *Blueprint* was a semi-religious school text with exercises on comprehension and creative writing. Brickhill never revealed who sent him the book – it may have been George Harsh, who became quite religious in his later years. Brickhill was much influenced by a poem by Sydney Carter in a section of the book that dealt with Jesus Christ. In fact, Brickhill said that it changed his life. Entitled *Anonymous*, Carter's poem condemned the Christian cult of personality. The poem told Brickhill that he was not alone in holding doubts. Taking up the Bible again, he'd used his talent for research to delve into the historical realities of its contents, a task that absorbed much of his time.

As Langsam quizzed him about his youth, Brickhill spoke of his childhood stutter. As they talked, the stutter returned, on just two words: Greenwich Point, a place which had meant so much to him. Although he spoke freely about the writing of his bestsellers, Brickhill wouldn't talk about *The Deadline*. As for new books, he said that for twenty-five years he'd been a literary cripple. 'Sometimes I would have a clear day and I'd be able to write a letter. But to structure a book and get down to it – impossible.'

When Langsam asked him what he was currently working on, Brickhill said he had a book eighty per cent written, but declined to go into detail. It was the Dodge biography, which had lain untouched since the Porter article. Porter's faith in him and the book had engendered massive self-doubt in Brickhill, and he'd set it aside to devote himself to answering his vast backlog of letters and fan mail which continued to roll in.

Yet, he told Langsam, he looked forward to completing the latest book, and was confident it would find a market. 'I'm determined to finish the job,' he assured the journalist. 'Properly.'

It would take him a while, he conceded. While he reckoned his mental health was now sound, physically he was declining, with his swims and walks less frequent than before.

Still, he remained upbeat as he escorted Langsam to the door. As they parted, he grinned, and, wagging the index finger of his left hand at him, reminded Langsam to confine his article to the facts: 'Now, mind, no line-shooting. Alright?'[322]

Six years later, *Superman* actor Christopher Reeve produced and starred in *The Great Escape II: The Untold Story*, a fictional four-hour NBC mini-series in which Johnny Dodge returned to Germany after the war to track down those responsible for executing the Fifty. Donald Pleasence was among the cast, this time playing a Gestapo man. Initially, Brickhill encouraged and advised Reeve, but as he learned more about what he was doing with Dodge, he was horrified.

'I fear they may use my name,' Brickhill wrote to Dodge's son Tony. 'Johnny would have been mortified.' He asked for his name to be removed from the credits.[323]

On the night of Tuesday, 23 April 1991, Paul Brickhill's heart gave out. He was seventy-four years of age. By the time of his death, debilitating back pain had forced him to give up swimming and walking. A battery-powered back brace had given him some relief. He died comfortably well off, lonely and unfulfilled. He never did submit the Dodge biography for publication.

From London to New York he rated brief obituaries. London's *Times* declared that he 'set a standard in the telling of popular war stories which has never been surpassed'.[324] The local press noted his passing, with only the *Australian* hinting at his later tormented years, headlining its obituary with 'War Writer's Ambition Unfulfilled', and quoting former *Sun* colleague Lionel Hudson, who recalled Brickhill's ambition to write the great Australian novel.[325]

Brickhill's children became the beneficiaries of his literary estate. After graduating from the University of Sydney, son Timothy worked in the UK. Later, he settled in New Zealand, land of his birth. In the 1990s, Tempe Brickhill became chief of the London operations of Japanese fashion designer Issey Miyake, before moving to Paris in 2010 to become CEO of Issey Miyake Europe and a director of the prestigious Fédération Française de la Couture.

29.

Upon Reflection

Many books have been written, and are still being written, in attempts to cash in on, or improve on, the products of Paul Brickhill's golden productive years of 1949–54. As if jealous of his enormous success, many others who have written about the same subjects have given Brickhill little or no mention, or credit. Few of these authors have shared Brickhill's insider experience or pain. Most have lacked Brickhill's focus on 'the guts' of a tale, and his skill to engineer a book that worked like an intricate self-propelled machine. None have possessed Brickhill's nose for a good story, his eye for detail, or his ear for humour. These skills were innate, born of a sensitive, stuttering child who could feel the pain of a lonely boy walking a dog around the streets of Greenwich Point. Skills which equipped him to construct tragedies that still leave the reader transported, inspired, uplifted. Brickhill made it look simple. It wasn't.

Many successful writers are unaware of their own formula for creating literary or screen gold, and are unable to replicate early successes. Similarly, when Brickhill attempted to emulate his novelist friends Jon Cleary and Morris West, his lone published novel contained a tolerably good story but lacked his earlier fascinating detail, the humour that had sustained desperate men in dark times, or the tragedy and sacrifice that had come hand in hand with victory in his nonfiction.

Brickhill himself felt that *Reach for the Sky* was his best work. In writing that biography, he'd discovered an additional string to his bow, the ability to show what made a man tick. From that springboard, he could have had a career writing illuminating biographies. Late in life he returned to the genre with his Johnny Dodge book, which was never published. Times had changed. Heroes were no longer in demand. The age of the antihero had arrived, just as it would in turn be overtaken in popular culture by the age of the superhero. Besides, Johnny had been dead for years by that stage, and there was no opportunity for Brickhill to spend eight months in combative but revealing interrogation of his subject, as he'd done with the juicily flawed Douglas Bader. After those draining Bader interviews, Brickhill had declared he'd never do that again; and he didn't.

Another factor would influence Brickhill's writing career. It is impossible to divorce a writer's personal life from their creative life. Each influences the other. Paul Brickhill's divorce ended his creative life, despite numerous attempts to subsequently kickstart it. Without the support of his mother, father and wife, he lacked the even emotional keel he so needed.

There is no doubt that Margot was his muse. Emotionally, during their marriage Margot and Paul come across as children posing as adults. When she was happy, he was happy, and produced his best work. He never married again, never found a new muse.

How then, after a space of more than sixty years, should we view Brickhill's work? All his books were born of different motives. *Escape to Danger* and *Escape or Die* were written essentially to please others. *The Great Escape* was a conscious attempt to honour the Fifty, and to create a full-time writing career. *The Dam Busters* was a means of maintaining employment as a full-time author. All were written quickly. *Reach for the Sky* was a much more studied work, an anxious entree into the world of the biographer, even though, following lengthy research, it too was relatively swiftly written.

Brickhill never consciously set out to create heroes. That was the by-product of his quest for central figures around which to build his narratives. And a product of the times. Michael Anderson, director of the screen version of *The Dam Busters*, explained the success of that movie with the view that, in 1955, the British public was in need of heroes.[326] Sixty years later, Australian critic Peter Craven recalled avidly reading Winston Churchill's history of the war along with *Reach for the Sky* and *The Great Escape* as he transitioned from King Arthur and Robin Hood to 'the remembered heroisms of the war'.[327] Such was the impact upon several generations of the hero Churchill, and the hero maker Brickhill.

Were the men and events that Brickhill wrote about truly heroic? British commentator Sinclair McKay said in 2013 that *The Great Escape* is now woven into Britain's cultural tapestry.[328] Yet this is a work embodying distortions and misrepresentations. It may have been a great escape, but it wasn't the greatest. The escape of 359 Japanese POWs from the Cowra camp in New South Wales was much larger. (All were subsequently killed or recaptured.) The greatest escape was the successful break by hundreds of American officers from Oflag 64 at Schubin in early 1945. And the Great Escape's three home runs were equalled by 1943's wooden-horse escape. Meanwhile, the Great Escape's tunnelling techniques, equipment and X Organisation departments such as forgery and tailoring were pioneered a year earlier at Schubin for the thirty-four-man Asselin tunnel escape.

Brickhill failed to tell his readers that half Stalag Luft 3's North Compound inmates wanted nothing to do with the mass escape, while many others had to be press-ganged into involvement. Brickhill estimated that five million Germans, directly and indirectly, were diverted from other duties to the search for the Stalag Luft 3 escapees. It's a figure without foundation, yet it's often been quoted over the years to justify the escape, its high cost in lives and its paltry success. A decade ago, British TV claimed 100,000 German troops were diverted to search for the escapees.[329] There is no proof of that claim, either.

The indications are that very few Germans devoted their sole energies to the search for the escapees. Most of the police, troops, home guard, farmers and Hitler Youth involved were already on the lookout for escaped forced labourers, German military deserters and the numerous downed Allied aircrew then falling to earth all over Germany.

In terms of tying up the military machine in Germany

and contributing to the defeat of the Nazis, the Great Escape had negligible, if any, effect. George Harsh never changed his view. In 1971, he said, 'I do not believe that what we did affected the eventual outcome of the war by so much as one tittle.' More than that, he was critical of the escape. 'I consider the Great Escape to have been an act of typical military madness, a futile, empty gesture and a needless sacrifice of fifty lives.'[330] Said Jimmy James, thirty-ninth man out of Harry: 'It seemed a high price to pay – three men gained their freedom and fifty were murdered.'[331] Les Brodrick, escapee number fifty-two: 'Was it worth it? No, with fifty men dead, I don't think so.'[332]

Was the Great Escape in fact the Great Folly? Henry Söderberg, Swedish international YMCA representative, regularly visited POW camps. He considered British officers at Stalag Luft 3 unreasonably 'arrogant' in dealings with their captors. Did this arrogance cloud thinking to a dangerous degree? At Schubin's Oflag 64, Söderberg found American prisoners much more pragmatic.[333] Most conserved their energy and resources for an escape with a genuine chance of success – their January 1945 break, when hundreds skedaddled east to join the Russians.[334]

No one disputes the courage of the Great Escapers. It's probable that, without Roger Bushell as the driving force, a record seventy-six RAF prisoners wouldn't have escaped the camp. Brickhill described Bushell as a brooding genius, absolutely autocratic and ruthless in his determination to get what he wanted, yet at times prone to bursts of charm. He could have been describing what psychologists characterise as a typical psychopath, people concerned with their own power and ends who charm and manipulate others to get what they want. Mind you, research by New York psychologist Paul Babiak suggests that one in twenty-five bosses in business and government today is a psychopath.[335]

In the end, it was Bushell's single-minded determination to himself be free that sent fifty men to their death. The night before the break, Sydney Dowse attempted to talk him out of it. 'Nothing doing, Sydney,' Bushell had irritably responded. 'I've lived for this, and I'm going.'[336] Was it incidental to Bushell's personal escape goal that the more escapees on the loose, the more the authorities would be tied up, and the more his own chances of making a home run would be maximised?

Brickhill knew exactly what Bushell was like. Yet to paint him as Machiavellian would have defeated his purpose of making *The Great Escape* a cracking read. Brickhill had tried a prosaic, journalistic approach to the escape with his BBC radio talk, then in his press articles and *Reader's Digest* piece, and lastly with the chapters about the escape in *Escape to Danger*. All to modest effect. To create a book readers couldn't put down, he had to portray all those who followed Big X into Harry as heroes. And in the process, Bushell, too, became a hero.

In writing *The Dam Busters*, Brickhill became aware that Guy Gibson grew big-headed following the dams raid, especially after the British Government sent him on an American publicity tour which culminated in his being treated like a film star in Hollywood. As a consequence, the government decided not to send any more of its 'heroes' on similar jaunts. And when Gibson arrived at a new command in 1944, he was so full of himself that to bring him down a peg or two his pilots stripped him of his trousers and tossed him out the door. Brickhill was likely to have also learned that Gibson was a philanderer who cheated on his wife. In *The Dam Busters*, he made no mention of any of this.

Meanwhile, some historians believe that Brickhill's influential book cast Bomber Command aircrew in such an heroic light that it made criticism of the morality of Bomber Command's bombing of German cities unpalatable.

As for Douglas Bader, was he a hero? By Babiak's definition, Bader, too, exhibited the traits of a psychopath. Even though Brickhill didn't hold back on Bader's dark side, many readers came to put the legless pilot on an heroic plinth. Was that more to do with them than with Bader, perhaps?

There's no doubting that Brickhill's legacy has staying power. *The Dam Busters*' movie theme has become part of the RAF band's repertoire. The theme of *The Great Escape* is the unofficial anthem of the England soccer team's band. Although why English football fans continue to jibe their German counterparts with 'Who won the war? We did!' is beyond Australian, New Zealand, American and Canadian sports fans, who have grounds to chant a similar refrain, but never do.

In 2005, Brickhill's son and daughter sold *The Dam Busters* film rights to British broadcasting icon Sir David Frost. He was partnered by Sir Peter Jackson, Kiwi producer and director of the *Lord of the Rings* and *Hobbit* movies, and a huge fan of the original film. Announcing production of a remake, they brought in British actor and TV personality Stephen Fry as scriptwriter. Jackson's Weta Workshop began construction of props. Jackson was then sidelined by production of the *Hobbit* movies, and David Frost passed away in 2013.

As recently as August 2014, Jackson said he still planned to make the movie. Today, twenty full-scale replica Lancaster bombers built by WETA sit in a warehouse in Wellington, New Zealand, waiting for Jackson's filmmakers to go to war. The film, if remade, will have to negotiate moral issues, not least the drowning of many innocent foreign workers as a result of the raid. Fry has already said that the name of Guy Gibson's labrador would be changed from Nigger to Digger, to address American sensibilities. Meanwhile, with 1963's *Great Escape* movie still a Christmas staple on British TV, in 2013 the BBC announced it would make a TV mini-series based on *The Great Escape*. There have been no subsequent announcements.

Paul Brickhill was no great intellectual. But he was a skilled and influential craftsman. He received no literary awards, and not a single honour was conferred on him by either the British or Australian governments – no OBE or Order of Australia for Brickhill the hero maker. He was a flawed man, who drank to excess, and raised his hand to his wife – for which he despised himself. Yet, if awards were restricted to those without flaws, few, if any, would be presented. Without Brickhill, the mass escape from Stalag Luft 3, the bombing of the Ruhr dams and the career of a legless pilot might have been swiftly forgotten in the post-war years. Because of him, they live on. So, too, should Brickhill's memory.

Appendix: The Works of Paul Brickhill

BOOKS
Escape to Danger (With Conrad Norton). Faber & Faber, 1946
The Great Escape. Evans Brothers, 1950
The Dam Busters. Evans Brothers, 1951. Revised, Pan, 1971
Escape or Die. Evans Brothers, 1952
The Sunburnt Country (Contributor). William Collins, 1953
Reach for the Sky: The Story of Douglas Bader. William Collins, 1954
The Deadline. William Collins, 1962. Published as *War of Nerves* in the USA, William Morrow, 1963

RADIO ADAPTATIONS
The Great Escape. Australasian Radio Productions, 1953
The Dam Busters. Australasian Radio Productions, 1953
Reach for the Sky. Australasian Radio Productions, 1954

TELEVISION & FILM ADAPTATIONS
The Great Escape, Philco-Goodyear TV Playhouse, NBC TV, 1951
The Dam Busters. Associated British Pictures Corporation, 1955
Reach for the Sky. Rank Organisation, 1956
The Great Escape. Mirisch Corporation-United Artists, 1963
War of Nerves. Bob Hope Chrysler Theater, CBS TV, 1964

Notes

1: Shot Down

1. JU to author, 2 December 2014.
2–5. Brickhill and Norton, *Escape to Danger*.
6. Bruckshaw's eyewitness account is in Squadron Leader Harper's 21 March 1943 report; Brickhill's Casualty File. Norman Franks, editor of *War Diaries of Neville Duke*, incorrectly states that Brickhill was shot down by an Me 109 flown by Oberleutnant Heinz-Edgar Berres of JG77. Berres shot down another 242 Wing Spitfire that day, at 13.23 hours.
7–8. *Escape to Danger*.
9-10. Squadron Leader Harper's report.
11–14. *Escape to Danger*.

2: Ink in the Blood

15. Launceston *Daily Telegraph*, 11 July 1908.
16. Launceston *Daily Telegraph*, 18 June 1883.
17. *North Western Advocate & Emu Bay Times*, 11 December 1903.
18. *Sydney Morning Herald*, 26 April 1905.
19. *Examiner*, 6 March 1905.
20. Brickhill mentions a white feather in 1939 when expressing no desire to enlist. Letter to Del Fox following Speedo Ball.
21–23. Sparrow, *Crusade for Journalism*.
24. Ibid. And *Table Talk*, Melbourne, 8 February 1917.

Notes

25. Sparrow.
26. Port Pirie *Recorder*, 17 March 1952.
27. *Recorder*, 27 April 1953.
28. Adelaide *Mail*, 12 November 1927.

3: Peter and Paul, the Apostles of Individualism

29. Dundy, in *Finch, Bloody Finch*, put Peter Finch's home on the corner of Lawrence and Wallace streets, but local historians believe it was on the corner of Lawrence and George.
30–32. Dundy, *Finch, Bloody Finch*.
33–34. *Sydney Morning Herald*, 8 December 1969.
35. Dundy. And *People*, 20 May 1953.
36. *Age*, 1 May 1982.
37. Dundy.

4: Wiped Out

38. Dundy.
39. *Sun-Herald*, 8 August 1954.
40. Dundy.
41. *Sun-Herald*, 8 August 1954.
42–43. Dundy.
44. *Australasian Post*, 20 May 1953.
45–46. Hetherington, *Forty-Two Faces*.
47–48. PB to DF, 1939.
49. Obituary, *Australian*, 25 April 1991.

5: Flying Officer Brickhill

50. Hetherington.
51. *Albury Banner, Wodonga Express & Riverina Stock Journal*, 11 April 1941. Sismey ended up piloting flying boats and was shot down off the Algerian coast flying a Catalina. Surviving the war, he captained the Australian Services cricket team that played in England in 1945.
52. *Daily Advertiser*, Wagga Wagga, 8 September 1941.
53–54. *Age*, 1 May 1982.
55. rcafuplands.blogspot.com.
56. *Ottawa Citizen*, 2 September 1941.
57. *Examiner*, 7 November 1941.
58–59. *Escape to Danger*. In reality, he probably said 'Christ!' rather than 'Gosh!'.

6: Spitfire Pilot

60. Dahl, *Over to You*, 'Death of an Old, Old Man.'
61. Obituary, London *Times*, 26 April 1991.
62. Johnson, *Wing Leader*.

63. *Escape to Danger.*
64. JU to author, 2 December 2014.
65. PB to DF, 28 January 1943.
66. AWM Oral History.
67. Duke, *War Diaries of Neville Duke*. Duke named none of the Australians at this party, but it's hard to imagine that hard-drinking Brickhill wasn't one of them, especially after Duke had noted Brickhill's earlier whisky donation in his diary.
68–70. PB to DF, 28 January 1943.
71. *Escape to Danger.*
72. Duke.
73. 'A Cobra in the Sky.'
74. Brickhill, footnote to *Reach for the Sky*. The lordly officer's identity is unclear; several Guards officers were captured in Tunisia.

7: In the Bag
75. Williams, *The Tunnel*.
76. Brickhill said little of his time at Dulag Luft. This account of the interrogation process is taken from George Harsh's experience, in *Lonesome Road*. Brickhill's interrogation likely took similar lines. The efficient Abwehr, German military intelligence, collected basic information about Allied servicemen from sources such as British newspapers and wire services. As for the greatcoat and scarf given to Brickhill, he certainly wasn't wearing these when captured in Tunisia, but was wearing them on arrival at Stalag Luft 3 from Dulag Luft – they are shown in the photograph taken of him by the Luftwaffe that day.
77. Williams.
78. Sydney *Sunday Telegraph*, 15 March 1981.

8: Welcome to Stalag Luft 3
79. Brickhill, 'POW Goes Back . . . How the Germans Have Changed!' Adelaide *News*, 24 December 1945.
80. In the singular, Brickhill spelled it 'kriegy', but 'kriegie' has become the norm.
81. This was how George Harsh was greeted when he arrived at Stalag Luft 3. Harsh, *Lonesome Road*.
82–83. Brickhill, *The Great Escape*.

9: The Tunnel Game
84. Sage, *Sage*.
85. *Escape to Danger.*
86. Sage.
87. *The Great Escape.*

Notes

88. Brickhill & Michie, 'Tunnel to Freedom', *Secrets & Stories of the War*.
89. *The Great Escape*.

10: In the Light of Day
90. Smith, *Wings Day*.
91. Sage.
92. *Escape to Danger*.
93. Harsh.
94–95. *The Great Escape*.
96. Brickhill made a point of mentioning that Van der Stock wore an RAAF greatcoat as part of his escape kit, and noted that another non-Australian escapee wore blue RAAF trousers during his escape bid. In writing *The Great Escape*, Brickhill made no mention of his own part in any aspect of the escape until the revised 1963 film tie-in edition. So it's no surprise he made no mention of personally sharing these items with colleagues.
97. Ash, *Under the Wire*.
98. Smith.
99. PB to DF, 27 November 1943.

11: The Great Escape
100. *Sydney Morning Herald*, 8 September 1945.
101. Differing accounts variously put the number purged at 19, 20 and 24.
102. Smith.
103. Without offering a source, Vance, in *A Gallant Company*, claimed that Brickhill voluntarily withdrew. This is contradicted by Brickhill's own accounts.
104. *The Great Escape*.
105. Smith.
106. *The Great Escape*.

12: Counting the Cost
107. 'POW Goes Back.' This was Brickhill's first take on Von Lindeiner's rant, written in 1945. Five years on, in *The Great Escape*, he would give a slightly different version of the commandant's words, apparently provided by one or more of the men caught at the tunnel exit.
108. Jack Lyon, *Great Escape: The Untold Story*. Granada TV, 2001.
109. Brickhill and others stated that Massey saw Oberst Braune, who shortly after became full-time commandant. Evidence presented at the Nuremburg War Trials on 4 March 1946 shows that it was actually acting commandant Cordes who Massey saw that day. Walton and Eberhardt, in *From Commandant to Captive*, give Cordes' first name as Erich.

110. Brickhill, Foreword to 1963 Crest edition of *The Great Escape*.
111. 'POW Goes Back.'
112. Brickhill, *The Dam Busters*.

13: March or Die

113. Brickhill said in *The Great Escape* that evacuation began on 26 January, but in his 22 June 1945 interview at 11PDRC he correctly gave the date as 27 January.
114. Gammon, *Not All Glory*.
115. *Escape to Danger*.
116. Hetherington.
117. Brickhill, 'POW Goes Back.'
118. Ash.
119. *The Great Escape*.

14: A Friendly Interrogation

120. JU to author, 2 December 2014.
121. Brickhill Casualty File.
122. *Age*, 1 May 1982.
123–124. PB to DF, 27 May 1945.
125. Brickhill mentioned this letter from home accusing Mary Callanan of 'consorting' with American servicemen during his divorce proceedings. See Divorce Papers.
126. Parliamentary Debates (Hansard), House of Commons, 23 June 1944.
127–128. 'Anzacs Calling: Tunnel Escape from Stalag Luft 3.'
129–131. JU to author, 2 December 2014.
132. Brickhill's own story, as Ted B, is in Chapter 18 of *Escape to Danger*. On 22 June 1945, he wrote the basic details of his own last flight and downing in the report he made during his RAAF debriefing at Brighton. Those details accord in every way with the story he wrote about 'Ted B's last sortie.
133. Transcript of BBC talk of 7 June 1945.
134. *Escape to Danger*.
135. *Sun-Herald*, 29 November 1959.
136. PB to ADF (undated), 1946.

15: The Man Who Came Back

137–140. 'POW Goes Back.'
141. Harris, *Bomber Offensive*.
142–148. 'POW Goes Back.'
149–150. Brickhill, 'Doctors Fight to Save Europe from 'Flu', *Newcastle Sun*, 22 December 1945.

Notes

151. Brickhill, 'Berlin Family's Drab Xmas Outlook,' Adelaide *Mail*, 22 December 1945.
152–153. Brickhill, 'Glassy-Eyed People of Berlin Have Now Ceased to Care,' *Newcastle Sun*, 28 December 1945.
154–155 Brickhill, 'No Home Here for Herr Laver,' Adelaide *Mail*, 12 January 1946.
156–157. Bean, 'SA Woman Returning from Berlin,' Adelaide *Mail*, 12 January 1946.
158. Brickhill, 'Do "Jungle Drums" Guide Jews?', Adelaide *Mail*, 12 January 1946.
159. Brickhill, 'Nazi Leaders Plotting to Rat on Mates,' Adelaide *Mail*, 16 February 1946.
160. *People*, 20 May 1953.
161–162. 'Nazi Leaders Plotting to Rat on Mates.'
163. *Newcastle Sun*, 12 March 1946.
164. Brickhill, 'Red Minority Has Hungary in Its Grip,' Adelaide *Mail*, 16 March 1946.
165. *Newcastle Sun*, 5 December 1946.
166. Brisbane *Courier Mail*, 3 May 1982.
167. *Sunday Mail*, Brisbane, 20 December 1953.
168. Hetherington.

16: Back in England

169. *People*, 20 May 1953.
170. *The Great Escape*, Crest 1963 edition.
171. *People*, 20 May 1953.
172. *The Dam Busters*.
173. *People*, 20 May 1953.
174. *The Great Escape*, Foreword to 1963 Crest edition.

17: Enter the Author and Wife

175–176. Harsh, Introduction to *The Great Escape*, 1963 Crest edition.
177. Divorce Papers. Margot disputed this.
178–179. Divorce Papers.
180. *People*, 20 May 1953.
181. Humphries obituary, London *Telegraph*, 21 February 2008.
182. London *Daily Mail*, 11 October 2011.
183. In *The Dam Busters*, for Wallis' security, Brickhill stated that Wallis lived at Weybridge, Surrey, location of the Vickers-Armstrong factory.
184. *The Dam Busters*, Pan revised edition, 1983.
185. Foreword to *The Dam Busters*.
186. Review extracts taken from *The Great Escape*, 1995 Sheridan edition.

187. 9 October 1950.
188. Review extracts taken from *The Great Escape*, 1963 Crest edition.
189. Dundy.
190. Divorce Papers.
191. *The Dam Busters*.
192. Brisbane *Sunday Mail*, 20 December 1953.
193. Divorce Papers.

18: Bader, the Man with Tin Legs
194. Brickhill, 'Getting to Grips with Amazing Bader.' *Examiner*, 27 March 1954.
195–196. Turner, *Douglas Bader*.
197. London *Daily Mail*, 14 March 2013.
198. Ashcroft, *Heroes of the Skies*.
199. Gammon.
200. 'Getting to Grips with Amazing Bader.'
201. Ramsden, *The Dam Busters: A British Film Guide*.
202. Turner.
203. Graham, *Memoirs of a Private Man*.
204. Greenfield, *A Smattering of Monsters*.
205. Embry, Preface, *Escape or Die*.
206. H. E. Bates, Introduction, *Escape or Die*.
207. *Australian*, 6 December 1969.
208–209. *Age*, 26 June 1954.
210–214. 'Getting to Grips with Amazing Bader.'
215. Dundy.
216. Starck, *Proud Australian Boy*.
217. Divorce Papers.
218–219. Ibid. This was Brickhill's version of events.
220–222. 'Coming to Grips with Amazing Bader.'
223–224. Turner.
225. *Age*, 26 June 1954.
226–227. Divorce Papers.

19: Reaching for the Sky
228. PB to WC, 28 January 1953.
229. *People*, 20 May 1953.
230. PB to WC, 28 January 1953.
231. *Age*, 26 June 1954.
232. *Sun-Herald*, 29 November 1959.
233–234. *Australian Women's Weekly*, 1 April 1953.
235. Divorce Papers.
236–238. *People*, 20 May 1953.

239. Mrs Dorothy Grace Joy.
240–241. PB to WC, 31 March 1953.
242. *Sydney Morning Herald*, 5 April 1953.
243. 'Getting to Grips with Amazing Bader.'
244. PB to WC, 22 June 1953.
245. 'Getting to Grips with Amazing Bader.'
246–247. PB to WC, 23 June 1953.
248. Turner.
249. Divorce Papers.
250. *Sunday Herald*, 12 July 1953.
251. From a 7 July 1953 letter by Collins to Brickhill.
252. PB to MBC, 24 April 1962.
253. PB to WC, 31 August 1953.
254. Adelaide *News*, 17 August 1953.
255. *Argus*, 20 August 1953.
256. PB to WC, 31 August 1953.
257. *Northern Champion*, 8 September 1953.
258. PB to WC, 31 August 1953.
259. DH to WC, 7 September 1953.
260. 'Getting to Grips with Amazing Bader.'
261. Divorce Papers.
262. 26 November 1953.

20: The Dam Busters Crisis
263. *Newcastle Sun*, 7 January 1954.
264. Adelaide *News*, 24 April 1954.
265. Divorce Papers.
266. Greenfield.
267. *Barrier Miner*, 27 May 1954.
268. PB to JP, 15 April 1954.
269–270. Divorce Papers.
271. PB to WC, 28 August 1954.
272. PB to WC, 7 August 1954.
273. MB to WC, 8 August 1954.
274. 9 September 1954.
275. *Daily Mail*, 2 November 1954.
276. Humphries obituary, *Times*, 21 February 2008.
277. *Daily Express*, 2 November 1954.
278. PB to WC, 2 December 1954.

21: A Slap in the Face
279. Divorce Papers.
280. *Borehamwood & Elstree Times*, 16 April 2013.

281–282. Ramsden.
283. *New Statesman*, 28 May and 9 July 1955.
284. Divorce Papers.

22: End of Exile
285–291. Divorce Papers.

23: Return to Oz
292. Lovell, *Escape Artist*.
293–294. Gulick, *Sixty-Four Years as a Writer*.
295. Lovell.
296. Divorce Papers.
297. ML to author, 4 November 2014.
298. Divorce Papers.
299. ML to author, 4 November 2014.
300. Divorce Papers.
301. PB to ML, 18 July 1960.
302. Lovell.
303–306. Divorce Papers.
307. PB to MBC, 24 April 1962.
308. MBC to WC, 1 May 1962.

24: John Sturges' Great Escape
309. PB to MBC, 10 July 1962.
310–311. Divorce Papers.
312. Review extracts taken from 1964 Fontana edition.
313. Court transcript, Divorce Papers.

25: War of Nerves
314. Divorce Papers.

26: The Artful Dodger
315. *Watertown Daily Times*, 15 March 1968.
316. *Canberra Times*, 27 January 1967.

27: Back, for Good
317. *West Australian*, 2 December 1969.
318. *Australian*, 6 December 1969.
319. *Daily Telegraph*, 6 December 1969.
320. *Sydney Morning Herald*, 8 December 1969.
321–323. *Age*, 1 May 1982.
324. *Sunday Telegraph*, 15 March 1981.

28: The Final Chapter
325. *Age*, 1 May 1982.
326. Carroll, *The Dodger*.
327. 26 April 1991.
328. 26 April 1991.

29: Upon Reflection
329. Ramsden.
330. *Sunday Age*, 15 February 2015.
331. London *Telegraph*, 19 February 2013.
332. 'Great Escape: The Untold Story.'
333. Harsh.
334. *Canberra Times*, 25 March 1984.
335. London *Telegraph*, 12 April 2013.
336. Diggs, *Americans Behind the Barbed Wire*.
337. *See* Dando-Collins, *The Big Break*.
338. Babiak, *Snakes in Suits*.
339. Smith.

Bibliography

BOOKS

Alomes, S., *When London Calls: The Expatriation of Australian Creative Artists in Britain*. Cambridge, CUP, 1999.

Ash, W., with B. Foley, *Under the Wire: The Wartime Memoir of a Spitfire Pilot, Legendary Escape Artist, and 'Cooler King'*. London, Bantam, 2005.

Ashby, J., and A. Higson (editors), *British Cinema Past and Present*. London, Routledge, 2000.

Ashcroft, M., *Heroes of the Skies*. London, Headline, 2012.

Babiak, P., *Snakes in Suits: When Psychopaths Go to Work*. New York, Harper, 2007.

Bevan, I. (editor), *The Sunburnt Country. Profile of Australia*. London, Collins, 1953.

Branson, R., *Reach for the Skies: Ballooning, Birdmen & Blasting into Space*. London, Virgin, 2010.

Brickhill, P., *Escape or Die*. London, Evans Brothers, 1952.

Brickhill, P., and C. Norton, *Escape to Danger*. London, Faber & Faber, 1946.

Brickhill, P., *Reach for the Sky: The Story of Douglas Bader DSO, DFC*. London, Collins, 1954.

Brickhill, P., and A. Michie, 'Tunnel to Freedom,' *Secrets & Stories of the War*. London, Reader's Digest, 1963.

Brickhill, P., *The Dam Busters*. London, Oldhams, 1952.

Brickhill, P., *The Dam Busters* (Revised edition). London, Pan, 1983.

Brickhill, P., *The Deadline*. London, Collins, 1962.

Brickhill, P., *The Great Escape*. New York, Norton, 1950.

Brickhill, P., *The Great Escape* (Movie tie-in edition). Greenwich, Fawcett, 1963.

Bibliography

Brickhill, P., *The Great Escape*. London, Random House, 1979.
Brickhill, P., *War of Nerves*. New York, Morrow, 1963.
Carroll, T., *The Dodger: The Extraordinary Story of Churchill's Cousin and the Great Escape*. Edinburgh, Mainstream, 2012.
Confoy, M., *Morris West, Literary Maverick*. Milton, Wiley, 2005.
Cooper, A., *The Dam Buster Raid: A Reappraisal, 70 Years On*. Barnsley, Pen & Sword Aviation, 2013.
Dahl, R., *Over to You*. Harmondsworth, Penguin, 1973.
Dando-Collins, S., *The Big Break: The Greatest WWII Escape Story Never Told*. New York, St Martin's, 2016.
Diggs, J. F., *Americans Behind the Barbed Wire*. New York, iBooks, 2000.
Duke, N., *The War Diaries of Neville Duke*. London, Grub Street, 1995.
Dundy, E., *Finch, Bloody Finch*. London, Michael Joseph, 1980.
Galland, A., *The First and the Last*. London, Methuen, 1955.
Gammon, V., *Not All Glory: True Accounts of RAF Airmen Taken Prisoner in Europe, 1939–1945*. London, Arms & Armour, 1996.
Gibson, G., *Enemy Coast Ahead*. London, Michael Joseph, 1946.
Graham, W., *Memoirs of a Private Man*. London, Macmillan, 2003.
Greenfield, G., *A Smattering of Monsters: A Kind of Memoir*. London, Little Brown, 1995.
Gulick, B., *Sixty-Four Years a Writer*. Caldwell, Caxton, 2006.
Harris, A., *Bomber Offensive*. London, Collins, 1947.
Harsh, G., *Lonesome Road*. Norton, New York, 1971.
Hetherington, J., *Forty-Two Faces: Profiles of Living Australian Writers*. Melbourne, Cheshire, 1962.
James, A. B., *Moonless Night: One Man's Struggle for Freedom 1940–45*. Barnsley, Pen & Sword, 2006.
Johnson, J. E., *Wing Leader*. Feltham, Hamlyn, 1979.
Kee, R., *A Crowd is Not Company*. London, Cardinal, 1982.
Killen, J., *The Luftwaffe: A History*. London, Sphere, 1969.
Kurowski, F., *Luftwaffe Aces: German Combat Pilots of World War II*. Mechanicsburg, Stackpole, 2004.
Lovell, G., *Escape Artist: The Life & Films of John Sturges*. Madison, University of Wisconsin Press, 2008.
Mackenzie, S. P., *The Battle of Britain on Screen*. Edinburgh, Edinburgh University Press, 2007.
Mayer, S. L., and M. Tokoi (editors), *Der Adler, The Luftwaffe Magazine*. London, Bison, 1977.
Meltesen, C. R., *Roads to Liberation from Oflag 64*. San Francisco, Oflag 64 Press, 2003.
Pearson, S., *The Great Escape: The Life and Death of Roger Bushell*. London, Hodder & Stoughton, 2014.
Price, A., *Luftwaffe Handbook, 1939–1945*. London, Ian Allan, 1977.

Ramsden, J., *The Dam Busters, A British Film Guide.* London, Tauris, 2002.
Rubin, J., *Combat Films: American Realism, 1945–2010.* Jefferson, McFarland, 2011.
Sage, J., *Sage.* Wayne, Standish, 1985.
Segaloff, N., *Stirling Silliphant: The Fingers of God.* Albany, Bear Manor, 2013.
Smith, G. (editor), *Military Small Arms.* London, Salamander, 1994.
Smith, S., *Wings Day.* London, Collins, 1968.
Sparrow, G. (editor), *Crusade for Journalism: Official History of the Australian Journalists Association.* Melbourne, AJA, 1960.
Stanley, P., *Commando to Colditz.* Sydney, Pier 9, 2009.
Stark, N., *Proud Australian Boy: A Biography of Russell Braddon.* Melbourne, Australian Scholarly Publishing, 2011.
Todd, R., *In Camera: An Autobiography Continued.* Hutchinson, London, 1989.
Turner, A. F., *Douglas Bader: A Biography of the Legendary World War II Fighter Pilot.* Shrewsbury, Airlife, 1995.
Vance, J. F., *A Gallant Company: The Men of the Great Escape.* New York, iBooks, 2003.
Walters, G., *The Real Great Escape.* London, Bantam, 2013.
Walton, M. J., and M. C. Eberhardt, *From Commandant to Captive: The Memoirs of Stalag Luft III Commandant Colonel Friedrich Wilhelm von Lindeiner genannt von Wildau.* Raleigh, Lulu, 2015.
Williams, E., *The Tunnel.* London, Collins, 1959.
Williams, E., *The Wooden Horse.* London, Collins, 1949.
Williams, L., *A True Story of the Great Escape.* Sydney, Allen & Unwin, 2015.

NEWSPAPERS & MAGAZINES
Advertiser, Adelaide, 1954
Age, Melbourne, 1954, 1982, 2015
Albury Banner, Wodonga Express & Riverina Stock Journal, 1941
Army News, Darwin, 1945
Australasian Post, 1953
Australian, 1969, 1991
Australian Women's Weekly, 1950–1963
Barrier Miner, Broken Hill, 1954
Borehamwood & Elstree Times, UK, 2013
Canberra Times, 1959, 1984, 1991
Chronicle, Adelaide, 1955
Courier-Mail, Brisbane, 1945, 1949, 1969
Daily Advertiser, Wagga Wagga, 1941
Daily Express, London, 1949, 1955
Daily Mail, London, 2010, 2013
Daily Mail Australia, 2013
Daily News, Perth (WA), 1943

Bibliography

Daily Telegraph, Launceston (Tas), 1881–1924
Daily Telegraph, Sydney, 1960, 1969
Dungong Chronicle/Durham & Gloucester Advertiser (NSW), 1953
Examiner, Launceston (Tas), 1880–1991
Flight, 1955
Goulburn Evening Post, 1954
Guardian, London, 1991
London Free Press, Canada, 2014
Mail, Adelaide, 1927
Mercury, Hobart, 1880–1991
Newcastle Morning Herald, NSW, 1953
Newcastle Sun, NSW, 1946, 1954
News, Adelaide, 1945–1959
New Statesman, London, 1955
New Zealand Herald, Auckland, 2015
North Western Advocate & Emu Bay Times, Burnie, 1903–1904
Northern Champion, Taree, 1953
Observer, London, 1951
Ottawa Citizen, 1941
Ottawa Journal, 1941
People, Sydney, 1953
Recorder, Port Pirie, 1922–1952
Register & Post Herald, Beckley, West Virginia, 1967
Sun-Herald, Sydney, 1950, 1954, 1982
Sunday Mail, Brisbane, 1945, 1953
Sydney Mail & New South Wales Advertiser, 1909
Sunday Telegraph, Sydney, 1981
Sydney Morning Herald, 1945, 1952, 1954, 1969
Telegraph, London, 2008, 2013–2015
Table Talk, Melbourne, 1917, 1919
Times, London, 1981, 1991
Watertown Daily Times, Wisconsin, 1968
West Australian, Perth (WA), 1953, 1969
Windsor & Richmond Gazette, NSW, 1950–59

NOTES & LETTERS
Paul Brickhill to Arthur Fincham, (undated) 1946. Private Collection, London
Paul Brickhill to Maria Lupp, 18 July 1960. Private Collection, Western Australia
Paul Brickhill to John Pudney, 14 April 1954. The Pudney Papers, Correspondence Index 3.11, (Ransom Center, University of Texas), Austin, Texas
Correspondence from Paul Brickhill to Del Fox, 1939–1945, PR03099, Australian War Memorial, Canberra
Correspondence between Paul Brickhill and Mark Bonham-Carter. University

of Glasgow Archive Services, William Collins, Sons & Co Ltd collection, GB248 UGD 243/1/11/1
Correspondence between Paul Brickhill and William 'Billy' Collins, University of Glasgow Archive Services, William Collins, Sons & Co Ltd collection, GB248 UGD 243/1/11/9
Correspondence from Paul Brickhill regarding *Escape to Danger*. Australian War Memorial, Canberra. AWM93, 50/2/23/349

OFFICIAL RECORDS
Brickhill Paul Chester Jerome 403313, AWM65 414. Australian War Memorial, Canberra
Brickhill P. C. J., A13950. National Archives of Australia, Canberra
Manifests Passenger – Outwards Ships, and Manifests Passenger – Outwards Aircraft/Sydney, April–June 1949, SP1148/2. National Archives of Australia, Chester Hill, NSW
NSW Electoral Rolls, 1930–1966
Parliamentary Debates (Hansard), House of Commons (UK), 23 June 1944
'Prisoners of War Bulletin', American National Red Cross, Vol 3 No 3, March 1945
Victorian Electoral Rolls, 1911–1920
World War II service record, P. C. J. Brickhill, A9300. National Archives of Australia, Canberra
World War II casualty file, P. C. J. Brickhill, A705, item 166/6/81. National Archives of Australia, Canberra

PAPERS
Divorce Papers, Margaret Olive Brickhill-Paul Chester Jerome Brickhill. NSW State Archives, Kingsgrove. 514/1962

ORAL HISTORY
Jack Donald. Australian War Memorial, Canberra, S00952

TELEVISION DOCUMENTARY
'Great Escape: The Untold Story.' Granada Television, UK, 2001.

ONLINE
'Brickhill, Paul Chester (1916–1991)', Craig Wilcox, Australian Dictionary of Biography, National Centre of Biography, Australian National University, http://adb.anu.edu.au/biography/brickhill-paul-chester-14647/text25780, published online 2014
'RCAF Uplands.' http://rcafuplands.blogspot.com.au/2012/10/course-31.html
'A Cobra in the Sky: 92 Squadron, Royal Air Force.' http://sirius1935.wix.com/92Squadron

Index

Advertiser, Bendigo 17
Age, the 19
American servicemen 155
Amos, Fred 28, 50
Anderson, Michael 375
Angel, Major Danny 280, 303
Ann Watkins Agency 193, 261
Argus, the 19
Army News, the 169
The Artful Dodger 350, 361
Asselin, Eddy 108
Asselin tunnel 108, 376
Associated Newspapers 153, 163, 168, 206
Australian Artists Association in London 250–1
Australian Journalists Association (AJA) 20–1, 22–3
Australian Militia 45

Bader, Douglas 233–6, 239, 246–50, 252, 253–5, 267–8, 278, 286–8, 303, 379
Bader, Thelma 233–4, 247–8, 255, 268, 275, 287, 303
Bates, Herbert Ernest 242–3

Baume, Eric 279
Bean, Keith 187
Bendigo Press Association 18
Berg, Dick 343–6
Bergsland, Per 'Peter' 136, 137
Berlin, post-war 174–88
  Soviet Zone 187–8
Bevan, Ian 226, 250, 251, 256
Bonham Carter, Mark 270, 271, 275, 324–5, 334
Bowes, Commander Wilfred 'Freddie' 205
Braddon (seat of) 15
Braddon, Russell 226, 251, 256, 261, 279
Bradshaw, John Walbourn 19, 26
Bradshaw, Louisa Adelaide 19, 26, 28
Brickhill, Ayde Geoffrey (Geoff) 21, 28, 32, 33, 194
Brickhill, Clive 26, 28, 37, 75, 195
Brickhill, Daisy 15, 17
Brickhill, Frank 17
Brickhill, George 15
Brickhill, George Russell 17–18, 19, 21–3, 24–6, 29, 37, 39, 40–1, 47, 48, 69, 81, 152, 168, 193, 204, 273, 324, 349

Brickhill, Hector 17
Brickhill, Izitella Victoria (Dot) (nee Bradshaw) 19, 21, 22, 24, 25, 26, 47, 81, 152, 193, 273, 324, 333, 349
Brickhill, James 13–14, 15–16, 17, 204
Brickhill, John 13
Brickhill, Lewis 15, 17
Brickhill, Lloyd 24, 28, 33, 37, 48, 50, 194
Brickhill, Margaret Olive (Margot) (nee Slater) 201–2, 205, 212, 215–16, 225, 227–8, 234, 240, 259, 261–2, 263, 266, 269–70, 271–2, 299, 300–1, 302, 306, 309, 375
  childbirth and motherhood 276–7, 283, 285–6, 307
  divorce 322–3, 325–6, 333–6, 338–42, 347–9
  marital difficulties 230–2, 244, 253, 255–8, 264, 273, 277, 295, 300–2, 307–8, 319, 322
Brickhill, Paul Chester Jerome 2–5, 21–2, 25, 28, 37, 45–6, 47, 48, 49–51, 52–8, 61–3, 64, 66–8, 69, 73–4, 92, 103, 115, 117, 118, 119, 146, 149–52, 153, 157–9, 161–2, 165, 166, 171, 178–83, 188–91, 192–4, 215–16, 231–2, 244, 264, 265–6, 267–8, 276, 281–3, 306, 309, 310–11, 315, 319, 321, 371–2
  92 Squadron 1–2, 68, 70–2, 76, 78
  childhood and school years 28–34, 36
  claustrophobia 103–4, 124–5, 172
  divorce 322–3, 325–6, 333–6, 338–42, 347–9, 374
  ill-health and breakdowns 212, 271, 283, 285, 301, 316, 319, 323, 335, 360, 365, 369
  marital difficulties 230–2, 244, 253, 255–8, 264, 273, 277, 295, 300–2, 307–8, 322
  prisoner of war 11, 78–9, 80–1, 85–9, 146–8, 158, 177
  shot down 2–11, 78, 159
  the *Sun* 39, 41, 43–4, 153, 161, 163, 194, 199
Brickhill, Rebecca (nee Emms) 14, 15, 17, 24, 47

Brickhill, Russell 21, 28, 37, 45, 50, 58–9, 60, 65, 74–6, 194, 279
Brickhill, Susannah (nee Hutley) 13
Brickhill, Tempe Melinda 307, 333, 334, 335–6, 349, 359, 369, 372, 379
Brickhill, Timothy Paul 283–4, 288, 305, 333, 334, 335–6, 349, 359, 372, 379
Brickhill, Walter 15, 17
Brickhill Publications Limited 169, 231, 278
British Air Ministry, Air Historical Branch 197
Broadhurst, Air Chief Marshal Harry 235
Bronson, Charles 328
Bruckshaw, Mick 2, 6, 8, 78
Bull, Leslie 'Johnny' 127–8, 135
Bushell, Squadron Leader Roger 90, 91–2, 93, 96–7, 99, 100, 108, 111, 119, 120, 122, 125, 135, 165, 178, 204–5, 207, 210, 211, 314, 328, 377–8
Buttrose, Ita 346

Callanan, Mary 45, 154–5, 315
Canberra 15
Canton, Norman 'Conk' 108, 125, 328
Cavanagh, Graham 356–7
Cheshire, Leonard, VC 197, 219, 222, 251, 304
Clark, Albert 'Bub' 100, 108, 117
Clark, Robert 237, 241, 243, 244–5, 256–7, 273, 290, 291, 295, 298
Clavell, James 327
Cleary, Jon 225–6, 276, 317–18, 351, 362, 374
Coburn, James 328, 329
Codner, Michael 95
Coe, Fred 223–4, 229–30, 273, 307, 311, 314, 318, 327
Collins, Sir William 'Billy' 239, 260, 267, 268, 269, 270, 282, 286–8, 289, 324, 325
Commonwealth Bank 15
Communism 192
Connolly, Roy 198, 229
Cordes, Oberstleutnant Erich 133

Index

Courier-Mail 169, 198, 212
Cradon, McGowan 197
Cunningham, Dan 217

Dahl, Roald 62, 193
Daily Express 212
Daily Telegraph 14, 15, 26, 358, 365
Dam Busters 197, 201–2, 205–6, 207–9, 217, 219–22, 252, 256–7, 298, 357
The Dam Busters 202, 217, 218–22, 228, 229, 231, 233, 359–61, 375, 378, 379
  film 237, 241, 243, 244–6, 262, 272–3, 280, 290–3, 295–8, 302–3, 375
  Pan paperback edition 284–5
Darwen, Wing Commander William 72
Darwin (seat of) 15
David Higham Associates 163
Davidson, James E. (Jed) 24, 25, 26
Davy, Elizabeth 156
Day, Wing Commander Harry 'Wings' 106–7, 110, 111, 118, 121, 123, 127, 136, 165, 209, 235, 314, 328, 351–3, 357, 362
D-Day Landings 140
de Niverville, Wing Commander Joseph 56
The Deadline 321–2, 324, 337, 358, 370
  War of Nerves 321, 337, 343, 343–6
Denison, Sir Hugh 37, 41–2
Department of Information 47, 48
Dimmock, Flight Sergeant Harry 56
Dodge, Major Johnny 109–10, 136, 209, 304, 328, 350, 357, 359, 364–5, 370, 374
Donald, Flight Lieutenant Jack 71, 151
Dowse, Sydney 118, 125, 136, 352–3, 359, 378
Duff, Gordon 229–30
Duke, Flying Officer Neville 68–9, 70–1, 72, 76, 77, 274
Dulag Luft 80–1, 82–4, 108, 165
Dunne, Pat 193, 325

Eden, Sir Anthony 155–6
Embry, Air Chief Marshal Sir Basil 240
escape from Stalag Luft 3 123–8, 130–2, 135–7, 155, 376–7

Escape Or Die 240, 241–3, 244, 375
Escape to Danger 167–8, 169, 188, 193, 194, 195, 196, 198, 199, 204, 234, 235, 375, 378
  writing 138–9, 155, 157, 163–5
Evans Brothers 198, 199, 206, 214, 240, 271
Evening News, the 26, 36, 37
Examiner, the 13–14, 17, 18, 57

Faber & Faber 167, 169, 194, 271
Fanshawe, Peter 'Hornblower' 101, 102, 118, 123, 328
Fifty, the 136, 137, 138, 156, 158, 159, 165, 187, 188, 203, 205, 210–11, 332
Finch, Kate 31, 33
Finch, Peter 30–2, 33–5, 36, 39, 40, 41–3, 202, 217, 226–7, 250, 251, 256, 364
Fincham, Arthur D. 169
Fincham, Vallance and Co 169
Fisher, Andrew 17
Floody, Wallace 'Wally' 97, 100–1, 103, 106, 110, 111, 123, 143, 206–7, 328, 331, 354, 362
Focke-Wulf 190 fighter 76–7
Fox, Del 46, 73–4, 119, 153–4, 156, 225

Gabes 2
Gades, Frau 180–1
Gaffney, James 16
Galland, Adolf 247
Gammon, Victor 235
Garner, James 328, 329, 330, 331
Gatty, Harold 34, 286
Geneva Convention 120
Gestapo 120, 132, 211
Gibson (Hyman), Evelyn 290, 291–2, 295, 297, 299
Gibson, Wing Commander Guy, VC 218–20, 223, 243, 257, 295, 329, 378–9
  Enemy Coast Ahead 219, 290, 295
Gieves Ltd 64, 116, 125
Glemnitz, Sergeant Hermann 99, 115, 122, 328

Goering, Reich Marshal Hermann 93, 133, 188, 189–90, 210–11
Gotfurt, Frederick 256
Graham, Winston 239
The Great Escape 198–9, 202–5, 207–10, 212, 213–14, 224–5, 230, 237, 339, 375, 378
    film 319–20, 326, 327–32, 338, 346
    film rights 223, 230, 273, 307, 311, 318
    United States television version 223–4, 230, 327
Greenfield, George 239
Griese, Corporal Karl 'Rubberneck' 99, 122
Griffin, Walter Burley 15
Guest, Tommy 98, 116, 328
Gulick, Bill 312, 313
Gullett, Sir Henry 47, 48

Hake, Albert 'Al' 89, 98, 126, 127, 135, 158, 173, 329
Harper, Squadron Leader William 78
Harris, Air Marshal Sir Arthur 'Bomber' 228, 296
Harsh, George 110–12, 113, 114, 117, 123, 143, 206–7, 213–14, 328, 354
Hartnell, Norman 258
Hastings, Hugh 250, 251
Hay, Bob 223
Herald 24
Herman, Joe 169
Higham, David 162–3, 166, 167, 196, 198, 199, 202, 214, 239, 241, 260, 278, 280, 283
Himmelpforten 208–9
Himmler, Heinrich 189
Hitler, Adolf 79, 140, 189, 190, 210
Hoffman, Dirk 186
Hoffman, Vera 185–6
Howard, Lance 223
Howe, Freddy 273, 276
Hudson, Lionel 'Bill' 45, 47
Hughes, Billy 17
Humphries, Adjutant Harry 218, 291
Humphries, Flight Lieutenant Peter 'Hunk' 2–5, 78

Hurricane IIb fighters 66, 67
Hyman, Jack 292

Isaacs, Sir Isaac 22–3
Italian First Army 11

Jackson, Sir Peter 379–80
James, Bertram 'Jimmy' 136
Jewish refugees, post-war Berlin 187–8
John Bull 274
Johnson, Johnnie 61, 64, 76, 234
Johnson, Norman 36, 39, 42, 44

Kee, Robert 203, 283
Kellow, Bob 223
Kenyon, Flight Lieutenant Ley 122, 166–7, 169
Ker-Ramsey, Robert 'Crump' 125, 127, 328
Kingsford Smith, Sir Charles 34
Kingsford Smith, Peter 151
Knight, Les 223
Krige, Uys 117

Labor Party 15
Langsam, David 367–71
Launceston, Tasmania 13, 17
Leggo, Jack 223, 291
London, post-war 151
Luftwaffe 3, 76, 93
Lupp, Nurse Maria 316–17

M19 118–19
McCormack, Bernard 219
McGarr, Neville 112, 135
McGill, George 112, 135
McGowan, Mac 210
McQueen, Steve 319, 328, 329, 332
Mail, Adelaide 25
Malan, Adolph 'Sailor' 234
Marks, George 'Doggie' 41
Marshall, Cuthbert 'Johnny' 127–8
Martin, Harold 'Micky' 219, 222, 223, 228, 246
Massey, Group Captain Herbert 89, 90, 107, 111, 125–6, 133–4, 156, 328

Index

Melbourne Press Bond 19
Messerschmitt Bf 109s 2, 64, 67, 71
Miller, Leonie 186
Milne, Dicky 113
Minchin, Devon 348–9
Mirisch Corporation 312, 318, 319
Mirisch, Walter 318, 327, 339, 350
Moehne dam 207, 228, 298
Moorehead, Alan 226, 251, 279
More, Kenneth 303–4
Morgan, Squadron Leader John 72
Morison, Walt 330
Mudge, Muriel 186
Muller, Jens 136, 137
Murdoch, Rupert 19, 25
Murdoch, Sir Keith 19, 20, 21, 47, 48
Murn, Cecil 24
Mycroft, Walter 237, 245, 296

Nebe, General Arthur 211
Nerney, John 196–7, 198, 206, 218, 223, 229
Newman, Walter 313, 319, 320
News, the 25
News Limited 25
newspaper business 13, 22–3
North Africa conflict 2–5, 65–70
Norton, Conrad 117–18, 138, 153, 154, 157, 167
Norton, Eve 227, 231
Norton & Co 207, 261, 275
Nuremberg trials 177, 182, 188–91, 210

O'Malley, King 15–16

Pearn, Nancy 162–3
Pearn, Pollinger and Higham 162
People magazine 264
Philpot, Oliver 95–6
Pieber, Hauptmann Hans 100, 135
Pollack, Sydney 345
Pollinger, Laurence 162–3
Prichard, Katharine Susannah 26
Prichard, Tom 26
Pudney, John 196–9, 202, 206, 214, 229, 240, 284

Quill, Norman 108

Reach for the Sky 233–6, 239, 246–50, 252, 253–5, 263, 267–8, 270–1, 273, 274, 275, 276, 278, 282, 283, 285, 286, 287, 303–4, 374
Recorder, the 24, 168–9, 212
Reeve, Christopher 371
Regia Aeronautica 3
Rimmer, Matron F. M. 60, 115, 116
Rommel, Field Marshal Erwin 65, 66, 79
Rose, Paddy 184, 186
Rowe, Hugh 118
Royal Air Force Escaping Society (RAFES) 240, 243
Royal Air Force Special Investigations Branch 205
Royal Air Force's Number 74 Squadron 63–66
Royal Air Force's Number 92 Squadron 1–2, 68, 70–2, 76, 78, 210
Royal Air Force's Number 145 Squadron 66, 69, 159, 160, 347
Royal Air Force's Number 617 Squadron 197, 201–2, 205–6, 207–9, 217, 219–22, 252, 256–7, 298, 357
Royle, Paul 138

Sage, Jerry 98, 101–2, 108, 109, 117, 329, 362
Schacht, Hjalmar 190
Schubin escape 96, 101, 107, 108, 353, 376
Scott, Paul 270
Second Battle of El Alamein 67
Shand, Alec, QC 339–41
Shannon, Dave 223
Sherriff, R. C. (Bob) 243, 244–6, 252, 256–7
Silliphant, Stirling 350–1, 361
Sinclair, Gordon 235
Slater, Edric 201, 252, 333
Slater, Jeanette 201, 212, 215, 216, 289
Society of Australian Writers (SAW) 251, 263
Sorpe dam 207

Spafford, 'Spam' 223, 297, 329
Speer, Albert 190
Spitfire fighters 55, 61–2, 64, 66, 77
SS *Largs Bray* 199, 200, 202, 206
Stalag Luft 3 83, 85–9, 91–2, 94–5, 108–9, 113–14, 119, 124, 130, 140–1, 142–6, 155, 168–9, 209, 362
   BBC broadcast on escape 156–7, 165
   Dick tunnel 106, 114, 115, 122, 139
   Eastern Compound escape 95–7, 120, 134, 376
   escape 123–8, 130–2, 135–7, 155, 376–7
   escape plans 91–2, 95–7, 109
   George tunnel 140
   the Fifty 136, 137, 138, 156, 158, 159, 165, 187, 188, 203, 205, 210–11, 332
   Harry tunnel 114, 115, 117, 120, 121, 123, 127, 166, 214
   Tom, Dick and Harry tunnels 97, 101, 103, 106, 111, 114, 115, 120
   tunnelling methods 96, 101–2, 103–4, 376
Steele, Ruth 212
Stockings, Henry 118, 127, 329–30
Sturges, John 230, 307, 311–13, 314, 326, 329, 332, 350, 356, 359, 364
Summers, Mutt 219–20
Sun, the 36, 39, 41, 43–4, 153, 161, 163, 194, 199
The Sunburnt Country 251–2, 278–9
Sunday Telegraph 365
Sydney Morning Herald, the 168, 290, 359, 367

tax and tax issues 169, 240, 258, 278, 281, 288
Taylor, Rod 276
Tedder, Lord 229
Telegraph, the 14, 15
Tiger Moth, De Havilland DH 82 51
Torr, Pat 212
Torrens, Dave 127, 328
Travis, Johnny 97
Tunis 1

Ulm, Charles 34
Ulm, John 47, 69, 149, 159–61, 195
Uplands, Ontario 52–57

Valenta, Arnost 'Wally' 98, 137
van der Stock, Bob 125, 137, 209, 329
VE Day 149
von Lindeiner, Oberst Friedrich 132, 328
von Massow, Hauptmann Günther 86
von Ribbentrop, Joachim 190

Waddell, William 57
Wadery, Flight Lieutenant William 157–9
Walenn, Gilbert 'Tim' 98, 100, 113
Wallis, Barnes 219–22, 243, 245–6, 257, 296, 299–300
War of Nerves 322, 337, 343, 343–6
Wareham, Edward 38, 39
Watkins, Mike 193, 207, 223, 292, 318
Welch, Lorne 330
West, Morris 275–6, 306, 351, 359, 361–2, 374
Whittaker, W. A. 'Bill' 245, 256
Wigmore, Lionel 'Wiggy' 47, 195
William Collins and Sons 239, 260, 282–3, 353
Williams, Doug 138, 140
Williams, Eric 83, 95–6, 198, 202
   The Wooden Horse 198–9, 202, 216–17, 239
Williams, John 'Willy' 98, 135
Willson, Robert 323
Wilmot, Chester 226, 251, 279, 281
Wilmot, Fred 57
Wilson, Group Captain Douglas 134, 135, 140–1
Wirth's Circus 18
Woman's Day 276
The Wooden Horse 198–9, 202, 239, 278
   film version 216–17
World War One 21
World War Two 45, 46, 47

Zeehan, Tasmania 15, 17